Geocritical Explorations

Geocritical Explorations

Space, Place, and Mapping in Literary and Cultural Studies

Edited by Robert T. Tally Jr.

Foreword by Bertrand Westphal

GEOCRITICAL EXPLORATIONS

First published in hardcover in 2011 by PALGRAVE MACMILLAN® in the United States—a division of St. Martin's Press LLC, 175 Fifth Avenue, New York, NY 10010.

Where this book is distributed in the UK, Europe and the rest of the world, this is by Palgrave Macmillan, a division of Macmillan Publishers Limited, registered in England, company number 785998, of Houndmills, Basingstoke, Hampshire RG21 6XS.

Palgrave Macmillan is the global academic imprint of the above companies and has companies and representatives throughout the world.

Palgrave® and Macmillan® are registered trademarks in the United States, the United Kingdom, Europe and other countries.

ISBN: 978–1-137–47110–9

The Library of Congress has cataloged the hardcover edition as follows:
    Geocritical explorations : space, place, and mapping in literary and cultural studies / edited by Robert T. Tally Jr. ; foreword by Bertrand Westphal.
        p. cm.
    Includes bibliographical references.
    ISBN 978–0-230–12080–8
    1. Space in literature. 2. Geocriticism. 3. Geography and literature. 4. Place (Philosophy) in literature. I. Tally, Robert T.

    PN56.S667G46 2011
    809'.9332—dc22   2011011125

A catalogue record of the book is available from the British Library.

Design by Scribe Inc.

First PALGRAVE MACMILLAN paperback edition: October 2014

10 9 8 7 6 5 4 3 2 1

Printed in the United States of America.

For Vancouver,
and for one who loves that place

Contents

Part III   Transgressions, Movements, and Border Crossings

Foreword

Bertrand Westphal

For a long period, time seems to have been the main coordinate—at least the main *scientific* coordinate—of human inscription into the world. Time was aristocracy. Space only was a rough container, a plebeian frame for time (see Kantian philosophy, for instance). Spaces were marginalia. Obviously there were exceptions, even strange ones. Ignatius of Loyola, founder of the Society of Jesus, wrote his famous *Spiritual Exercises* (1522–1524), and there already were previous links between geography or topography and hagiography (here we might recall the medieval Irish *Navigatio Sancti Brendani*), but in Loyola's *Exercises* the connection matched spatial representation and prayer—prayer as an elaboration of a fantasy world, a global and abstract framework of faith's eternity. Ignatius indeed worked out the concept of *compositio loci*. Describing a prelude to one exercise, he said, "The First Prelude is a composition, seeing the place. Here it is also to be noted that, in a visible contemplation or meditation [...] the composition will be to see with the sight of the imagination the corporeal place where the thing is found which I want to contemplate. I say the corporeal place, as for instance, a Temple or Mountain where Jesus Christ or Our Lady is found, according to what I want to contemplate."[1] This exercise deserves a lot of commentary, but we do not have the space to develop it here. Suffice it to say that such a baroque representation could be said to announce what Gaston Bachelard terms *topoanalysis*—that is, "the systematic psychological study of the sites of our intimate lives."[2]

Does this mean that there is a link between Ignatius and Bachelard, between the baroque and psychoanalysis? Why not? Anyway, for both of them, what matters is not so much the thing in itself, *in se*, but the idea it suggests, its composition, almost in a rhetorical and iconic sense, whether through a direct observation or through an abstract effort of reconfiguration (i.e., prayer in Ignatius's times was a means of constructing things with the mind, and psychoanalysis in Bachelard's was another one). On the eve of a new reading of the world, in which the Renaissance vision is no longer considered as a global and homogeneous space, Ignatius admitted that the world's unity, in a realm that hitherto was said to be *scriptus per digito Dei* (as Pier Damiani wrote in the eleventh century), was to be overcome. Maybe the world was still the playground of the soul, but the rules had to be rethought or at least adapted by Man—and by Woman also: we should not forget that Teresa de Avila concretely mapped her visionary projections on paper.

Yet if these considerations point out that space might have been more than a mere container, they do not imply that it was theorized in humanities, especially not in literary studies. I suppose that we had to wait for twentieth-century literature scholars to put forward spatial conceptions of literature and literary theories of space—maybe even until the second half of that century, after the end of World War II's *decompositio loci*. The first half of last century was still dominated by temporal studies (à la Henri Bergson, Martin Heidegger, Georges Poulet, and so on). In localized spots, here and there, maybe some isolated names might be mentioned—Joseph Frank and his notion of spatial form and then Bachelard with his poetics of space—but for the most part, we would have to wait until the 1960s to see significant changes. As I have only a brief space and little time to explore the subject here (which once more shows that time and space are closely interrelated), I refer to only three or four different approaches that emerged in that era.

In literary theory, the first systematic approach was *imagology*, which was born in the wake of a passionate debate within comparative literature. During the first congress of the International Comparative Literature Association, René Wellek accused the so-called French School (including Marius-François Guyard and Jean-Marie Carré), which had started an interdisciplinary reflection upon "images" and "mirages" of the Other, of promoting national points of view and an extrinsic approach at the expense of pure literary scholarship. Consequently, when Hugo Dyserink coined the term *imagology* in 1966, he boldly entered an already perilous field. Without going into detail, I would add that if imagology (at least as conceived by Dyserink) pays attention to questions of space, it is mainly in order to refer to the Other's imagined territory. The location in itself, as understood by Homi Bhabha and other postcolonial theorists, has a very little relevance in imagology. Moreover, it is only thanks to such scholars as Daniel-Henri Pageaux and Jean-Marc Moura, among others, that imagology managed to get rid of its purported Eurocentrism (which, it always seemed to me, would have been more aptly described as Western-centric). There was actually a kind of African adaptation of imagology, which Bonny Duala-M'bedy, a Cameroon-born anthropologist, formalized; his approach was called *xenology*,³ and he tried to show how a so-called foreigner systematically gets included in a mythological scheme that stages him instead of giving him a particular identity. Like imagology, xenology consecrates the alienation of the Other without considering a possible overcoming of Otherness. Imagology, like xenology, studies the insurmountable gap between a looking subject and an observed object and presumes that their respective places cannot merge in a global human space. Mind the gap!

Two other authoritative literary and global approaches to space have been developed more recently: *geopoetics* and *ecocriticism*. Geopoetics has been elaborated by Kenneth White, a Scottish poet who has been living in France since the 1970s. Geopoetics focuses on the intertwining of the biosphere, poetry, and poetics, foregrounding these in a somewhat systematic endeavor. Geopoetics goes along with a certain ecological view of life, a certain inclusion in world culture. Obviously it has a global range, and White's favorite references prove it: Heraclitus, Thoreau, Emerson, Stevens, Whitman, Tchouang-tseu, Matsuo Bashô, Hölderlin, and so on. White likes invoking "a geography of the poetic spirit." However, even if geopoetics has almost become a common term, I am not sure that it rests on a clearly defined theoretical base. Frequently, geopoetics offers a hodgepodge of ideas, without the systematic theoretical framework it might have aspired to provide.

As for ecocriticism, it is even more fashionably up to date since it developed and spread beginning in the 1990s in the United States and Canada, without any named individual source (if I am not mistaken). Although there are a number of key scholars—ecocritics—who have made important contributions to the theory and practice, ecocriticism is not really associated with a founding figure—quite rightly, it seems. Ecocriticism, which also may be called *ecoliterature*, has proved to be a collective and progressive achievement. Allison B. Wallace, in defining the term *ecoliterature*, explains, "When I talk about ecoliterature, I'm talking about any writing that focuses on *place*, on the thousands of local landscapes that make up not scenery through car windows, not Sierra Club calendars nor slick ads for hiking gear, but rather our daily contexts, what David Quammen calls our 'matrices for destiny.' Writing that examines and invites intimate human experience of place's myriad ingredients: weather, climate, flora, fauna, soil, air, water, rocks, minerals, fire and ice as well as all the marks there of human history."⁴ It escapes nobody that ecocriticism covers the same fields as geopoetics but with much more concern for theory. And emerging after the era of structuralist dominance had ended, ecocriticism has reintroduced the question of the referent, a reflection upon the eventual links between *realia* and representation.

Most of those approaches allot some room for questions of space, but none directly addresses the spatial turn that has recently been pinpointed by theoreticians as different as Michel Foucault (who, alongside Henri Lefebvre, is perhaps the most influential promoter of this "turn"), Edward Soja, or Paul Zumthor. In the literary area, writing about space did not involve a rethinking of the relationship between the so-called objective referent and its artistic representation, between the real world and fictitious words. As we know, the structuralist view held overwhelming sway for more than two decades in France; it was certainly no easy task to fight back against its predominance. I believe that structuralism's credo might be summed up in Jacques Derrida's laconic formula: *Il n'y a pas de hors-texte*. There is nothing outside the text, and a text is a text is a text. A text may be a Steinian rose, who knows, but anyway a text should have no concrete link with the actual world. In his famous and almost revolutionary *Fictional Worlds*, Thomas Pavel denounced structuralism's worship of paper as "textolatry" and proposed to expound a logical, formalist "possible-world theory" in literature. A text was no more a mere text; a text opened a new world in a constellation of worlds, some real, some less real, some clearly fictitious— even if these adjectives were losing part of their sense under the pressure of a weakening definition of reality (see, for example, Gianni Vattimo's notion of *pensiero debole*, or "weak thought"). Globality becomes a compound of heterogeneous representations in a fully postmodern meaning.

Another characteristic of spatial literary analysis refers to the status of the world's occupants. In most approaches, one is supposed to watch and another has to be watched, according to a model that turns out to be more entomological than ontological. A subject called "One" observes an object called "Other," taking note of characteristics that seem to delineate the outlines of his or her strangeness. The "exotic" frame is the result of a naïve attempt to rationalize strangeness and to integrate it into something that may be mastered. Traditionally, "One" is a Westerner and "Other" is not. Most imagological studies are one-way, European, or North American streets. Otherness is the hallmark of minorities according to such an approach. It would probably be fairer to say that the Other is part of a majority that is given a minor role by One or, to parody the title of a now aging movie, the Other becomes a child of a lesser god. Here, the globe looks like a halved orange with section lines running horizontal or vertical—that is, following a north/south or east/west axis. You may easily guess which of the halves has for a long time been supposed to be the better one (and I would not affirm that nowadays such a hierarchy has really been overcome). Postcolonial studies have tried to introduce new perspectives since even before the era of decolonization, and they managed to make significant changes, sometimes by running the risk of establishing another centric point of view, the former Other becoming an ongoing One. In fact, is it possible to consider an overcoming of Otherness, an overtaking of the Other's alienation, whoever he or she is? Is it possible to remove those multiple lines that split space and short-circuit globality? Is it possible to address globality as the target of a *heterarchic* focus (to use Douglas Hofstadter's terminology)?

These issues are absolutely critical in today's worldwide, geographically oversized society. To a large extent, they exceed literature and even culture—unless culture be viewed as ubiquitous, which seems quite reasonable to me. In any case, both literature and culture are of concern here, in a way and in a proportion that still has to be defined. In my opinion, the era when "fictitious" narrations can be definitely cut off from the "real" world is long over. Culture, the arts, and, more specifically, literature have assumed a renewed responsibility, such as they had in earlier centuries. Let us not forget that ancient Greeks did not separate history from what we call literature; they had no appropriate word for "literature" simply because they did not need it. The Homeric *Odyssey* was literature, geography, history, theology, anthropology, and something more: a book, a *biblion*, a universal topic. At the very start of a new millennium, there is no doubt that literature has to be reinstated within a discourse on the world. What we call "world literature" should imply a double openness on literary productions: first, that they be regarded as wholly universal and freed from any discrimination between supposed centers (they always have been plural) and peripheries, and second, that they be linked to "real-life" referents, a coupling that allows them to hold their own position in the global discourse about modern society.

Geocriticism is an approach whose purpose is to explore some of the interstices that until recent times were blank spaces for literary studies. Geocriticism is clearly affiliated with those theories that unleash spatial perception and representation in a nomadic perspective, which have made for a very stimulating background. In the 1970s, mainly in France, several theoretical achievements led to a new dynamic of space and reading in philosophy, sociology, and anthropology: among others, the most important might have been Foucault's heterotopias, Deleuze and Guattari's deterritorialization process, and Lefebvre's production-of-space hypothesis. In the1980s, Baudrillard's analysis of the simulacra inspired such scholars of postmodernism as Brian McHale, who draws upon Fredric Jameson and many other earlier theorists, especially those who elaborated possible-world theories (e.g., Goodman, Walton, Pavel, Doležel, etc.). Also influential have been the postmodern cultural geography of Cosgrove, Gregory, Brosseau, and above all Edward Soja and his notion of *thirdspace*.[5] Last but not least, geocriticism entertains a close relationship to most minority discourses: Deleuze's once again, and of course postcolonial theory (Bhabha, Spivak, Rabasa, etc.), gender studies (Anzaldúa, Rose, etc.) and whatnot. It is probably necessary to combine all these cross-disciplinary inputs in order to open up a truly literary approach to spaces, one that is closer to contemporary postcolonial and globalization theory than to imagology, for instance.

Having already written a book and some shorter theoretical essays on geocriticism,[6] I will avoid going into detail here, but I can list a few of the main methodological features. First of all, as I underscored previously, geocriticism enters an interdisciplinary field. By interdisciplinarity, I do not mean a utilitarian piling up of heterogeneous notions, but a process that produces true interactions among disciplines like literary studies, geography, urbanism and architecture, with pathways to sociology and anthropology. So geocriticism expresses a comparativist concern, but it is not limited to the traditional disciplinary concepts and practices of comparative literature. As for more precise elements of definition, let me just add the following points:

1. Geocriticism is a geo-centered rather than an ego-centered approach; that is, the analysis focuses on global spatial representations rather than on individual ones (a given traveler's, for example). Thus one may undertake a geocritical study of a city, a region, a territory, and so on, rather than studying a given author's treatment of that place.
2. Geocriticism ceases to privilege a given point of view in order to embrace a broader range of vision regarding a place. Three main perspectives may be identified (endogenous, exogenous, and allogeneous), and this hybridization of the different focuses (multifocalization) tends to relativize Otherness and to identify stereotypes.
3. Geocriticism promotes the empire of the senses, a polysensuous approach to places—*places* meaning concrete or realized spaces. Most of the time, places are perceived with our eyes, but it seems most appropriate to diversify sensing to include the sounds, smells, tastes, and textures of a place.
4. Geocriticism associates both geometric and philosophical coordinates of life—time and space—in a spatiotemporal scheme. A geocritical analysis locates places in a temporal depth in order to uncover or discover multilayered identities, and it highlights the temporal variability of heterogeneous spaces. Spatial analysis reveals that present is asynchronic: our vision of time is not necessarily the same as our neighbor's. Globality implies polychrony.

All this is in line with three fundamental concepts: *spatiotemporality* (no spatial analysis may avoid temporal concerns); *transgressivity* (no representation is stable; on the contrary, as in Deleuze's deterritorialization process, permanent fluidity is the characteristic of representations and, consequently, of identities); and *referentiality* (any representation is linked with the referential world).

Geocriticism has been theorized, certainly, but it will continue being a work in progress. This is coextensive with its very nature. This volume is a testament to the fact that more scholars are beginning to work on geocritical projects in Europe and on other continents (e.g., Robert Tally's discussions of "literary cartography" and geocriticism), as well as in both literature and the human sciences. A geocritical approach should be particularly helpful in postcolonial and globalization studies as well. Geocriticism, like space itself, offers infinite opportunities for further examination and exploration.

Notes

1. Ignatius Loyola, *The Spiritual Exercises of St. Ignatius of Loyola*, trans. Father Elder Mullan (New York: Cosimo, 2007), 35–36.
2. Gaston Bachelard, *The Poetics of Space*, trans. Maria Jolas (Boston: Beacon Press, 1969), 8.
3. Bonny Duala-M'Bedy, *Xenologie: Die Wissenschaft vom Fremden und die Verdrängung der Humanität in der Anthropologie* (Freiburg: Verlag Karl Alber, 1976).
4. Allison B. Wallace, "What Is Ecocriticism?" *Defining Ecocritical Theory and Practice*, Western Literature Association Meeting, Salt Lake City (October 6, 1994), http://www.asle.org/site/resources/ecocritical-library/intro/defining/wallace.
5. Bertrand Westphal, "Edward Soja and the Poetics of Decentering," in *Centquatrevue* (paper version, May 2009), http://www.104lerevue.fr.
6. See Bertrand Westphal, *La Géocritique: Réel, fiction, espace* (Paris: Minuit, 2007); in English, *Geocriticism: Real and Fictional Spaces*, trans. Robert T. Tally Jr. (New York: Palgrave Macmillan, 2011). Also see "Pour une approche géocritique des textes: esquisse," in Bertrand Westphal, ed., *La géocritique mode d'emploi* (Limoges: Presses Universitaires de Limoges, 2000), 9–39; "Géocritique," in *La Recherche en Littérature générale et comparée en France en 2007*, ed. Anne Tomiche and Karl Zieger (Valenciennes: Presses Universitaires de Valenciennes, 2007), 325–34; "Oltre la torre d'avorio: Genesi della geocritica," in *Lezioni di dottorato 2007*, ed. Roberto Baronti Marchió (Santa Maria Capua Vetere: Edizioni Spartaco, 2008), 251–71.

Acknowledgments

Like the space of a place itself, in which the present configurations of things are shaped by what comes before and are ceaselessly reconfigured in anticipation of future developments, a book is what it is largely because of a heterogeneous mélange of textual and material circumstances. *Geocritical Explorations* has benefitted from many other texts and contexts. This project undoubtedly began long before it crystallized in the form of a Modern Language Association panel on geocriticism in December 2009. That panel, which featured presentations by several contributors to this volume (and had another contributor in the audience), already revealed the diversity of approaches that could be called "geocritical," but it also reinforced my sense that a large and growing number of scholars working in literary and cultural studies were interested in geocriticism. I hope that this collection supplements and encourages current and future research in this field.

I would like to thank the contributors for their excellent contributions, and I want to especially thank my former panelists (Christine Battista, Rachel Collins, Eric Prieto, and Bertrand Westphal) for revising and elaborating their presentations for inclusion here. Let me single out Professor Westphal for special thanks. I have come to know him well through our efforts to characterize and to promote geocriticism (see his *Geocriticism: Real and Fictional Spaces*), and I have found him to be generous, patient, and enthusiastic. When I first issued a call for proposals, I received a large number of excellent ones that, for various reasons, could not be included in this collection, but I am grateful to all who submitted abstracts and who are engaged in such intriguing research. I am also grateful for the well wishes from others who, while not directly involved in *Geocritical Explorations*, have nevertheless contributed in ways they may not themselves realize. These include Eric Bulson, Tom Conley, Peter Hulme, Fredric Jameson, Franco Moretti, Ricardo Padron, John Protevi, Edward Soja, and Amy Wells. My colleagues at Texas State University, in particular Michael Hennessy and Ann Marie Ellis, have provided unflagging support. I owe a debt of gratitude to Brigitte Shull of Palgrave Macmillan, who has been indefatigable in her support for both the *Geocriticism* translation and this project, and I appreciate her endless patience and hard work.

Above all, I want to thank Reiko Graham for her love and support. She also introduced me to her hometown and one of the most beautiful places on the planet, which has enlarged and improved my own affective geography and quality of life.

Introduction

On Geocriticism

Robert T. Tally Jr.

In the early 1990s, I started to use the term *geocriticism* to refer to an aspect of my research project through which I hoped to bring a greater emphasis to space, place, and mapping in literary studies; this ultimately resulted in a much narrower dissertation topic. At the time, I imagined geocriticism as the critic's counterpart to what I viewed as the writer's literary cartography. Using *literary cartography*, a writer maps the social spaces of his or her world; a geocritic would read these maps, drawing particular attention to the spatial practices involved in literature. Although I thought I may have coined the term, I was not so bold as to think I had come up with the idea of geocriticism, as a large number of scholars, critics, and theorists had been producing works that might be considered geocritical. Among those I had in mind, Kristen Ross's fascinating work on Rimbaud in *The Emergence of Social Space*, Edward Said's "geographical inquiry into historical experience" in *Culture and Imperialism*, and Fredric Jameson's expanded notion of cognitive mapping in *The Geopolitical Aesthetic* provided current examples. But I also considered earlier works, such as Raymond Williams's *The Country and the City*, Walter Benjamin's writings on Paris (especially his unfinished *Arcades Project*), and Mikhail Bakhtin's study of "chronotopes." And this list could be expanded in many different directions once one allows for figurative uses of space and mapping. In using the word *geocriticism*, I also wanted to indicate an analogue in literature to what Deleuze and Guattari had termed "geophilosophy" in *What Is Philosophy?* But even as I wished to give the neologism definition, I wanted to make sure it remained broad enough to encompass a number of different spatial and critical practices. Geocriticism, at least as much as ecocriticism and other emerging approaches, needed to be flexible.

After experiencing my own spatiotemporal displacements, I returned to these preliminary studies recently. In completing my book on Herman Melville's literary cartography,[1] I was pleased to discover or rediscover a number of critics engaged in geocriticism, including one employing the term *géocritique*. Reading Bertrand Westphal's foundational essay on the subject,[2] I realized that his view of geocriticism was not the same as mine but that he was clearly a kindred spirit. I contacted Westphal just after his book-length theoretical explication of geocriticism (*La Géocritique: Réel, fiction, espace*) was published, and we began our efforts to produce the English translation.[3] *Geocriticism: Real and Fictional Spaces* now makes Westphal's theory of geocriticism available to a wider audience, and I hope that it will provoke further discussion about other geocritical practices. As I noted in my translator's preface to *Geocriticism*, the title is deceptively categorical. Although Westphal clearly wants to distinguish geocriticism from other critical practices or schools, he does not want to define it so narrowly that it would overlook useful materials or approaches that could benefit our greater understanding of literature, space, and place. Hence that book's frequent recourse to a tentative or provisional language, where one can see Westphal's desire to encompass a variety of methods and texts without losing sight of the expressly geocritical project he has in mind. This requires a balancing act. We had originally thought of giving the English version of Westphal's book a more tentative title, like "A Theory of Geocriticism" or "Toward a Theory of Geocriticism," as a way to register that there are other, perhaps even opposed, versions of geocriticism out there. Yet in the end, we decided that the simplicity of the title was preferable, as it might spur discussion about the nature of geocriticism or related critical practices. By suggesting that *this* is what geocriticism is, the book invites others to engage in a debate, to argue and to disagree as well as to listen and to concur; perhaps a more productive discussion may ensue. In any case, the *Geocriticism* of Westphal provides an excellent point of departure for the multiple geocritical explorations to come.

Indeed, in the final line of *Geocriticism*, Westphal writes that geocriticism "operates somewhere between the geography of the 'real' and the geography of the 'imaginary' . . . two quite similar geographies that may lead to others, which critics should try to develop and explore." It is fitting that Westphal's study ends with the word "explore," because the active exploration—in every sense of the word, for better or worse—of the real and imaginary spaces of literature is the goal of geocriticism. Geocriticism certainly does not provide all the answers, and it is more likely to generate further questions. Geocriticism explores, seeks, surveys, digs into, reads, and writes a place; it looks at, listens to, touches, smells, and tastes spaces.

The essays in *Geocritical Explorations* offer a sampling of the sort of work and play that geocriticism may entail.

Thus *Geocritical Explorations* serves as both a companion and a counterpoint to Westphal's *Geocriticism*, demonstrating the heterogeneity of geocritical practices. Many of the essays in this volume challenge Westphal's views, and many offer positions quite different from his. And yet all the essays maintain that spirit of geocritical exploration that Westphal and I wish to foster and promote, and the diversity of approaches—as well as the nearly global representation of the contributors, places, and texts—befits the overall enterprise of geocriticism. Undoubtedly, as more scholars and critics explore the spaces, places, and mappings of literature, geocritical practices and readings will multiply. Such, in any case, is my hope, and I think that, even if it appears in hitherto unseen and unforeseeable forms, geocriticism will be a vital part of literary and cultural studies in the years to come.

*   *   *

As a relatively new name for a critical practice or for an ensemble of related critical practices, *geocriticism* requires some definition. In Part I, "Geocriticism in Theory and Practice," Eric Prieto and Sten Pultz Moslund present their own definitions of geocriticism while also exploring the variety of ways that geocritical practices may be deployed. One may say that this part helps to establish a groundwork for the essays that follow, as long as it is also understood that this groundwork is less a solid, stable foundation than a provisional and mutable site for further exploration and construction.

Eric Prieto takes up the challenge of defining, as well as extending and questioning, the geocritical approach in "Geocriticism, Geopoetics, Geophilosophy, and Beyond." Building on Westphal's *Geocriticism*, Prieto emphasizes the ongoing interplay between text and world—the ability of literature not only to reflect the world around us or even to shape our understanding of it but also to inflect the history of the places in question in a reciprocal relationship akin to a positive feedback loop. Examining the ways in which literary representations participate in the construction of our world, Prieto focuses on a number of important geographical tasks to which the imaginative vocation of literature is particularly well suited, such as the identification and analysis of emerging geocultural and geosocial formations. Explicating and extending Westphal's version of geocriticism, Prieto reveals how geocriticism, broadly understood, can invigorate literary criticism and open it up to new areas of inquiry.

In "The Presencing of Place in Literature: Toward an Embodied Topopoetic Mode of Reading," Sten Pultz Moslund offers a perspective on reading that emphasizes matters of place over the more celebrated transcultural migrations, movements, and displacements. Using a kind of lingua-topo-analysis, as he terms it, Moslund reads literature as geography (as from the original Greek, meaning "earth-writing"), looking at the *lang*scaping of the novel or reading the novel's *land*guage to signal the integral connection in literature between land, earth, place, and language. *Langscaping* the novel discloses how places and landscapes are *presenced* in literature—that is, how they are brought before our senses so that we may actually experience the spatial setting of a novel. Drawing on Heidegger and Deleuze as well as a number of literary texts, Moslund describes a *topopoetics* that would supplement geocriticism by focusing on the embodied character of textuality and place.

Part II, "Places, Spaces, and Texts," expands upon the theory and practice of geocriticism by using a wide variety of texts to explore not only different geographical locations but also different types of space in literature and in the world. Ranging from Australia to South America, northern Africa, the Mediterranean, and the United States, these essays demonstrate how a geocritical approach opens up literary and cultural studies to an array of representational practices, offering new and intriguing models for further interrogation and presenting novel ways of looking at places and texts around the world.

In "Redrawing the Map: An Interdisciplinary Geocritical Approach to Australian Cultural Narratives," Peta Mitchell and Jane Stadler argue that a geocritical approach, taking its lead from literary cartography's analysis of locational data within cultural narratives, provides an interdisciplinary framework for identifying tropes across geographic regions and across media representations. Space, place, and landscape are longstanding themes in Australian literary and cultural studies. Drawing on examples from Australian cinematic, literary, and theatrical narratives, this chapter surveys published work in the field and argues for a more refined geocritical mapping and analysis of the cultural terrain. Mitchell and Stadler conclude by looking at the possibilities for future research emerging from recent technological developments in interactive cartography.

Maria Ortiz, in "Textual Forests: The Representation of Landscape in Latin American Narratives," analyzes the rainforest as a socially constructed place, intertwined with race, ethnicity, and gender and linked to the history of the so-called rubber boom (1879–1912). Ortiz examines how the rainforest is variously portrayed in selected narratives according to the process of rubber extraction and to nation-building discourses. Initially, the rainforest is seen as the garden of Eden and a virgin land, but when climate and disease began to devastate the labor force, it became a curse of God and an overwhelming power that controlled human lives. The rainforest was also used as a metaphor to express the anxieties of the nation toward its uncontrolled peripheries and to criticize the peripheral modernity that was imposed on Latin America by means of the extractive economy.

Crossing the Atlantic, Michael Walonen finds the Mediterranean to be a site of social and radical fluidity in "Land of Racial Confluence and Spatial Accessibility: Claude McKay's Sense of Mediterranean Place." While recent scholarship has questioned the notion of a coherent, overarching Mediterranean regional identity, Walonen argues that the pioneering work of the modernist writer Claude McKay—in novels, short stories, poems, and autobiographical writings that portray life in Marseilles, Morocco, and Spain—envisions these places, for all their local points of specificity and distinctiveness, as sites of racial and social class convergence that can be approached and entered into by foreigners, racial minorities, the poor, and the working class with greater fluidity than more rigidly zoned spaces, such as those of New York City. McKay's Mediterranean is a place of refuge and fellowship, one that, tainted as it was at times by the specter of imperialism, offers glimpses of the closest he was to come in his life and work to finding an ideal spatio-racial order.

Staying in the Mediterranean zone, Antoine Eche examines the spatial representation of Cyprus in "The Shores of Aphrodite's Island: Cyprus and European Travel Memory." Eche focuses on travels narratives, geographical texts, drama, poetry, and maps produced in the epoch of the Turkish occupation (1572–1880). On the maritime road to Jerusalem, Cyprus is situated on the conceptual dividing line of Occident and Orient, where, as Voltaire put it, "Europe ends and Asia begins," and the island activates an *imaginaire du lieu* reminiscent of the Greek eschatological idea of the limits of the known world. But limits can be infringed, and the end is also a threshold. Drawing on Westphal's theory of geocriticism, Eche analyzes this space in relation to the dynamics of cultural memory and diachronic movement, thus showing how the real and imaginary spaces of this place affect historical and narrative experience.

Drawing on a rather different narrative form, but one that draws force from the travel narrative's desire for epistemological and scientific dominance, Christine Battista reads Thomas Jefferson's *Notes on Virginia* as a harbinger of the political and ecological problems we face today in the era of globalization. In "Jefferson's Ecologies of Exception: Geography, Race, and American Empire," Battista notes that our current postmodern situation represents an ecologically precarious moment in which borders are increasingly redefined and threatened by environmental disasters. Emphasizing the relationship between the geocritical and the ecocritical, Battista analyzes the ways in which theories of space and geography intersect with theories of ecology. Specifically, she reveals how Jefferson's desire to orient and produce an American national narrative is predicated on a spatialized code of ethics that neglected the actual "living" portion of the land itself. In establishing a geographic Virginia that also could be coded as a national space, Jefferson anticipates the geographical metaphysics associated with globalization and discloses an ecological unconscious of the processes involved.

The chapters that make up Part III, "Transgressions, Movements, and Border Crossings," all deal with some aspect of that "transgressivity" that Westphal had argued was a fundamental characteristic of space and hence a crucial aspect of geocritical analysis. These chapters deal less with the theory of space or with a particular place or type of place than with the movements across territories and domains. Some of these movements may be understood broadly as migrations or colonizations, whereas others may involve the apparently simpler or subtler border crossings within a society or a language. In any event, the transgressive movements of subjects within space relate to the mobility of spaces themselves.

In "Geopolitics, Landscape, and Guilt in Nineteenth-Century Colonial Literature," Rebecca Weaver-Hightower examines nineteenth-century Australian, South African, Canadian, and American frontier literature. Weaver-Hightower shows how such works participated in colonization by creating narratives that managed to contain or limit the guilt associated with taking land from indigenous populations. This chapter focuses on depictions of the landscape, since these narratives often describe the settler's interaction with the natural world (stories of farming, surviving natural disasters, being immersed in the landscape) and adaptation (building houses, fences, forts, and other structures). Weaver-Hightower categorizes three types of narrative that each function as ways of managing guilt for both settlers and readers a generation later, who then use the myth of the settler to deal with their own qualms about colonial expansion.

Narrowing her focus to the urban space of a single novel, Rachel Collins nevertheless reveals how rich and complex the representations of personal, social, and spatial transgressions can be in her chapter, "'Amid all the maze, uproar and novelty': The Limits of the Other-Space in *Sister Carrie*." Collins notes that in producing a literary cartography, novels often depict social space by setting their particular plots against a tangle of spatial networks that embody social relations and by focusing on the ways individual characters negotiate those spaces. In her geocritical approach, Collins argues that Theodore Dreiser's *Sister Carrie* does not merely reproduce static perceptions of Chicago and New York but that its representations of social and spatial engagement precipitated shifts in the ways Americans understood cities. Collins's spatially oriented reading demonstrates that by inviting readers to rethink popular ideas about urban danger, the controversial novel's representation of social space was just as transgressive as its depictions of sexuality.

Of course, transgressive movement is never strictly one way. In "Furrowing the Soil with His Pen: Derek Walcott's Topography of the English Countryside," Joanna Johnson looks at the way the Caribbean writer "writes back" to and against the metropolitan space of England. Given Walcott's concern for physical and geographical aspects of his native Caribbean and other North American locations, it is perhaps surprising this is largely absent from his poetical depictions of England. Walcott engages with English pastoral tradition in less direct ways. In an essay on V. S. Naipaul, Walcott comments on England's literary landscape: "Press one foot on the soil of England and the phantoms spring. Poets, naturalists and novelists have harrowed and hallowed it for centuries with their furrowing pens as steadily as its yeomen once did with the plough." But whereas Walcott's own pen furrows the soil just as steadily, it does not reify the myth of the so-called purity of the countryside; rather, it exposes that myth. By closely examining Walcott's depictions of England's countryside, Johnson explores the nature and significance of his resistance to engage directly with that zone where "topography delineates its verse."

In "Global Positioning from Spain: Mapping Identity in African American Narratives of Travel," Maria C. Ramos shows how twentieth-century African American narratives of travel to Spain (including accounts by Langston Hughes, Claude McKay, Nella Larsen, Richard Wright, and Frank Yerby) create a geographic imaginary. Spain's liminal position geographically (between Europe and Africa), historically and culturally (between East and West), and politically (between liberal secularism and the religious state or totalitarianism) provides these writers with a variety of routes into discussions that revise the dominant North Atlantic geographic imaginary and expand the theoretical discourses of the politics of location and identity, at times challenging the stability of such categories or suggesting alternative conceptions of them. Using the idea of global positioning systems, Ramos argues for an updated metaphor for mapping identity—one that moves beyond the common us/them or core/periphery binary structure and that takes into account the recent focus on the multiplicity and intersectionality of identities—a metaphor more closely linked to the mapmaking process than to the physical map itself.

The questions of exile and identity also inform Brigitte Le Juez's chapter, "The Space of Transgression: A Geocritical Study of Albert Camus's 'The Adulterous Wife.'" Camus's "The Adulterous Wife" ("The Adulterous Woman" in Justin O'Brien's English translation) appears in a collection called *Exile and the Kingdom*, two terms that designate an experience both physical and spiritual. Describing the journey of a *pied-noir* couple from their coastal city to the desert, far away from their comfortable French routine and into a world inhabited by Arabs—a space silent, empty and seemingly hostile—Camus exploits all those possibilities, playing with the natural environment, the topography, and the architecture of different places as the journey develops. Using Westphal's theory of geocriticism, Le Juez examines the spatial transgressivity inherent in the protagonist's adultery: crossing boundaries of the norms according to which she has lived (a world to which she will have to return) to establish a new relation with a space she is now conscious of, a limitless space that fulfills her desires. Here, the geographical transgression overlaps with the emotional or personal, and geocriticism reveals how the spatial transgressivity permeates the other aspects of lived experience.

Although geocritical analysis has focused more closely on narratives, Heather Yeung's "Affective Mapping in Lyric Poetry" shows how geocriticism may extend beyond the novel, film, travelogue, or documentary. As Yeung points out, the poet—like the naturalist, the cartographer, or the surveyor—uses visual and aural engagement with a landscape in an effort to map and determine spaces. However, the poet's eye may observe, react to, and record sensations in addition to those that make up the concrete landscape. The poet thus communicates with a freedom of affect that the geographer or naturalist cannot always notate, bridging the gap between the ready-to-hand of the observer in the natural setting and the present-at-hand of the geographer or naturalist's detachedly observed phenomena or specimens. Through this freedom of vision, the "eye" and the "I" of the poem become necessarily interchangeable: poetic landscape and poetic voice blur in a process that Yeung calls *affective mapping*. In this final chapter, Yeung shows how affective mapping provides a richer understanding of the poetic *topos*.

Geocriticism, whatever else it may be, is a way of looking at the spaces of literature, broadly conceived to include not only those places that readers and writers experience by means of texts but also the experience of space and place within ourselves. That is, geocriticism can examine how the ways in which we are situated in space determine the nature and quality of our existence in the world. With geocriticism, one emphasizes this inherent spatiality while also focusing one's critical gaze on those aspects of literature (and other texts not always deemed literary) that give meaning to our spatialized sense of being. In their diversity and scope, the essays in *Geocritical Explorations* offer examples of how geocriticism may be used to ask new questions, to read differently, to engage with other disciplinary methods, and to interpret the ways that we make sense of our own spaces, of our own mappings. These essays suggest some of the directions that geocriticism and geocritics may take in the future, as readers and writers—some lost in space, some at home in the world—continue to explore.

Notes

1. See my *Melville, Mapping and Globalization: Literary Cartography in the American Baroque Writer* (London: Continuum, 2009).
2. See Bertrand Westphal, "Pour une approche géocritique des textes: esquisse," in *La Géocritique mode d'emploi*, ed. Bertrand Westphal (Limoges: Pulim, 2000), 9–39.
3. See Bertrand Westphal, *La Géocritique: Réel, fiction, espace* (Paris: Minuit, 2007); see also Bertrand Westphal, *Geocriticism: Real and Fictional Spaces*, trans. Robert T. Tally Jr. (New York: Palgrave, 2011).

Part I

Geocriticism in Theory and Practice

1

Geocriticism, Geopoetics, Geophilosophy, and Beyond

Eric Prieto

Those who study the representation of space and place in literature are well aware of the debt this subfield owes to work done in the social sciences. Many of the most exciting recent developments in this burgeoning area of literary studies have involved an interdisciplinary turn toward themes and analytic tools that borrow from fields like cultural and social geography, urban sociology, environmental studies, and the phenomenology of place. Such tools have greatly enriched the study of literary space. But what does literature have to offer in return? That is, how can the literary study of space and place contribute to the work being done in these other fields and in so doing enrich our broader understanding of and interactions with the natural and built environments through which we move? How can we, as literary critics, build on these developments, helping to bring literature into the larger conversation on space and place? My answers to these questions will be centered on a consideration of Bertrand Westphal's *La Géocritique: Réel, fiction, espace.*[1] Informed by postmodern, postcolonial, and poststructuralist theories of space, Westphal's book argues forcefully for the strategic role that imaginative literature plays in a world marked irrevocably by postmodern epistemological and ideological uncertainty.

As Westphal notes, literature in our postmodern era seems to be finding its way back to the center of our discussions of space and place. This is true not only of literary critics eager to explore the spatial capacities of literary representation but also of many in other disciplines who have recognized the strategic role that literary representations play in shaping our conceptions of human spatiality. We could cite as examples Henri Lefebvre, Nicholas Entrikin, Edward Soja, David Harvey, and Derek Gregory, all spatial thinkers who emphasize the inherent instability of all representations of space and place. For these thinkers, the need to question the authority of spatial representations extends even, and perhaps especially, to the scientific disciplines. Who speaks? From what position? On what authority? With what presuppositions? In a postmodern era characterized by what Jean-François Lyotard famously called our "incredulity with regard to metanarratives," geographers and other spatial thinkers have showed a renewed sensitivity to the fact that narrative, metaphor, and the other paralogical modes of discourse that we often associate with literature are also at work in the social and even the physical sciences. Thus although a more traditional geographer, sociologist, or urban planner might consider the hypothetical or counterfactual status of fictional and metaphorical language a liability, these writers have come to appreciate the potential epistemological and ethical value of such paralogical modes of discourse. Rather than drawing a sharp line between imaginative, theoretical, and empirical discourses, they explore the borders and zones of overlap between them.[2]

Given this interpenetration of scientific and imaginative modes of thinking, it is possible to see literature's relative freedom from documentary concerns and the scientific principle of falsifiability as an advantage. It is precisely the imaginative dimension of fictional narratives and metaphorical language that gives them their peculiar form of power over the real. The "fictive imagination" (to borrow Timothy Reiss's expression) seems to be more sensitive to those qualities of spatial and geographical formations that are most difficult to detect from within the established, formalized explanatory frameworks of the physical and social sciences. This aspect of literary discourse, which Paul Ricoeur emphasizes in terms of the *indirect referentiality* of metaphor and fiction, enables them to act as a kind of midwife, drawing nebulous spatial intuitions out of their conceptual purgatory and making them available for other, nonliterary uses.[3] Literature, in other words, can insert itself at a critical phase in the process of concept formation between that of the vague intuition and that of the established concept.

In what follows, I would like to build on this insight, looking for tools that leverage this exploratory, hypothetical, indirectly referential quality of literature in ways that enable it to contribute to the evolution of spatial thinking in ways that have an impact on debates going on outside of literature and the humanities, including those in the social sciences and also in the more casual forms of knowledge that we apply in our daily lives. Of particular importance for my purposes is the concept of place, which has come to play an important role in the modern era as it seems to have come

under threat by the delocalizing forces of modernization and globalization. *Place*, in the sense that interests me here, extends beyond the restrictive definitions used in cartography (i.e., as a point or shape on a map)
or geometry (that of locus, an intersection of lines defining a point in a
space). I emphasize the human, subjective dimension of place, which gives
rise to expressions like "a sense of place" and has an inherently experiential
dimension that has often gone missing from geographical analyses, especially since the advent of the post–World War II "quantitative revolution"
in geography and the abstractive, spatializing tendencies of poststructuralist social theory. This perhaps questionable but nonetheless intuitively
obvious sense of the term *place* has attracted the attention of those who
worry about the transformations that modernity (and *a fortiori* postmodernity) have wrought on our built and natural environments and the consequences of these transformations for the ways in which we relate to the
world around us.

Theoretical Orientations

Within the field of literary criticism, much of the work on place has
remained wedded to the traditional tools of literary history, the history of
ideas, and philological exegesis.[4] But I would argue that many of the most
exciting recent developments in place studies have involved an interdisciplinary turn toward tools that reach beyond the scope of conventional
literary criticism. At the risk of oversimplifying, I would break these tendencies into four main groups: phenomenological, poststructuralist, identitarian, and environmental.

The phenomenological approach, which emphasizes the subjective
experience of place, is no doubt the one that is most familiar to literary
scholars. In France it is associated with the work of Gaston Bachelard, who
adds a distinct psychoanalytic twist, and Georges Poulet's small but important book on Proust.[5] This approach has been renovated and revitalized in
recent years by philosophers like Edward Casey and Jeff Malpas, both of
whom are primarily phenomenologically inspired. Casey seeks to restore
the philosophical dignity of the concept, which he considers to have been
progressively marginalized by the scientific revolutions begun in the seventeenth century under the dual aegis of Descartes and Newton.[6] As for
Malpas, his attempt to delineate a topography of the conceptual field of
place begins with the Heideggerian concept of *Dasein*, with an emphasis on
the importance of the *Da* in *Dasein*, which is to say the embeddedness of
human subjectivity in the environing world. He subjects this Heideggerian
conception of human being to a critique that strengthens it by exploring

the place-bound nature of human subjectivity as it has been developed by Anglo-American philosophers like Tyler Burge, Hilary Putnam, and Donald Davidson.[7] In another vein, the self-proclaimed neurophenomenologist Francisco Varela couples Husserl's insight about the intentionality of human consciousness (which is necessarily consciousness *of* something) with work on the nature of human consciousness being done in evolutionary biology, neuroscience, and cognitive theory. For Varela, the relationship between consciousness and world is one of ongoing "mutual specification," a fact that has great importance for our understanding of the relationship between self and place, since the self is always defined in and through its explorations of the place in which it finds itself.[8]

The phenomenological approach to place has evolved, then, from the more or less impressionistic accounts of Bachelard and Poulet into something that is much more firmly grounded in empirical scientific research while also finding common ground with Anglo-American ways of doing philosophy it had heretofore tended to eschew. This modified phenomenological approach shows great promise as a way to use literature to better understand how the insights of these writers into the nature of human consciousness both benefit from and contribute to progress in our scientific understanding of the interface between mind and world. By emphasizing the embodied, environmentally constrained nature of human consciousness, such analyses help to overcome the age-old philosophical problem of mind-body dualism (which runs back through Kant and Descartes to Plato) and the paradoxes of radical doubt that have accompanied it. Such phenomenologically oriented approaches are less well adapted, however, to the study of the social and political dimensions of place. It is at this point that the poststructuralist approach to place has an important contribution to make to the literary study of space and place.

The poststructuralist approach to place has one important point in common with the phenomenological approach: both emphasize the importance of doubt and link it to the epistemological problem of mediation, the indirectness of so much of our knowledge of the world. For the phenomenologists, it is the fallible nature of our sensory and cognitive apparatus, which mediates between the world "out there" and our subjective beliefs, that is the source of doubt. For the poststructuralists, on the other hand, doubt is necessitated by the socially mediated nature of knowledge, the fact that we are born into institutionalized power networks and impersonal social structures that shape the information that comes to us and restrict our access to counterhegemonic forms of knowledge. For this reason, the thinkers that I'm calling poststructuralist are less interested in the subjective experience of place than in the semiotics of spatial representations (à la Barthes and Bourdieu), the spatial distribution of power (as emphasized, for example, by Foucault), and, more generally, what Edward Soja, following Lefebvre (following Marx), calls the social *production* of space. For all these thinkers, space is not a neutral featureless void within which objects and events are situated but a dimension that has been produced by social forces that in turn constrain future possibilities.

The poststructuralist emphasis on impersonal networks of power and discourse helps to understand why the poststructuralists tend to emphasize the concept of *space* over that of *place*. In a word, they reject the humanist presumption of the priority of individual experience and subjective consciousness that forms the basis of the phenomenological concept of place. For the poststructuralists, the individual subject may be no more than a kind of epiphenomenal construct, "a simple fold in our knowledge," as Foucault famously put it.[9] Place, in this view, is the product of a corollary perspectival error, the erroneous belief that the individual's experience of its local environment provides an adequate starting point for understanding the significance of that environment and its place in the totality. This critique can be found in essays like Foucault's "Of Other Spaces" and Blanchot's "The Conquest of Space," which argue for the need to emancipate ourselves from the almost superstitious belief that the world is best understood in terms of relations between places.[10]

The poststructuralist deconstructions of the human subject and place, it should be noted, rely on a logic that owes much to the Marxist theory of mediation. Both question the truth value of our subjective representations of the world with respect to the underlying material reality.[11] It is not surprising, then, that there is much overlap between the thinkers associated with these two movements. It is nonetheless important to distinguish between the two tendencies, because the emphasis on structure in poststructuralism tends to weaken the claims for individual and/or collective (class-based) agency made by Marxists. For this reason poststructuralism has been, with some justification, associated with a tendency toward political quietism. This distinction leads me to consider a third category of approaches to the study of place, which I will call activist. This is, admittedly, somewhat of a catch-all category, but it nevertheless captures an important tendency in contemporary spatial thinking.

If, for the sake of convenience, we restrict ourselves to those modes of activist thinking that have had the greatest influence in literary studies, we can organize them into several clear tendencies. We have already begun to consider the first of these, the Marxist tradition, whose geoliterary dimension is most clearly evident in works like Walter Benjamin's *Arcades* project,

Raymond Williams's *The Country and the City*, and David Harvey's *Social Justice and the City*. Three other important tendencies must be mentioned here: postcolonial studies, feminist studies, and environmental studies. Postcolonial studies has consistently emphasized themes like territorial identity, intercultural contact, dispossession and displacement, exile and migration. From Aimé Césaire and Frantz Fanon to Edward Said, Homi Bhabha, and Edouard Glissant, spatial thinking has played in integral role in postcolonial studies. The link between feminism and geography is perhaps less evident, but it has taken on an important role in the study of concepts like home and community in the work of bell hooks, Doreen Massey, and Lucy Lippard. Moreover, many of these writers combine feminist and postcolonial themes in their work while developing their spatial implications. Gloria Anzaldúa's *Borderlands* is perhaps the iconic example.[12]

As for environmentalism in literary studies, it has given rise to movements like ecocriticism and the geopoetics of Kenneth White. In its purest or most extreme forms, environmentalism implies a need to radically relativize human subjectivity by thinking of it within the larger context of what Lawrence Buell has called the "agency of nature."[13] In this it moves beyond the poststructuralist and Marxist critique of individualism and humanism and suggests a radical dissemination of the human throughout the larger order of nature. In this sense, it links up with the materialist or vitalist epistemology of Deleuze and Guattari and their quest to explain human consciousness as one plane in a self-immanent material realm. Perhaps the clearest statement of this tendency in their work is in *What Is Philosophy?* Deleuze and Guattari's use of the term *geophilosophy* in that volume is picked up by Bonta and Protevi in *Deleuze and Geophilosophy*, which they use to draw out the geographical implications of the philosophy of Deleuze and Guattari.[14]

Significantly, then, although environmental activism might seem to have brought us far away from the phenomenological concerns with which we started, the epistemological implications of any thoroughgoing environmentalist position bring us back full circle to the equally materialist view promoted by Casey, Malpas, and Varela: that human subjectivity and agency are embodied and, therefore, inextricably intertwined with the material environment from which the dualist tradition has tended to separate it. This may indeed be one of the main lessons to draw from the resurgence of interest in spatial studies: no matter what the starting point—whether psychological, social, identitarian, political, or environmental—and no matter how much of a tendency we have to forget this basic fact, human identity, indeed the very ability to be the kind of creature who has an identity (to paraphrase a recurrent refrain of Malpas) is inextricably bound up with the places in which we find ourselves and through which we move.

Situating Westphal's Geocriticism

What precedes is a necessarily schematic overview of three distinct yet intertwining approaches to the relationship between humans and their various environments. But it seems important to have these matters in mind in order to understand what Bertrand Westphal attempts to achieve in *La Géocritique: Réel, fiction, espace*, which proposes nothing less than the establishment of a new field of literary studies, focused on a systematically geocentric or geocentered approach to the study of literature.[15]

Echoing the spatializing theses of Fredric Jameson's book on post-modernism, although his evaluation of postmodernism is more positive, Westphal argues that space has become more important than time and geography has become more important than history as a guiding metaphor for the postmodern era: "We are entering into a temporality where the synchronic seems to be getting the upper hand over the diachronic."[16] Like Adorno, Westphal identifies the epistemological rupture of the contemporary period with the historical rupture of World War II and the emblem of its dehumanizing brutality, Auschwitz. World War II, Westphal reminds us, destroyed the Enlightenment metanarrative of progress (conceived as a linear process) and led immediately to the fracturing of the myth of history as a single unified narrative. For Westphal, "time had been deprived of its structuring metaphor" (24). Indeed, Westphal reads the resistance narratives of the anticolonial movements of the postwar years as confirmation of this thesis (23): the single, unified "line (of history) broke down into lines; time would henceforth become a surface" (26). Much of chapter 1 is devoted to establishing this point: that, in our postmodern era, the multipolar, nonlinear spatial metaphor of the map replaces the single teleological arrow of history as the dominant interpretive paradigm.

Having established this point, Westphal gets down to exploring the key components of his theory of spatial representation and its implications for the study of literature in chapters 2 and 3. Of particular importance is the figure of the border as the site of reflection (e.g., in his chapter titled "Transgressivity"). For Westphal, the postmodern world has already been fully explored; the task that remains to us is that of going back and reexamining the interstices between established domains. It is, therefore, "transgressive" thinking (conceived, etymologically, as a crossing of borders) that provides the most significant examples of spatial thinking in the postmodern era. This leads him into a quick overview of postcolonial criticism (Bhabha, Anzaldua) and postmodern geography (Soja, Gregory). For Westphal, these two movements—postcolonial theory and postmodern geography along with the Deleuzo-Guattarian philosophy of deterritorialization and reterritorialization—provide the surest guides for this kind of work.

Central to Westphal's conception of literary criticism is the conviction that it is only by emphasizing the referential force of literature—the ability of the fictive imagination to interact with and meaningfully shape the real world in which we live—that we can understand the essential function of true literary creation. This is the subject of chapter 3, "Referentiality." Westphal emphasizes in particular the importance of possible worlds theory, as exemplified by Thomas Pavel and Lubomir Doležel, which he sees as an important corrective to the structuralist and poststructuralist emphasis on textuality and autoreferentiality. If it is in the interstices between established places that the most interesting discoveries are to be made, then what we need are new ways of seeing what we thought we already knew, new tools for seeing what had remained unnoticed because it was caught in the cracks between known entities. It is for this reason that Bhabha's *entredeux* plays such an important role in Westphal's thinking, and it is also why literature is considered to have such an exalted status in the temporally flattened world of postmodern space. "I will never get tired of repeating that fiction does not reproduce the real, but actualizes new virtualities that had remained unformulated, and that then go on to *interact* with the real according to the hypertextual logic of interfaces [. . .] fiction detects possibilities buried in the folds of the real, knowing that these folds have not been temporalized" (171).

This brings us to chapter 4 of Westphal's book, "Elements of Geocriticism," which sets forth his understanding of the specificity of geocriticism as a mode of literary criticism. The central proposition of Westphal's definition of geocriticism involves what he calls its geocentered outlook. For Westphal, the geocritical study of literature is not organized around texts or authors but around geographic sites. Rather than studying, say, the representation of Dublin in *Ulysses* or Thomas Hardy's Wessex, the geographical space itself will become the focus of attention and the texts of Joyce or Hardy will be brought into dialogue with as many other texts as possible that deal with that space. As Westphal puts it, "The study of the point of view of the author or of a series of authors from the same identitarian space will be left aside in favor of the analysis of a multiplicity of points of view, preferably heterogeneous, which will all converge towards a given site, prime mover of the analysis. This multifocal dynamic will be the indispensable object of this analysis. Without hesitating we can affirm that that is the defining characteristic of the geocritical approach" (199). Westphal emphasizes that it is crucial to bring in as many authors as possible, including both insider and outsider perspectives, and also to include, when possible, nonliterary texts, which might range from tourist brochures to official reports and records. Moreover, texts from different historical periods and different cultures should be referenced in order to create an archeological, or as he puts it, "stratigraphic," reading of the places in question. The overarching goal is to create as complete as possible an image of the chosen place, one that transcends the point of view of individual authors and cultural communities considered in isolation.

As a way to demarcate geocriticism from other modes of spatially oriented literary criticism, the advantages of this approach are clear: the specificity of geocriticism is to be a truly geocentric or geocentered mode of analysis, focused on understanding a given place (through the problematics of representation) rather than studying a given set of representations (through the thematics of place). The traditional tools of literary criticism and interpretation have a role to play in such an investigation (they help to reveal the complex relations between the mode of representation and the object of representation), but the ultimate objective is spatial.

For Westphal, the comparative mode of analysis is crucial to this task. The goal is to get at a kind of dialogical understanding of the chosen place, one that is not, to be sure, *objective* (since absolute objectivity is an epistemological impossibility) but one that is able to transcend the limited (subjective, ethnocentric, self-interested) perspectives of individual authors and the interpretive communities to which they belong. By, for example, focusing attention on the ideological presuppositions of authors and the representational and argumentative choices they make, this kind of comparative analysis can reveal much about the meaning and significance of the places in question that would not otherwise be evident. It is not a matter of achieving the more complete understanding of the insider but, on the contrary, of escaping altogether from the perspectival limitations of individual viewpoints. As Westphal puts it, "The space is extracted from the isolated gaze [...] the bipolar relationship between alterity and identity is no longer governed by a simple action but by an interaction. The representation of the space grows from a creative back-and-forth and no longer from a single trajectory coinciding with a single perspective. [...] The principle of geocritical analysis resides in the confrontation of several outlooks which correct each other" (187). The goal, then, is to get as close as possible to what he calls "the identitarian essence of the space in question" (188).

Because of the challenge it poses to the more familiar author-and-text focus of traditional philological and literary historical methods, this approach might seem to call into question the value of studies of the "Joyce's Dublin" or "Hardy's Wessex" type. But actually, Westphal does not present his proposal in a doctrinaire way that would delegitimize such studies. Rather, he wants to build on them in a way that would make geocriticism a kind of metacritical endeavor, one that extends literary studies into the domain of the geographical referent in a way that transcends literature's aesthetic function and seeks to show how it can actually participate in and inflect the history of the places in question.

The Limits of Geocriticism

The boldness and straightforwardness of Westphal's proposal are refreshing, and it brings the dual problem of subjectivism and ethnocentrism into focus in a powerful way. Moreover, whatever we might think about whether such an approach can really afford us access to "the identitarian essence of a place" (which, like absolute objectivity, seems a rather idealistic notion), it shows great promise, both as a mode of comparative literature able to bring divergent literary traditions into contact with each other in an illuminating way and also as a way to explore the enormous significance that some places have taken on in world culture. Having said that, however, it seems important to consider some of the things that get left out of Westphal's account and to think of ways to extend and/or complement the theory of geocriticism. This is a question of the *limits* of geocriticism— not its *limitations* (in the sense of that which it is unable to do) so much as its self-imposed outer limits (the methodological boundaries through which it defines and delimits itself). Consideration of these boundaries will enable us to resurrect some of the legitimate subjects that seem to have been unwittingly excluded from the purview of geocriticism.

As we saw, for Westphal, the specificity of geocriticism is to maintain a geocentric focus, with a variety of texts gathered around a single place. To illustrate the kinds of place he has in mind, Westphal gives a list of cities and regions: Lisbon, Venice, Rome, Paris, Trieste, San Francisco, and so on. In other words, what he has in mind is above all the *hauts lieux* of the literary tradition: places that have a distinct cultural and topographical profile and that have given rise to a whole body of literature. He extends his list to other, less canonical locations (the Dalmation Islands) and even includes imaginary places like Poldevia and Atlantis (193), which have, by virtue of their cultural notoriety, a certain geographical reality despite their fictional or mythological status. He also extends the focus on specific places to generic topographical features like deserts, archipelagoes, and ice floes (194), but he does this primarily as a prelude to the study of singular, named geographical sites. What he does rule out is what he calls "reference to nongeographical places" ["*le renvoi à des lieux non géographiques*"] (194), by which he seems to mean places whose significance is too intimate to find their way onto a map. He refers explicitly to the domestic spaces described in Bachelard's *Poetics of Space* as an example of what *Géocritique* does not cover (194). The implication, if I've understood him correctly, is that such places are not legitimately "geographical places" because they are not singular places. They are not the unique, one-of-a-kind, generally recognized places that have names and can be found on maps.

This seems fair enough, and the emphasis on cultural *hauts lieux* certainly enables his theory to target many of the most notable examples of literary representations of place. Still, I'm not convinced that this is really the only or the best way to guarantee the geographical rigor of a geocentric study of literature.

Another way to lend rigor to a study of literary place would be to focus not on singular places but on particular *types* of place. In this case, the texts studied would deal with sites that might be spread around the globe. The unity of such a study would be guaranteed not by the site-specific singularity of a place but by the shared traits that make it possible to conceive the sites as part of the same category. For example, my research has led to me to develop an interest in squatter cities and shanty towns, marginal places that don't often appear on maps, may not even be named, and remain relatively inaccessible to outsiders. Despite these divergences from Westphal's criteria, I think it would nonetheless be geographically and literarily worthwhile to pen a study on literary representations of the squatter city, which might lead to interesting comparisons between, for example, Vikas Swarup's Mumbai, Athol Fugard's Soweto, Paulo Lins's Rio, Steinbeck's California, Azouz Begag's Lyon, Patrick Chamoiseau's Fort-de-France, and so on. Such a study would have the kind of broad historical and perspectival sweep envisioned by Westphal and could also tie into the many scientific or documentary studies of such places that have been conducted by social scientists, urban planners, economists, and others. Similar projects could be imagined for many other kinds of interstitial geographical entities, such as American-style suburbia, which Robert Beuka studied in *SuburbiaNation*.

Another, more abstract but also more far-reaching extension to Westphal's approach would be to focus not on places nor even kinds of places but on modes of spatial practice. After all, some branches of geography are less interested in mapping out the physical distribution of spatial entities than in the study of the various modes of spatial awareness and activity. The field of behavioral geography, for example, studies spatial reasoning, decision making, and behavior. It focuses on the ways we use and evaluate our environments as well as on the needs, abilities, and goals that explain that behavior. This kind of approach suggests a mode of literary analysis that would organize the study of literary texts in a way that converges neither on singular places nor on categories of place but on behavioral aptitudes and strategies. Take for example the theme of *orientation*. This is not only a fundamental geographic skill (being able to situate oneself and find one's way) but also a universal theme of literature that has important psychological, sociological, and philosophical implications. It takes on particular importance in texts as diverse as the overture to Proust's *In Remembrance of Things Past*, Joyce's *Ulysses*, Samuel Beckett's wandering fictions, Salman Rushdie's *Satanic Verses*, Paul Auster's *New York Trilogy*, and many other texts where spatial orientation is linked to the theme of personal identity. The comparative study of spatial orientation in such texts has much to teach us about the links between spatial awareness and self-awareness, much of which could contribute to the studies of cognitive scientists, architects, and urban planners, not to mention the kinds of philosophy done by Casey, Malpas, and others. What roles do the cues that enable individuals to orient themselves in space play in the constitution of human subjectivity? What are the costs and benefits of uniformity and variation, predictability and surprise, and grids and curves in different kinds of environments? Why are the techniques of spatiotemporal disorientation used by CIA interrogators so effective? Might the standardization and increasing uniformity that give rise to the nonplaces described by Marc Augé (airports, motels, rest stops, fast-food restaurants) disrupt something essential in the spatial practice of those who use them?[17] Is there such a thing as an ecological unconscious?[18]

Having considered these two alternatives to Westphal's focus on individual places (types of places and spatial aptitudes), it is clear that there are many others. We could also focus on a particular kind of geographical technique or tool. Franco Moretti's work on maps provides an important model for this kind of work.[19] We could also build a geocentric study of literature around a consideration of literary techniques that examine, for example, the geographic implications of different modes of description (as Philippe Hamon does in *Expositions*), of different narrative modes and perspectives (as Michel de Certeau does in his opposition between the itinerary and the map), and even of different patterns of rhythm and rhyme (as the French poet Jacques Réda does).[20]

Conclusion

The previously mentioned list clearly could be extended at will. I prefer to end by returning to my basic point: we can agree with Westphal on the importance of juxtaposing literary texts in a geocentric fashion without necessarily concluding that the only or even the best way to do this is to converge on a single place. I have argued that it is equally useful to focus on types of places, spatial practices, geographical modes of analysis, and literary techniques that are not site specific but that are nonetheless integral to the field of geography and to our understanding of the human experience of space and place. Westphal and I agree that the geocentered study of authors or works should lead away from the individual author and work and toward a more general kind of knowledge, one that breaks through the aesthetic frame that sets works of literature off from the world and seeks to use the study of literature as a way to better think about the world around us.

Westphal, as we've seen, is most concerned with using literature to break through to some kind of essential truth about singular places. My work has led me to focus more strongly on the impact that the environmental constraints of place have on the human psyche. I have been struck by the precious resources that literature provides for understanding the human relationship to the environment in terms that would enable a Deleuzian deterritorialization/reterritorialization that is able to see human consciousness as part of nature (the material world) without reducing it to mere structure or epiphenomenon (following the argument of Bonta and Protevi). Whereas Westphal uses textual representation as a lens for focusing attention on individual places, conceived as freestanding, isolated entities, I propose to put the emphasis on place as a manifestation of the dynamic interpenetration of consciousness and world, one that can teach us much about the nature of man's place within the natural order, considered in a thoroughgoing material sense. This implies not declaring the end of man, as the poststructuralists were tempted to do, but knocking humankind off the pedestal that places humanity somehow outside of or above the natural order. Conceiving of such a thing is not difficult; it has now become, I would dare say, the consensus position. But understanding how to represent the human experience of place in a way that reflects this understanding and makes it possible to extend its reach has remained an elusive goal. Taken alongside Westphal's book, then, I believe that the suggestions sketched out in this chapter have the potential to contribute to an even more powerful, inclusive approach to the geocentric study of literature.

Notes

1. Bertrand Westphal, *La Géocritique: Réel, fiction, espace* (Paris: Minuit, 2007).
2. For Lefebvre, artistic representations of space play an important role in overcoming the limitations of the representations created by the "spatial practices" of individuals and the normative "representations of space" that reflect the imperatives of the dominant relations of production. Soja and Harvey, whose work builds in part on Lefebvre's, also emphasize the importance of

social mediation, as does Derek Gregory's *Geographical Imaginations* (Oxford: Blackwell, 1994). Entrikin's *The Betweenness of Place* (Baltimore: Johns Hopkins University Press, 1991), looks to narrative as a way to mediate between scientific representations of space and the subjective experience of place.

3. See Ricoeur's *Time and Narrative* (Chicago: University of Chicago Press, 1984) and Reiss's *Against Autonomy: Global Dialectics of Cultural Exchange* (Palo Alto, CA: Stanford University Press, 2002).

4. An excellent example of this approach would be Richard Lehan's *The City in Literature: An Intellectual and Cultural History* (Berkeley: University of California Press, 1998), which is impressive in its historical scope.

5. See Bachelard's *Poetics of Space* (Boston: Beacon Press, 1994) and Poulet's *Proustian Space* (Baltimore: Johns Hopkins University Press, 1997).

6. See Casey's important series of books on place: *Getting Back Into Place* (Bloomington: Indiana University Press, 1993), *The Fate of Place* (Berkeley: University of California Press, 1997), and *Representing Place* (Minneapolis: University of Minnesota Press, 2002).

7. See Malpas's *The Experience of Place* (Cambridge: Cambridge University Press, 1999) and *Heidegger's Topology: Being, Place, World* (Cambridge, MA: MIT Press, 2007).

8. See Francisco J. Varela, Evan T. Thompson, and Eleanor Rosch's *The Embodied Mind* (Cambridge, MA: MIT Press, 1991).

9. Michel Foucault, *The Order of Things: An Archaeology of the Human Sciences* (New York: Random House, 1970), xxiii, translation modified.

10. See Foucault, "Of Other Spaces," *diacritics* 16 (Spring 1986): 22–7; Maurice Blanchot's "The Conquest of Space," in *The Blanchot Reader* (Oxford: Blackwell, 1995), 269–71; and Michel de Certeau's "Spatial Stories," in *The Practice of Everyday Life* (Berkeley, CA: University of California Press, 2002), which make related arguments also emphasizing the primacy of space over place. Place in these works is dismissed as the product of an excessive reliance on established landmarks and fixed points of reference in the search for meaning.

11. As Marx wrote in *The German Ideology*, "The class which has the means of material production at its disposal, has control at the same time over the means of mental production, so that thereby, generally speaking, the ideas of those who lack the means of mental production are subject to it."

12. Gloria Anzaldúa, *Borderlands/La Frontera: The New Mestiza* (San Francisco: Aunt Lute Books, 1987).

13. Lawrence Buell, "Crosscurrents of Urban Theory," *Configurations* 7, no. 1 (1999): 117.

14. See Deleuze and Guattari, *What Is Philosophy?*, trans. Hugh Tomlinson and Graham Burchell (New York: Columbia University Press, 1994) and Bonta and Protevi, *Deleuze and Geophilosophy* (Edinburgh: Edinburgh University Press, 2004).

15. Robert Tally's translation now makes this important book more readily accessible to English speakers; see *Geocriticism: Real and Fictional Spaces* (New York: Palgrave Macmillan, 2011).

16. Westphal, *Géocritique*, 27; compare the introductory essay of Jameson's *Post-modernism, or, The Cultural Logic of Late Capitalism* (Durham, NC: Duke University Press, 1991). Further references to Westphal's *Géocritique* appear in parentheses.

17. Marc Augé, *Non Places* (London: Verso, 1995).

18. On this last question, see Daniel B. Smith's "Is There an Ecological Unconscious?" (*The New York Times Magazine*, January 27, 2010), which focuses on the possible psychological disorientation caused by disruptions to the natural environment in which we, as a species, evolved. Smith's article focuses on the work of the environmental studies scholar Glenn Albrecht, who coined the term "solastalgia," which is defined as "the pain experienced when there is recognition that the place where one resides and that one loves is under immediate assault [. . .] a form of homesickness one gets when one is still at 'home.'"

19. See, notably, Moretti's *Atlas of the European Novel, 1800–1900* (London: Verso, 1998) and *Graphs, Maps, Trees* (London: Verso, 2005).

20. Philippe Hamon, *Expositions: Literature and Architecture in Nineteenth-Century France* (Berkeley: University of California Press, 1993); Certeau, *The Practice of Everyday Life* (Berkeley, CA: University of California Press, 2002); Jacques Réda, *Le vingtième me fatigue* (Genève: Dogana, 2004).

2

The Presencing of Place in Literature

Toward an Embodied Topopoetic Mode of Reading

Sten Pultz Moslund

One of the most remarkable developments within cultural and literary studies within the last fifty years has been the liberation of notions like movement, migration, multiplicity, difference, and displacement from a subordinate status as mere exceptions to an archaic thinking of individual and cultural life as matters of identity and sedentary settlement. However, the drawback of the successful reassertion of these notions is that matters of physical places and human experiences of emplacement have been generally overlooked or too hastily devalued as less significant. Hans Ulrich Gumbrecht is not off the mark when he identifies the dominance of a Cartesian worldview in the humanities, the body and the physicality of the world being eliminated by the cerebral tenet of *cogito ergo sum*. The study of globalization in particular has become the story of increased detachment from space and physical existence: we are developing a "largely 'digital' relationship to the material world" where "specific physical places" and "the position of [our] bodies" have become entirely irrelevant for "information transfer" and "the activities of [our] minds."[1] Or as Nigel Thrift puts it, nearness has been replaced by distribution as "a guiding metaphor and ambition."[2] These tendencies are also evident in the triumphant language of transcultural mobility within the later development of postcolonial studies, where place, to the extent that it is noticed at all, is something the migrant hero merely passes through, if it is not reduced to the stasis of an oppressive monoglossia of origin and rootedness. In parallel, the renaissance of the idea of world literature has started out with a keen inclination to read texts as cosmopolitan or as detached from the specifics of place. In David Damrosch's view, for instance, world literature as a mode of reading is sometimes talked about as "a form of detached engagement" and in order for a work to "achieve a successful life as world literature," it must be easy to delocalize: its "cultural assumptions" must travel well rather than being steeped in "regional realism."[3]

But the corporal body, locality, place, and experience of physical emplacement have always mattered and continue to matter, in literature, too, even in these times of flux, uprooting, and great speeds of mobility. And paradoxically, as Gumbrecht argues, their significance becomes all the more apparent the longer they are neglected or remain unsatisfied.[4] This may explain the increasing interest in spaces and places that is under way these years: "We are longing for languages that open up and that are shaped by the specific spaces that we call ours."[5] In response to this, the present article will sketch a geocritical approach to literature—a kind of *topopoetic* mode of reading that revives the power of *platial* experiences in literature, to use a term inspired by Edward Casey's study of the rendition of place in the visual arts. In a manner of speaking, this is a reading not for the plot but for the setting, where the setting of the story is not reduced to an expendable passive or ornamental backdrop for the story's action. Rather, place is experienced as one of the primary events of the story and any action is experienced as being shaped, at least partially, by the event of place.

There are numerous approaches to the study of place in literature—place as mapped by discourses and power; place as a transplatial contact zone; place as a dynamic process or event; place as emotional, imagined, remembered, or experienced by the senses. Ideally, our readings will bring all these approaches together, but in the present study, due to the comparative neglect of the body and physicality in contemporary literary studies, I intend to concentrate on the corporal experience of place, or geographies as sensuous geographies, along Paul Rodaway's lines of thinking about geographies as constituted by our senses of smell, taste, touch, hearing, and seeing.[6] This corporal strand of topopoetics, then, which I will isolate for the sake of experiment, reads for the production—or the *poiesis* or *presencing*—of place in literature through the enduring interconnections between place, language, and bodily sensation. Whenever the question falls on literatures of a more place-specific nature (as in the examples I will provide later), we may even be speaking of topopoetics as a *lang*scaping of literature or a reading that maps the work as a *land*guage. The fusion of "language" with "land" or "landscape" points to the way a work's language may be laden with the natural and cultural symptomologies of its setting, endowed with sensory energies that are intricately evocative of things like the topography, flora, fauna, and climate of the place, and, in that way, place may be said to have a form-giving influence on the work—not unlike the way Édouard Glissant believes every landscape to have its specific language.[7] Whenever we move away from landscapes to langscapes, we also move from the detached contemplation of place as scenery and enter into the complex cultural and sensuous experiences of place as a lived-in world. I shall offer a few brief examples of this, but before that, I will venture some theoretical considerations of how we may arrive at an appreciation of the physicality of place in language and literature.

The Presencing of the Physical World in Language

Most significantly, the bodily side to the topopoetics in question involves a mode of reading that moves away from the *representation* of place in literature to a direct presencing of place or sensation of place. The physicality of place in this mode of reading is not something absent to the reader, some passive "out there" that is only textually represented. Place is experienced as present within language and made present by language, if not also, at times, making language possible at all. It involves an approach to literature and language not as meaning and discourse but as phenomena that are capable of triggering a disorganized intensity of sensory experiences or sensory memories of taste, color, smell, touch, warmth, cold, and so on.

To many philosophers and literary scholars, this is precisely the property of the language of art and literature. To Maurice Merleau-Ponty, for instance, the work of art "thrusts us once again into the presence of the world of lived experience," and he speaks of how art "resembles the object of perception" as "its nature is to be seen or heard."[8] George Steiner speaks of visceral and tactile "echoes of sensibility" in the work of art and how "speech is edged in reach of materiality" and capable of translating matter into bodily sensation.[9] Recently, Gumbrecht has argued for a return to such ideas to complicate our disembodied fixation on the sheer "meaning-effects" of literature—as in the preoccupation with discourse and politics of representation in sociocultural analyses or as in the antimaterial varieties of deconstruction that leave behind only the textuality of the signifier. Gumbrecht promotes what he refers to as a "presence-based" way of thinking.[10] An aesthetics of presence is about bringing back to our consciousness and bodies the experience of the *thingness* of the world—the dimension of physical closeness and tangibility in works of art. It is a body-centered experience of art that registers its "presence effects"; that is, how a work *makes a world present* or how it *produces a presence* in the literal sense of "production" as a physical "bringing forth" of something. Presence effects "exclusively appeal to the senses" the way art, in "moments of intensity," touches our bodies and brings "the things of the world close to our skin."[11] Gilles Deleuze coins a useful term in this regard. To Deleuze, a sign always has a meaning, but it also always has an effect, a "sense-effect."[12]

Clearly, the notion of *presence* depends on an idea of language as something other than a medium of representation or a discursive conveyor or imposer of meaning: to reroot art in the substance and materiality of the world, we need a theory of the sign that is capable of bringing back an experience of "the exteriority of the signifier."[13] A topopoetic approach to literature follows Gumbrecht, among others, in returning to Martin Heidegger's philosophy of language.

Heidegger says thus about the linguistic work of art that it does not represent but makes present: "The work as work, in its presencing, is a setting forth, a making."[14] In this connection, Heidegger speaks of language as a naming—language speaks names. And rather than a meaning-centered determination of identity, this naming is really a primordial calling forth: "The naming calls." It calls into appearance: "by naming beings for the first time," language "first brings beings to word and to appearance."[15] We may say that it causes *phusis* to emerge: "It clears and illuminates" and causes "[t]ree and grass, eagle and bull, snake and cricket [to] enter into their distinctive shapes."[16] It is a calling that brings the thingness of the world "into nearness," brings it close to our senses.[17] Precisely because naming things brings things forth or close, as if standing them up before our senses, the word opens toward a prelinguistic sensation that compares with the sensation of the thing itself. This is not a mimetic copy or a true reflection of the object of the thing-world but a triggering of the sensations of that object—as when art, in Deleuze and Guattari's terminology, brings before us "not the resemblance but the pure sensation" of an object, when "the material [is] passing completely into the sensation" or into sense energies.[18] This is also why language as a naming in Heidegger's sense is not necessarily a discursive matter of appropriation, territorialization, or ordering people about, although it can be. Rather than denotation, meaning, and designation, the word opens as a matter of irreducible connotation, association, and sensory experience: like the work of art, language at its poetic depths (in the original Greek sense of *poiēsis* as creation or production) "holds open the Open of the world."[19] Deleuze expresses the same point a little differently. In his opinion the most productive readings happen when words cease to *represent* something else, when they cease to *stand for* something else and instead become pure sense-effects—affects or percepts—that provoke asignifying "intensive states" within the reader.[20] More recently, Fauconnier and Turner have spoken of words as powerful *compressions* of infinite meanings and sensations that may be released through *decompression*.[21] In his Nobel lecture, Derek Walcott made such a decompression of the noun "Antilles," which he said "ripples like brightening water, and the sounds of leaves, palm fronds, and birds are the sounds of a fresh dialect, the native tongue."[22] But for all the sensations this locative triggers in Walcott's experience, his opening of the Open of the word "Antilles," his release of its sense-effects immediately obscures other experiences (tornadoes, earthquakes, destitution). This is one account of what Heidegger means when he says that the calling of a word may conceal as much as it may unconceal. Another way in which the open of the Open is concealed, or reduced, is through cultural mediations of words, which discursively channel our sensuous experiences. Here Heidegger makes a basic distinction between earth and world. Whereas earth refers to a precultural or preconceptual experience of being-in-the-world or the rock bottom *poiesis* of language where it connects directly with *phusis*, Heidegger's "world" refers to all that is less immediate and less fundamental. It is the meaning-based, cultural mediation of a purely sensory experience of the world, a lessening of the immediacy of "earth." However, earth and world are always interconnected in Heidegger. Cultures condition and precondition sensuous experiences, but since sensuous experiences give shape to cultural meaning making in the first place, we may say that the "world," or culture, ultimately "grounds itself on the earth."[23] For this reason Gumbrecht is right in arguing that a "world," or cultural mediation of Being, can in fact be a starting point for a sensory-based presencing of earth, or unconcealment of Being.[24]

The Presencing of Place and Earth

The presencing of the physical dimensions of a text and its signs through sensory experience is relevant to the appreciation of any matter the text may raise (movement, violence, desire, horror, or intimate spaces of cupboards and drawers). As regards the presencing of the physicality or physical experiences of geographical places in literature, Heidegger makes a fundamental connection between art and earth (or nature) when he speaks of earth as the "thingly character" or "thingly substructure" in art: above all, it is earth that gives art existence, and, indeed, language itself, as they both dwell or rest on the ground.[25] Heidegger's "earth" has nothing to do with any neo-romantic ideas of ecological harmony or nationalist territorialization (or it need not be read that way). Rather, it may be read as an expression of how all our "cogitos," our disembodied concepts and abstract ideas and culturally mediated worlds connect deep down with an immediate, precultural sensory experience of the physicality of the thing-world. Or, in Josephine

Machon's words, how the preconceptual or corporal dimension of language "refers human perception back to its own primordial, or *chthonic* (from the Greek 'of, or to, the earth') impulse."[26] So for instance, when Lakoff and Johnson's famous study of how language is fundamentally built on metaphors that are "shaped and constrained by our bodily experiences in the world," by "our interactions in the physical environment,"[27] we are dealing with a tracing of the earth of language in Heidegger's vocabulary.

In Casey's philosophy, Heidegger's earth translates as place and emplacement; we are fundamentally emplaced beings. We impulsively and incessantly establish places through our sensuous and orientational interactions with the world, which makes our envelopment in the physical dimensions of place "the bedrock of our being-in-the-world."[28] Our awareness of this ever-present and fundamental physical grounding or emplacement is lost on our daily communicative uses of language because of the silent workings of the senses, the taken-for-grantedness of place and the dominance of practical, discursive, or meaning-based uses of language. But whereas our "everyday language is a forgotten and therefore used-up poem, from which there hardly resounds any call any longer,"[29] the poetic language of art is capable of revealing "the silent call of the earth" in all things: it may be experienced as no less than a presencing or "setting forth of earth."[30] A topopoetics, then, is sensitive to the *silent* calls in the artwork's language of the physicality of place (poetry as *poiesis*) and the sensory experience of place and physical emplacement (poetry as *aesthesis*). And it is sensitive to the ways in which the language and the culture of the work (including movements and transcultural dynamics) dwell in the *physicality* of the world, or, more precisely, the ways in which the physicality of place may give shape to or affect the language of the work and its cultural worldviews, as well as the processes of cultural transformation it may engage or involve. A topopoetic reading is sensitive to how "[t]he world grounds itself on the earth and [how] the earth juts through the world."[31] Or, in geographic terms, whenever we are dealing with a work of a particular platial setting (wild, rural, or urban), a topopoetic reading examines how physical dimensions and elementals (such as topography, horizontality, verticality, earth, wind, water, light, vegetation, density, or scarcity of matter) fill out the work through its language.[32] The following examples are only a few random illustrations of how a topopoetic reading may engage with specific textual features.

Examples of Topopoetic Appreciation

In a topopoetic reading, a simple place name may unleash a rush of presence effects, as in the case of Walcott's Antilles, and the same goes for any other vocabular feature such as names of place-specific plants and animals, geological and topographic features, names of climactic characteristics and weather phenomena, names of rain and rock, and so on. In this respect, as Casey observes, landscapes, as well as artistic renditions of landscapes are *panperceptual*; they appeal "to the full bodily sensorium."[33] A topopoetic reading involves a panperceptual appreciation of the work: we read the work's geography with our entire body, and as in Rodaway's sensuous geographies, all odorous, haptic, auditory, and visual evocations of place combine as the presencing of a great synesthetic experience or event of place. Smells, tastes, hardnesses, softnesses, temperatures, sounds, and sights hit us all "at one stroke."[34] In Harold Sonny Ladoo's novel of the Indian diaspora in the Caribbean, *No Pain Like This Body*, we find ourselves in the midst of a rural area of rice fields and small plots of sugar cane, surrounded by tropical forest with hills and mountains in the distance. There is a small settlement of mud huts. We are in the rainy season. The air is humming with insects: black and blue flies and crickets. If read topopoetically, these words are not just flat, textual signifiers: all of them are names that trigger or presence an inner image of shapes and colors and blended with sounds, smells, and haptic sensations of the heat and moisture of the climate. No object in the text is too small to dwell on: the name of a single tree may open a complexity of sensations, such as the sound of its rustling leaves, the touch of its trunk, the movements of its branches, the multiple smells of leaves, wood, and fruit, the colors of shifting greens and browns, the warmth or coolness it gives off. Or try listening to how it is in fact the sound that brings out the contours of the place, as when the rain beats the mango trees ("wish wish wish"), the grass roof ("par par par"), and other objects close to the hut ("tarat tat tat tarat tat tat" and "clat clat clat").[35]

A topopoetics may appreciate the ways in which the vocabulary of a text is affected by, or sometimes produced by, the environment of its setting. In this regard, a topopoetics within a language like English will be particularly sensitive to the presencing of place through the untranslatability of local varieties of English, or englishes: how a variety of English, such as Australian English or Scots (or even local variations of these), may be experienced at the same time as part of the soundscape of the work's place, like any sound imagery, and part of a local naming, not least through loan words, or untranslatable chunks from aboriginal languages (Warlpiri, Celtic, etc.) that speak of earlier or coexisting languages of emplacement. In Ladoo's novel, the *sound* of "skopian" and "wadder" for "scorpion" and "water" are particular sounds of this place, the sounds of human voices in the landscape, just as loan words in Australian texts, like "goanna," "syllabub," "cockatoo," "wallaby," "kangaroo," or "billabong" create a bind between the text and the specificity of place. As Derrida says, the "symptomology" of accent—or dialect or style—in this way actually "invades" the infinite errantry of writing, like the untranslatability of proper names.[36]

However, as much as specific place names or individual place-specific words or the particular sound of a dialect or language variety may call forth the presence of places in themselves, a topopoetic reading of literatures in English will also be sensitive to how the setting of a story affects universal or standard words in English; how, for instance, the embodied perception of common nouns like "tree" or "grass" are inevitably conditioned by the geographical setting of the text. Think of how we automatically sense the word "tree" or "bush" in radically different ways when appearing in an African setting and an English setting, respectively, or in a text from the jungle in British Guyana—an entire hidden heterogeneity is produced in a word by the physiognomic differences of different places, surroundings, and contexts. The English language is already being affected by the specifics of place, in invisible or silent ways, from the moment it enters into or speaks from a particular landscape. The Kalahari chapter in Coetzee's *Duskland*, for example, may be read as the drama of a colonialist language as it sets out to subdue a place by naming it, but contrary to the objectives of the novel's colonialist conqueror, a self-proclaimed "tamer of the wild,"[37] the desert soon takes over and starts speaking the names he speaks. Just as the place inevitably enters the main character through his body, nose, ears, eyes, and heart,[38] the place inevitably enters the language of the book, issuing forth the smells of this place, its tastes and its sounds, its heat, its colors, its shapes and its temporal dimensions—the signified of the words "bush" or "buck" or "cow" are not the same anymore; they are no longer issuing forth from any familiar English ontology. In a radical topopoetics, they are not even mediating a foreign world through a known language; they are issuing forth directly from the Kalahari: merging with this place, once familiar words are turning into foreign words for a distant reader.

A reading that is place sensitive is not to be equated with an argument for place-boundedness. Any literature of any place also carries the traces and memories of other places in the depths of its language. The landscape of the English language may very well be read as the language of the "meadow," as Glissant mockingly does,[39] but the deeper poetry of English calls forth the peregrination of a heterogeneity of landscapes and places from all over the world. The very word "meadow," for instance, has arrived over the Proto-Germanic *mædwon* from the Indo-European *metwa*. The word "jungle," so crucial in Glissant's poetics of the Caribbean, has travelled from the Hindi *jangal*. A topopoetic reading may therefore appreciate how the language of emplacement in one place is full of languages of emplacement from other places (with new ones continually arriving), and, consequently, how a language can therefore never be said to be fully in place or to be *naturally* of a place. Such difference or *Unheimlichkeit* is integral to any language, place, or place experience, and yet the bodily thrust of a topopoetics will remain sensitive to how language is always caught up in a process of emplacement: words from other languages of emplacement are continually domesticated to become, in this moment, distinctively of this place or caused, in this moment, distinctively to be speaking this place— the word "jungle" in Wilson Harris's novels of Guyana uniquely presences the jungle of the Amazon basin before anything else. As in Casey's philosophy, any accent of emplacement in a topopoetic reading is not to be equated with stasis or finality but with a continual process of *reemplacement*: changing languages of emplacement are always in the process of getting back into changing physical places.[40]

The processes of linguistic emplacement are intimately connected with processes of cultural emplacement, or reemplacement. Engaging the blending of world and earth, a topopoetic reading may register how place is presenced in language as the product of interactions between human bodies and the world, between culture and nature—for instance, in the ways in which human experience, actions, movements, and features are described or perceived through metaphors drawn from the local climate, flora, and fauna. On the surface of things, the characters in Ladoo's novel of Indo-Caribbean displacement are constantly chased around by the harsh conditions of the landscape and the weather. Indeed Ladoo's book seems to enact the breathlessness Glissant has noted as a remarkable feature of the Caribbean folktale, where an inhospitable landscape typically offers no time to rest, no time for characters to root themselves or "gaze on things."[41] However, at a silent, nonexplicated level of the novel, at the poetic level of the text that emerges if we take the time to dwell on it, the characters, as well as the work itself, are clearly becoming *of* this place. Human features, actions, movements, and sensations turn out to be understood almost exclusively through the natural features of the place, its flora and fauna, and its weather. Eyes are "bulging like ripe guavas," a man is "strong like a carat tree," Pa is pulling at Ma "as if he was uprooting a sapodilla tree," Ma is "quiet as a mango skin," and the shaking of a rice bag sounds like "opening a dry coconut with a dull cutlass."[42] In a Deleuzian reading, the characters of the place no longer differ from the wind blowing or the colors of the landscapes or its sounds. Everything enters into composition with everything else.[43] Or from a Heideggerian perspective, the physical world in Ladoo ceases to be an unreceptive element that is outside the characters or observable from a state of exteriority. Rather, the characters are subject to it and transported into its Being.[44] And it is not that this emplacement has been deliberately fashioned in language or forged. Rather, this place, and the unconscious reciprocal process of human embodied emplacement in it, produces the language in the first place: the language of the text becomes entirely place-saturated as a local landguage. Appreciating the novel's language as a landguage is an appreciation of how the physiognomy of the place is not external but interiorized into the local self-perception, becoming part of the unconscious "perceptual infrastructure" of the characters as it is indeed part of the "perceptual infrastructure" of the text itself:[45] so the physicality of the earth of this place starts jutting through the cultural world of the deracinated characters, just as the earth of the place juts through the cultural world of the novel itself.

Appreciating the earth of the novel's language, its poetry, means that the novel comes to stand in a place,[46] dwelling in it, or *on* it, and that any intercultural and interplatial relations and changes, as much as they are shaping a place, also take shape within and in relation to the physicality of this place. Topopoetically, we approach the novel and its signifiers, not as standing *for* the place, representing the place from some outside view that dwells nowhere and everywhere, but as standing *in* that very place that comes through or ushers in to the reader's nearness. We may even be said to enter the platial dimensions of the work, experiencing our own emplacement within the scene. The landscape in the work, or the place, seems to open up in front of us, behind us, above us, and beneath us; "it sweeps us in" and engages us in "full body participation."[47] We are taken "beyond the words," as Merleau-Ponty puts it; we no longer notice the words on the page; the language of the text "sweeps [us] on from the signs" and "throws us toward the things it signifies."[48] The words of sky or mountain or rain metamorphose into sensations, into the wordlessness of all substance. Semantic interpretation and outside readings no longer apply, presence takes over. We enter into what Deleuze and Guattari refer to as "close vision." In close vision, "no line separates earth from sky [. . .] there is neither horizon nor background nor perspective nor limit not outline or form or center; there is no intermediary distance." When close enough, "space is not visual, or rather the eye itself has a haptic, nonoptical function."[49] And as for the appreciation of the processes of cultural emplacement, we get to sense a culture from within its perceptual framework rather than judging it from the outside: we get closer to the way locals may be said to apprehend their reality more aesthetically than conceptually.

Conclusion

Although the names and images that populate the languages of the literary examples in this chapter clearly gravitate to the place experiences of specific settings or localities, a topopoetic reading that ushers in the presence of a place as a synesthesia of colors and shapes and sounds and temperatures is not easy at all. To appreciate the poetry or the earth or physicality or the platial depths of language—to reopen the sensory experiences of words that have been closed off by our cerebral and discursive preoccupations—is almost like resuscitating a dead language within a living language. This is mainly because we live in what Gumbrecht calls a meaning culture as opposed to a presence culture, and hence we keep falling out of the experience of physical presence of things or places to consider them rationally from the outside.[50] We cannot help but interpret and look for meaning, which is when sensation wanes and discourse and rationality reemerge. We do not dwell on the trees of a work; we tend to scan over such phenomena to get on with the story, the meaning, the intention, or the politics of representation. Art unconceals "the silent call of the earth" in all things, but in everyday life only the discursive, communicative, or meaning-based utility of words remains visible, while the subterranean sensory dimension of our interaction with the world, and the words of the world, continues unnoticed.

Second, there is the problem of distance. The assumption goes without saying that the experience of the sense-effects of a langscape will be most intense if the reader lives in the place and the climate of that langscape or is somehow endowed with a sensory memory of the place—you will almost automatically comprehend a work set on your childhood street in an aesthetic or sensory mode of reception rather than, or at least alongside, a conceptual and analytic mode. This is also where I, as an outsider of the place in a novel like Ladoo's, who may never even have been to the Caribbean, cannot experience the intensity of the presencing of the place the way a local reader is likely to. I do not have the sensory memory from the immediate physical contact that inhabits the language of the book. My physical sensation of the place may travel along the English words that I recognize and bring "the presence of what was previously uncalled into a nearness."[51] Yet the English words, or words from any other language that have travelled to this place ("bandicoot," "jumbie moko," "meri," "kola"), have also come to grow into the landscape of this place and now grow out of this place again as foreign words, so that I may feel left without the signified of a simple, common signifier in English like *tree* (let alone the fact that I have no idea of what a specified signified like *carat tree* looks like or feels like or smells like). Ladoo's landguage "brings the presence of what was previously uncalled into a nearness," yet "the call does not wrest what it calls away from the remoteness, in which it is kept by the calling there."[52] But I can choose to do without the sensory dimensions of Ladoo's novel—that is the easiest thing.

Imagination travels more freely than the trades of local specificity and embodied experience, which makes it very easy to read literature from other, distant settings. But the more boundless imagination rules my reading (which by itself is one of the most wonderful aspects of literature), the more I distance myself from the physical experience of the particularity of place or the physical background of the imagined dimension of the text or "the work's perceptual qualities."[53] As Casey says, there are no "genuine locations in imagined space [...] only transitory *locales*, which do not last from one imaginative presentation to another."[54] This is no problem at all in a purely literary discussion, but whenever our engagement with literature and language in one way or another involves questions of geography, cultural capital, and human relations, which is certainly the case in postcolonial studies and world literature, there is a danger that the liberties of free imagination come to work as the primary drive of popular paradigms like uprootedness, displacement, and transculturation. Likewise, when all literature is uprooted from context, it lends itself beautifully as a suggestion of the effortlessness of global multicultural distribution and flux. As Casey continues, there is a "lack of background" or *Hintergrund* in "imagined content": the "imaginative presentation" has an "insistently frontal character" that "dominates the spatiality of all that we imagine."[55] That is why it is so easy from a placeless and disembodied imaginative point of view to speak of distribution and free cultural flows as the primary forces of the contemporary world while dispensing entirely with the friction of places and processes of human emplacement. Things become far more complex the moment we equip human beings with bodies and see the imagined dimensions of their cultures and transcultural processes as interacting with physical dimensions and local environs.

Whereas the implications of a notion like "detached reading" seems to make it hard to enter into any serious engagement with place, the geographical impulse of a topopoetic reading turns directly to *place* as a primary paradigm of reading. Yet entering into the place of a text or into its landguage, or its "regional realism," still brings in questions of the globe, not only because all places are "contact zones" of local and global forces of change,[56] but also in terms of reception: after all I am reading of one place in the world from the distance of a completely different place. But here a topopoetics operates with a different epistemology of the globe than the discourse of globalization. It aligns with Spivak's idea of *planetarity*, which is far more sensitive to the gravitational nearness of the *earth* of local worlds than the disembodied communication highways of globalization. "The globe is on our computers. No one lives there," and "everyday cultural detail, condition and effect of sedimented cultural idiom, does not come up into satellite country."[57] Planetarity is a "learning to learn from below" toward a view of or an imagining of the earth that "undergirds" the global.[58] Like this, a topopoetics does not dissolve places into an abstract globalized *space* but sees the world and processes of change as coming forth within specific places.

So moving into the platial depth of the novel, as in a Deleuzian close vision, is really a moving out, too. We may be going so deep that we emerge through the bottom to the other side, not into the privileged "satellite country" of globalization but into place's position on the earthy surface of the planet, where the embodied experience of reality is shared by all humans. In spite of the fact that our experiences of and thus our sensitivity to different climates and topographies differ widely, we all share fundamental sense memories of the elementals of the world that fill out all places: vegetation, earth, rock, water, weather, light, sound, temperature, color, and so on. Our memory of how these elementals fill out the environs we live in or are near to may stretch into a kind of sense-based imagination that is capable of appreciating how the elementals and the bodily experience of elementals fill out or shape languages, cultural processes, and literatures of distant places in other ways than our own. Hence in a topopoetic approach, it is not so much the work that is uprooted from its locality and distributed to the nearness of a distant reader as much as it is the distant reader who stretches toward the place or the nearness of the work. It is not a matter of experiencing a location inside our "present here," to paraphrase Heidegger, but to let our thinking, our embodied thinking, "get through, persist through, the distance to that location," to the nearness of the place from where the work "*begins its presencing.*"[59]

Notes

1. Hans Ulrich Gumbrecht, "A Negative Anthropology of Globalization," in *The Multiple Faces of Globalization*, ed. Francisco González et al. (Madrid: BBVA, 2009), 234, 239, 231.
2. Nigel Thrift, "Space," *Theory, Culture and Society* 23, no. 2/3 (2006): 145.
3. David Damrosch, *What Is World Literature?* (Princeton, NJ: Princeton University Press, 2003), 4, 281, 289, 217.
4. Gumbrecht, "Negative Anthropology," 232.
5. Ibid., 240.
6. Paul Rodaway, *Sensuous Geographies: Body, Sense and Place* (London: Routledge, 1994).
7. Édouard Glissant, *Caribbean Discourse: Selected Essays* (Charlottesville: University Press of Virginia, 1999), 146.
8. Maurice Merleau-Ponty, *The World of Perception* (London: Routledge, 2008), 69, 71.

9. George Steiner, *Real Presences: Is There Anything in What We Say?* (Chicago: University of Chicago Press, 1991), 9, 15, 16.

10. Hans Ulrecht Gumbrecht, *The Production of Presence: What Meaning Cannot Convey* (Stanford: Stanford University Press, 2004), 18, 19.

11. Ibid., xiii–xiv, xv, 9, 19, 97, 106.

12. Gilles Deleuze, *Essays Critical and Clinical* (Minneapolis: University of Minnesota Press, 1997), 138.

13. Gumbrecht, *Production*, 19.

14. Martin Heidegger, *Poetry, Language, Thought* (New York: HarperCollins, 2001), 42, 44.

15. Ibid., 196, 71.

16. Ibid., 41.

17. Ibid., 196.

18. Gilles Deleuze and Félix Guattari, *What Is Philosophy?* (London: Verso, 2003), 166–67; see also 164, 168, 182–83.

19. Heidegger, *Poetry, Language, Thought*, 25, 44; see also 71.

20. See Deleuze, *Essays Critical and Clinical*, 141; and Gilles Deleuze and Félix Guattari, *Kafka: Toward a Minor Literature* (Minneapolis: University of Minnesota Press, 1986), 21–23.

21. See Gilles Fauconnier and Mark Turner, *The Way We Think: Conceptual Blending and the Mind's Hidden Complexities* (New York: Basic Books, 2003), 92–96, 101–9, 182–83.

22. Derek Walcott, "The Antilles: Fragments of Epic Memory," *What the Twilight Says: Essays* (London: Faber and Faber, 1998), 79.

23. Heidegger, *Poetry, Language, Thought*, 48.

24. Gumbrecht, *Production*, 77.

25. Heidegger, *Poetry, Language, Thought*, 37, 41, 68.

26. Josephine Machon *(Syn)aesthetics: Redefining Visceral Performance* (New York: Palgrave Macmillan, 2009), 5, 6.

27. George Lakoff and Mark Johnson, *Metaphors We Live By* (Chicago: University of Chicago Press, 2003), 246–47.

28. Edward Casey, "How to Get from Space to Place in a Fairly Short Stretch of Time: Phenomenological Prolegomena," in *Senses of Place*, ed. Steven Feld and Keith H. Basso (Santa Fe: School of American Research Press, 2003), 21, 22; Edward Casey, *Getting Back into Place. Toward a Renewed Understanding of the Place-World* (Bloomington: Indiana University Press, 1993), xvii.

29. Heidegger, *Poetry, Language, Thought*, 205.

30. Ibid., 33, 46.

31. Ibid., 47.

32. Edward Casey, *Representing Place: Landscape Painting and Maps* (Minneapolis: University of Minnesota Press, 2002), 32–37.

33. Ibid., 6.

34. Sartre quoted in Merleau-Ponty, *World of Perception*, 48.

35. Harold Sonny Ladoo, *No Pain Like This Body* (Toronto: House of Anansi Press, 2003), 19, 120, 19–21, 124.

36. Jacques Derrida, *Monolingualism of the Other; or, The Prosthesis of Origin* (Palo Alto: Stanford University Press, 1998), 46.

37. J. M. Coetzee, *Dusklands* (London: Vintage, 2004), 77.

38. Ibid.

39. Édouard Glissant, *Caribbean Discourse*, xxxvi, 146.

40. See Casey, *Getting Back into Place*, 297.

41. Glissant, *Caribbean Discourse*, 131.

42. Ladoo, *No Pain Like This Body*, 6, 14, 77, 13, 54, 41.

43. Deleuze, *Essays Critical and Clinical*, 169.

44. Heidegger, *Poetry, Language, Thought*, 43.

45. Casey, "How to Get from Space to Place," 19.

46. Casey, *Representing Place*, 19, 75, 89.

47. Ibid., 29, 261.

48. Maurice Merleau-Ponty, "The Prose of the World," *Tri-Quarterly* 20, no. 9 (1971): 16.

49. Gilles Deleuze and Félix Guattari, *A Thousand Plateaus: Capitalism and Schizophrenia* (London: Continuum, 2003), 494.

50. Gumbrecht, *Production*, 106, 79–89.

51. Heidegger, *Poetry, Language, Thought*, 196.

52. Ibid.

53. Edward Casey, *Imagining: A Phenomenological Study* (Bloomington: Indiana University Press, 2000), 141.

54. Ibid., 156.

55. Ibid.

56. Mary Louise Pratt, *Imperial Eyes: Travel Writing and Transculturation* (London: Routledge, 1992).

57. Gayatri Chakravorty Spivak, *The Death of a Discipline* (New York: Columbia University Press, 2003), 16, 72.

58. Ibid., 94, 100.

59. Heidegger, *Poetry, Language, Thought*, 152, 156.

Part II

Places, Spaces, and Texts

3

Redrawing the Map

An Interdisciplinary Geocritical Approach to Australian Cultural Narratives

Peta Mitchell and Jane Stadler

Space, place, and landscape are long-standing themes in Australian literary and cultural studies and, from the colonial era to the present day, Australian cultural narratives have proven fertile ground for spatial analysis. In his influential 1986 book on Australian film and literature, *National Fictions*,[1] Graeme Turner argues that narrative forms are, in the Australian context, profoundly tied up with national myths of land, landscape, and identity. Moreover, Turner argues, Australian filmic and fictive texts "invite us to accept that the land is central to a distinctively Australian meaning."[2] This concept of the "land producing its literature" has, he continues, in turn influenced both Australian literary and film criticism, though the former more strongly than the latter.[3] This carries through into theater for, as Joanne Tompkins argues in her landmark study *Unsettling Space*,[4] spatial tensions driven by anxieties about contested land, nationalism, colonial settlement, and Aboriginal reconciliation play out as narratives on the Australian stage, where the performance of nationhood and identity is dramatically enacted: "Australian theatre not only contests conventional Australian history and culture; it also stages alternative means of managing the production of space in a spatially unstable nation."[5]

One reason for this emphasis on spatial enquiry in Australian cultural studies is the fact that, as Allaine Cerwonka has noted, Australian history has traditionally "been imagined in relation to geography. Its history testifies to how colonization largely depended on spatial practices that shaped the landscape."[6] In his *Geographical Imaginations*,[7] Derek Gregory points out the interrelationship between imagination, geography, and spatial politics, and nowhere has this been more evident than in the mapping, naming, and colonization of the Australian continent. Certainly, the iconic nature of Australia's landform—its status as the "island continent"— affords it a singular place in the cultural-geographic imaginary, and one that has invited a textual-geographic reading of its history of colonization.

In his seminal 1988 "essay in spatial history," *The Road to Botany Bay*,[8] Paul Carter argues that the continent's "discoverers, explorers and settlers were making spatial history. They were choosing directions, applying names, imagining goals, inhabiting the country."[9] This process was, in itself, an exercise in spatial imagining, for, as Carter describes it, his concept of "spatial history" cannot simply be equated to the "geographer's space"; rather, he says, what spatial history evokes "are the spatial forms and fantasies through which a culture declares its presence. It is spatiality as a form of nonlinear writing; as a form of history."[10] Following Carter, Simon Ryan argues that the process of Western exploration effectively reified the Australian landscape as a "blank text, ready to be inscribed by the impending colonial process."[11] This "textualization" of the landscape has in turn been played out in Australian cultural narratives, particularly in Australian literature. Indeed, according to Martin Leer, the "evocative power" of Australia's cartographical image may be the reason "Australian literature has been more diligent in literally, metaphorically, and self-consciously mapping the continent than almost any other old or emerging national literature."[12]

Carter and Ryan's work exemplifies the spatial focus that has typified Australian cultural studies, a focus that received new impetus with the "spatial turn" identified by Edward Soja and Fredric Jameson in the late 1980s and early 1990s.[13] Across Australian film, literary, and theater studies, spatial enquiry—or approaching texts from a spatial/geographical perspective as well as from a temporal/historical one—has become increasingly important since the 1980s. Yet despite the centrality of space as a theme in Australian film, literature, and theater research over the past thirty years, very little research has been done to bring these strands of spatial enquiry into dialogue. In this chapter, we trace the largely separate—and until now unmapped—traditions of spatial enquiry in literary geography; film geography; and Australian film, literature, and theater studies; and we suggest ways in which the concept of geocriticism might provide a unified approach to examining how place is depicted and translated across media forms. Finally, we discuss how a geocritical method might be applied to an interdisciplinary and multimodal research project examining representations of Australian landscape and locations.

Geocritical Traditions: Literary Geography, Film Geography, and Traditions of Spatial Enquiry in Australian Literary, Film, and Theater Studies

In 1947, geographer John K. Wright made an appeal in the *Annals of the Association of American Geographers* for a new breed of geographers trained in literary studies whose "research and teaching would be directed toward the discovery and the interpretation of geographical truth, belief, and error as they find and have found literary and artistic expression."[14] These aesthetic geographers, or "geosophers," Wright argued, would open the discipline up to new kinds of evidence and new ways of thinking about geography. Certainly geographers had been employing literary texts to support more traditional geographical research much earlier than the 1940s,[15] but Wright's is one of the first explicit calls for defined literary geography.

It took some decades for Wright's call to be heeded in any way that might resemble the formation of a subdiscipline, but by the late 1970s and early 1980s a number of geographers were either doing literary geography (in the form of studies of regional novels) or making cases for its validity as an area of study.[16] What is clear from both Wright's 1947 appeal and the studies that appeared in the 1980s is that one kind of aesthetic text is clearly privileged: the novel, which J. Douglas Porteous argues has "reign[ed] supreme" as literary geographers' genre of choice.[17] According to Douglas C. D. Pocock, poetry does not offer itself so readily to geographical analysis, for it "is less concerned with the observation of landscape than with its use to set in motion the writer's subjective response," while in theater, any concentration on setting "would detract from its prime study of character."[18] Noticeably absent from any analysis of aesthetic or literary geography through to the 1990s is any mention of film as a cultural form for analysis.[19] Indeed, in 1994 Stuart C. Aitken and Leo E. Zonn noted that film had been virtually ignored by the discipline of geography.[20]

Moreover, as Joanne P. Sharp argues, these foundational studies in literary geography have been characterized by a certain naïveté toward the literary text, which is viewed as universal, "unproblematic, and self-evident in its immediate beauty."[21] This insistence upon universality marks a clear distinction between the aims and assumptions of literary geography and of cultural geography more broadly, for, as Sharp argues, although "universalist positions have been heavily critiqued in other parts of geography," they remain "strangely underexamined for literature and other arts."[22] What seems at first an odd incongruence between literary and cultural geography becomes less perplexing when considered in the context of the former's history. As Marc Brosseau astutely points out, literary geography did not arise out of "research on discursive, semantic, or symbolic

structures—with the corollary rejection of the subject and/or history"—
research that was re-forming and reframing literary studies at the time—
but rather "within a humanistic project designed to restore 'man,' meaning
and values in geography."[23]

In this sense, then, there has been little to connect literary geography
with the discipline of literary studies as it developed over the same period,
and this is perhaps partly because what is a strength in one has been considered a weakness in the other. Andrew Thacker argues that, although literary
studies has a long tradition of engaging with spatio-geographical aspects of
literary works, literary scholars have "quite often [. . .] read these texts by
subjugating their spatiality to that of an aesthetic theme or trope."[24] Similarly, Fabio Lando makes the point that, while literary geographers have
often overlooked the literary context of the novels they analyze, literary
scholars have often "interpret[ed] the man/environment relationship only
in clumsy, deterministic terms."[25] According to Thacker, this all changed in
1989, when he says, with self-conscious hyperbole, "literary and cultural
critics all read David Harvey's *The Condition of Postmodernity.*"[26] Harvey's
work, along with that of Soja and Jameson, among others, enabled the
development of a kind of "geographical criticism," one that "enabled questions of space and geography [to] become recognized as legitimate and
important topics in many areas of literary and cultural studies."[27]

Certainly in the mid- to late 1980s, Martin Leer and Graham Huggan
were beginning to hold Australian literature up to a dual geographical/
postcolonial view, with Huggan in his seminal 1989 essay "Decolonizing
the Map" invoking both cartographic historian J. B. Harley and Edward
Said.[28] In his 1994 book, *Territorial Disputes*, Huggan argues that the prev-
alence of maps and mapping in contemporary Australian and Canadian
writing must be understood as an active engagement in the "politics of
cultural representation," shifting the countries' spatial paradigm from a
"cartography of exile" to a "cartography of difference."[29] Following Huggan's book and starting in the mid-1990s, a stream of major literary studies
devoted to space and spatiality emerged,[30] but of these publications, virtually none has been cited in the published literature on literary geography
post 1995, and vice versa, bearing out the clear disconnect between literary
geography and geographically inflected literary studies.

When film geography began to emerge within the discipline of geography in the early 1990s,[31] it not only responded to the comparative lack of
attention to cinema by geographers, but it also diverged from literary geography's universalizing tendencies. This divergence between literary and
film geography—the two streams of geography that directly engage with
narrative fiction—has meant there has been very little dialogue between
the two. They appear to exist as two different subdisciplines with different

histories, approaches, and assumptions. By 2006, Christopher Lukinbeal and Stefan Zimmermann were calling for film geography to be recognized as a new subfield of geography.[32] Under the banner of film geography, Lukinbeal and Zimmermann posit four trajectories: geopolitics (examining mise-en-scène and narrative), cultural politics (revealing contested sociospatial meanings), globalization (exploring the impact of economic and pragmatic imperatives on film production, distribution, and reception in terms of selecting, representing, and visiting film locations) and, finally, concerns about film's capacity to mimic or accurately reflect real landscapes and locations in accordance with scientific and aesthetic models of realism. These trajectories broadly correspond to approaches to film within Australian cinema studies, and they speak to the development of film geography out of an engagement with existing scholarship in cinema studies.

Within Australian cinema studies itself, what Lukinbeal and Zimmermann describe as the "globalization trajectory" corresponds to pragmatic approaches that examine the political and spatial economy of production logistics;[33] the "cultural politics trajectory" corresponds to accounts of land rights, immigration, indigeneity, and belonging;[34] and "geopolitics" encompasses not only the very large body of work on mise-en-scène criticism but also studies that focus on regionality[35] and cinematic cartography.[36] With the exception of debates around the use of CGI to alter the physical landscape in Baz Luhrmann's 2008 film, *Australia*, Lukinbeal and Zimmermann's fourth trajectory, the concern with "science, representation, and mimesis," appears to be the focus of geographers rather than film scholars. Nevertheless, unlike literary geography's relationship to literary studies, film geography's approaches and assumptions are much more closely aligned with those of film studies. Further, with respect to Lukinbeal and Zimmermann's trajectories, Australian cinema studies has been dominated by concerns with the cultural politics of location. Indeed, this focus unites the only analyses of Australian cinema by film geographers and the wideranging analyses by film scholars with an interest in landscape.[37]

Because film studies first took root in the Australian university system as an offshoot of more established modes of literary and cultural criticism, it is unsurprising that critical approaches to cinematic geography within film studies have until recently been dominated by studies of structural dichotomies, narrative symbolism, and postcolonial critiques of *terra nullius* derived from literary analysis and informed by aesthetic approaches to representations of landscape, such as mise-en-scène criticism drawn from art history and theater studies. Within this tradition of criticism, many scholars have examined how Australian cinema has tended to locate colonization and experiences of survival and belonging in the physical environment in relation to an ideal of identity and nation-building associated with European masculine endeavor. Much contemporary research still approaches cinematic representations of landscape in this manner; however, fresh approaches to landscape informed by disciplines such as tourism studies and geography are emerging within film studies.

This shift away from understandings of film narrative based in literary criticism toward a more geographic and cartographic, historicized conception of screen space can be traced, in the Australian context, to Ross Gibson's influential research in the 1990s. Gibson took up a perspective often advanced by geographers and geocritical theorists and distinguished between the omniscient viewing position of the modern map and pre-Renaissance maps that "like medieval icon paintings, presume the existence of a reader who is *inside* the scene, not separate and voyeuristic of it at all."[38] Gibson compares these European representations of landscape with the view of the land offered in cinema and in non-Western systems of representation such as Aboriginal paintings. In *Australian National Cinema*, Tom O'Regan follows Gibson in describing the recently colonized landscape as taking on an emblematic identity in Australian cinema to the extent that film narration is a way of staking a claim on the land: "A sense of youth and beginning anew is paradoxically associated with an ancient landscape, a unique flora and fauna and, more lately, Aboriginal people and their heritage."[39] In an important contribution to the turn toward films that engage with indigenous perspectives, Felicity Collins and Therese Davis's book *Australian Cinema after Mabo* draws out the cultural politics and contested significance of postcolonial representations of land.[40]

Unlike literary and film studies, theater studies has no direct counterpart within geography—there is no "theater geography" *per se*, and, indeed, very few studies of theater, drama, or theatrical performance exist that are written from within geography as a discipline.[41] Although space has been subject to critical analysis within theater studies, such research principally engages with staging space and representations of landscapes.[42] Most studies of space in Australian theater analyze set design and mise-en-scène or dramaturgical uses of stage space, or they take a postcolonial approach to contested narrative spaces.[43] The postcolonial framework of analysis has been particularly fruitful, leading to Tompkins's concept of "unsettlement" and Helen Gilbert's work on spatial histories within indigenous theater and cartographies of the stagescape and landscape in what she terms settler/invader plays in *Sightlines: Race, Gender, and Nation in Contemporary Australian Theatre*.[44] Geographical approaches to theater are rare, yet, as Stephen Carleton's work suggests, drama studies is ripe for geocriticism: "Theatre not only represents space, it enacts space. It reads, politicizes and activates the ways in which we imagine cultural geographies. It brings

Australian landscapes to the fore and populates and physicalises them in conscious and frequently metaphoric or metonymic ways."[45]

The approaches outlined previously can broadly be termed geocritical and interdisciplinary in the sense that they take a critical approach to geographical representation in narrative fiction. However, as we have noted, literary geography and film geography are distinct traditions within geography, each with its own histories and assumptions. Similarly, although spatial enquiry has been a preoccupation for Australian literary, film, and theater studies since the 1980s, very little research exists that brings these strands into dialogue to examine how spaces are depicted and translated across media forms. Aside from Roslynn Haynes's *Seeking the Centre*,[46] there has been little sustained intermedia analysis of representations of Australian space beyond edited collections or themed journal issues.[47] As with film geography's relationship to literary geography, this lack of intermedia spatial analysis within Australian cultural studies is partly a question of disciplinary politics, and again the question of literature's "primacy" is at the fore, particularly in regard to film studies. As Turner argues, "[t]he problem of making links between film and fiction [. . .] lies in the fact that historically, film has [. . .] been treated as a literary text," and the "application of literary criticism to the analysis of film" has resulted in the privileging of "the literary text—by valorising those of its functions which are difficult to reproduce on screen."[48]

Each of these disciplinary traditions brings its own particular strengths to the study of narrative fiction: literary geography brings a close and sustained engagement with geographical and environmental knowledge; literary studies enables a more complex discussion of relationships between language, representation, space, and place; film geography brings critical distinctions between land and landscape and theoretically informed understandings of the production of place as spectacle, metaphor, and cultural artifact; film studies brings questions about screen aesthetics, spectatorship, and the cinematic articulation of varied, ideologically charged perspectives on landscape; and theater studies brings the staging of space into the frame. If we accept, broadly speaking, that all the approaches have developed in response to the "spatial turn," that in their current forms they all hinge on the same body of theoretical knowledge and yet that they have had little or no direct bearing upon one another, then the focus must turn to methodology. In the next section, we outline the ways in which a defined geocritical method that draws on the combined strengths of geographical, filmic, literary, and theatrical analysis might bring these traditions into mutually beneficial dialogue with one another in order to realize the potential for spatial theory to illuminate the study of Australian narrative fiction.

Geocriticism, Interdisciplinarity, and (Re)mediated
Geographies: A Cultural Atlas of Australia

Given the long history of critical spatial analysis, the term *geocriticism* is a surprisingly recent coining, arising out of the work of Bertrand Westphal (2007) and Robert T. Tally Jr. (2008).[49] As Tally defines it, geocriticism is a predominantly literary-critical methodological "framework that focuses on the spatial representations within [literary] texts" while also "explor[ing] the overlapping territories of actual, physical geography and an author's or character's cognitive mapping in the literary text."[50] Acknowledging that his approach differs in some respects from Westphal's, Tally explains their shared interest in examining the relationship between the dimensions of the real and the imagined, between the referent and the representation.[51]

In Westphal's *Geocriticism*, geocriticism emerges as a multifocal and dialectical method of analysis. Indeed, the principle of geocritical analysis, Westphal argues, lies in "the confrontation of several optics that correct, nourish, and mutually enrich each other."[52] Geocritical representation "emerges from a spectrum of individual representations as rich and varied as possible." and each representation must be treated in a "dialectical process" in keeping with geocriticism's plurality of viewpoints.[53] This dialectical process carves out a "common space, born from and touching upon different points of view"; "we come closer to the essential identity of the referenced space," and in doing so, simultaneously "confirm that any cultural identity is only the result of incessant efforts of creation and re-creation."[54] Finally, Westphal is adamant that geocriticism is a fundamentally interdisciplinary approach. Although it finds its drive in the field of comparative literary studies, this discipline is itself "often driven by the desire to mobilize distinct but compatible methodologies," and, as such, it may illuminate a range of aesthetic forms.[55]

We see the value of a geocritical approach in the way that it moves beyond the examination of space in literary narratives or the analysis of location in film or theater. It is a theoretical framework that informs various modes of textual analysis and foregrounds the significance of geography to culture without privileging any particular textual form. Geocriticism, therefore, enables us to grapple with adapting spatial representations across various media forms. As such, a geocritical approach may prove germane to media geography, itself a recent development within the interdisciplinary field of human geography, which has undergone, as Tristan Thielmann puts it, a "media turn" to complement media studies' spatial turn.[56]

In the context of Australian narrative fiction, we are interested in investigating the ways in which film, literature, and theater are at once mediated and remediated. Cultural narratives not only mediate and represent space, place, and location, but they are themselves mediated representational spaces. Furthermore, films, novels, and plays also open themselves up to further remediation in the form of cross-media adaptation, or, as we will argue, spatial analysis in the form of geovisualization. In order to examine and map the ways in which spatial representation in Australian film, literature, and theater is translated within and across media forms, we have embarked upon a project, entitled "A Cultural Atlas of Australia," that blends geocritical and media geography approaches with digital cartographic technologies. This project, which investigates the cultural and historical significance of location and landscape in Australian narrative fiction, presents the first national survey of narrative space spanning Australian novels, films, and plays.

Moreover, this project is the first to employ geovisualization—in the form of an interactive online map—as a means by which to map representations of iconic landscapes and sites within Australian narrative fiction. A prototype of the interactive map component of "A Cultural Atlas of Australia" can be accessed at the following website: http://australian-cultural -atlas.info/CAA/. Where geocriticism offers a response to the striking lack of dialogue between different traditions of spatial research, many of which focus on common texts and locations, recent technological developments in digital cartography make it possible to visualize some of these intersecting concerns and varied perspectives and to map the ways in which spatial storytelling enacts, produces and translates space across different media.

Mashing Up the Map: Digital Cartography and Geocriticism in Practice

Interactive online mapping, we argue, is one way in which geocriticism can put into practice its capacity to reframe understandings of place and space by revealing connections between separate strands of spatial enquiry. Over the past decade, interactive online mapping—what D. R. Fraser Taylor has called "cybercartography"[57]—has become a particularly salient issue within cartography and, more broadly, geography.[58] This is particularly the case since Google released the Google Maps API in 2005, allowing users free access to the Google Maps code as long as the resulting map "mashup" remains nonproprietary and in the public domain. According to William Buckingham and Samuel Dennis, the development of open source mapping tools, such as Google Maps, has generated much interest in the use of maps for "understanding 'non-mapped' phenomena (e.g., qualitative data or localized community information and knowledge)," and this, they continue, articulates well with the sociological perspectives that have influenced the discipline over the past two decades.[59] This is, as Buckingham and

Dennis argue, a "new world of spatial information," promising increased dialogue among professionals in cartography, geography, and the humanities and other interested citizens.[60]

At the same time, there has been a surge of popular and critical interest in linking online mapping with narrative. This manifests most obviously in a rash of "movie maps" and online spatial resources such as History Pin (http://www.historypin.com), which uses Google Maps as a bulletin board on which to pin multiple layers of stories and photographs documenting particular places over time. While the disciplines of geography and cartography are increasingly engaging with new media studies, the digital humanities, and fields such as literary geography, researchers working in the digital humanities have also become interested in the possibilities afforded by interactive mapping technologies. This, in turn, has resulted in a number of cultural mapping initiatives and projects, notably the "Map of Early Modern London" (http://mapoflondon.uvic.ca) at the University of Victoria, Canada (1999–); Matthew L. Jockers's Google Maps project "Beyond Boston: Georeferencing Irish-American Literature" (https://www .stanford.edu/~mjockers/cgi-bin/drupal/?q=node/19) at Stanford University; the "Atlas of Early Printing" (http://atlas.lib.uiowa.edu) at the University of Iowa (2008–); and HyperCities (http://hypercities.com) at the University of California–Los Angeles (2001–).

Recent interactive mapping initiatives in cinematic and literary cartography are also symptomatic of both recent developments and ongoing challenges in the field. For example, Lorenz Hurni and Barbara Piatti's "Literary Atlas of Europe" (http://www.literaturatlas.eu) project is led by a genuinely interdisciplinary research team at the Eldgenössische Technische Hochschule (ETH) Zürich,[61] and it aims to employ literary geographical methods as the basis for "an entirely new, spatially structured, cartographically supported literary history."[62] Similarly, but from a film perspective, Sébastien Caquard's work on cinematic cartography in the Canadian Cinematographic Territories Atlas (http://www.atlascine.org) traces the history of animated maps and virtual globes such as Google Earth through cinema, examines the technological interface connecting cinema and cartography, and maps the locations of cinemas across Canada.[63]

In Australia, interest in interactive cultural mapping is demonstrated by preliminary progress on the National Film and Sound Archive's (NFSA) film-location map on the Australian Screen Online site (http://aso.gov.au) and by efforts by two national scholarly arts databases, AusStage (http:// www.ausstage.edu.au) and AustLit (http://www.austlit.edu.au), to begin indexing literary, cinematic, and theatrical texts against place of composition, performance, and narrative setting. Drawing in part upon these ready-made but at present discrete and fairly raw datasets, our cultural atlas of Australia uses an interdisciplinary geocritical method—blending film, literary, theater, and media geography methods of textual analysis—to interpret, situate, and contextualize the representation of location within and across texts, genres, and media forms. Our project, in turn, remediates that information in the form of an online, interactive map, which we anticipate will be valuable not only to spatio-cultural researchers but also to cultural professionals and the general public.

As spatio-cultural researchers, our main interest is in the way in which the map has the potential to suggest new ways of thinking about location and landscape and to break down traditional typologies of Australian space. We anticipate that this geocritical work in the digital humanities will advance on traditional cartographic explorations and representations of space, making it possible to visualize new perspectives on, intersections between, and layerings of geographic and textual information. This will enable us to identify regional tropes, patterns, and gaps in spatial representations that may not have previously been evident in research that focused on isolated case studies of individual texts, whether literary, cinematic, or theatrical.

Where geocriticism encourages dialogue among discrete traditions of spatial analysis, geovisualization and interactive mapping have the added benefit of rendering this work accessible to a broader audience. We envision not only that the map will be a cultural information resource but also that it will be participatory, incorporating user-generated content. As a research tool, the map is fully searchable (by medium, location, author, and text) and in its developed version will enable users to generate and export their own maps with information they require. For instance, users of the cultural atlas might generate a map of all locations featured in the novels of David Malouf for a cultural tour of literary sites, or they might make a map of plays, novels, and films set in central Australia. The map's temporal dimension will enable users to plot successive adaptations of a text and identify multiple texts set in the same place. These functions have the capacity to reveal how cultural meanings accrue on the landscape and how our relationship with and understanding of the natural and cultural environment changes over time. The possibilities for incorporating participants' photographs, videos, and textual accounts of Australian places via mobile social computing technologies opens up still more opportunities for the representation of multiple perspectives.

Geovisualization, as we have argued, offers the potential to open up new questions for spatial analysis and to encourage broader public engagement in cultural geography. However, as a form of remediation, it does carry its own representational problems. As Piatti et al. have noted, the geography of fiction is an imprecise one.[64] Piatti is speaking specifically about literary fiction, but the point can be made for all forms of narrative fiction. In film, literature, and theater, the representation of space and place can never simply be mimetic, but it always, to a greater or lesser degree, creates an imaginative geography that may correspond to what Piatti calls the *geospace* (or map space) directly, only loosely, or not at all.[65] Bringing film and theater space into the analytical frame carries its own set of complexities and ambiguities: film requires attention to the relationship between narrative locations and shooting locations, while drama brings questions of performance and dramaturgical space. Beyond the question of impreciseness, we must also remain aware that the remediation of narrative locations is not simply a matter of re-presenting narrative locations in map form, difficult though that process might be in itself; the process of re-presenting narrative locations, too, is a process of imagining and reimagining geography that, by its very nature, must also be political. In creating our cultural atlas, we continually ask questions of it: Whose geography does it represent? How can we foreground multiple perspectives, given that the map space privileges an omniscient viewing perspective? How might the technology and database structure both enable and limit forms of spatial representation? A vital question for our project is considering what spaces, locations, and forms of spatial knowledge might be overlooked. Especially in regard to indigenous perspectives, it is not a straightforward matter of making visible the invisible because complex issues surround the representation, naming, and mapping of sacred or culturally sensitive sites. These questions are themselves all geocritical ones and they cannot, and should not, be elided.

Ultimately, then, we argue, geocriticism offers itself as a metacritical methodology that is particularly relevant for Australian cultural studies but is also applicable to interdisciplinary spatio-cultural research more broadly. It recognizes literature, film, and theater texts as being more than representations, more than containers for narrative symbolism and ideological views and values, and this extends to any geovisualization strategy that seeks to map those texts. Such texts are also generative—productive of meanings, social relationships, and subject positions. Conley argues in *Cartographic Cinema* that cinematic images "produce space through the act of perception";[66] similarly, theater stages and enacts space, and literature imaginatively invokes space in ways that subsequently inflect the meanings readers associate with actual places. Where geocriticism enables analysis of locational information in narrative fiction informed by insights from geography as well as literary and cultural studies, it also builds from the premise that such texts intervene in the cultural field and alter the perceptual, ideological, political, and practical orientation of readers and audiences in relation to the physical environment.

Notes

1. Graeme Turner, *National Fictions: Literature, Film and the Construction of Australian Narrative,* 2nd ed. (St. Leonards, NSW: Allen and Unwin, 1993).
2. Ibid., 30.
3. Ibid.
4. Joanne Tompkins, *Unsettling Space: Contestations in Contemporary Australian Theatre* (Basingstoke: Palgrave Macmillan, 2007).
5. Ibid., 5.
6. Allaine Cerwonka, *Native to the Nation: Disciplining Landscapes and Bodies in Australia* (Minneapolis: University of Minnesota Press, 2004), 6.
7. Derek Gregory, *Geographical Imaginations* (Cambridge: Blackwell, 1994).
8. Paul Carter, *The Road to Botany Bay: An Essay in Spatial History* (London: Faber and Faber, 1987).
9. Ibid., xxi.
10. Ibid., xxii.
11. Ibid., 126.
12. Martin Leer, "Imagined Counterpart: Outlining a Conceptual Literary Geography of Australia," *Australian Literary Studies* 15, no. 2 (1991): 1.
13. See Edward Soja, *Postmodern Geographies: The Reassertion of Space in Critical Social Theory* (London: Verso, 1989); and Fredric Jameson, *Postmodernism, or, The Cultural Logic of Late Capitalism* (Durham, NC: Duke University Press, 1991).
14. John K. Wright, "Terrae Incognitae: The Place of the Imagination in Geography," *Annals of the Association of American Geographers* 37, no. 1 (1947): 15.
15. See Allen G. Noble and Ramesh Dhussa's "Image and Substance: A Review of Literary Geography," *Journal of Cultural Geography* 10, no. 2 (1990): 49–65 and Marc Brosseau's "Geography's Literature," *Progress in Human Geography* 18, no. 3 (1994): 333–53 for a review of literary geography's early history.
16. See, for instance, Douglas C. D. Pocock, "Introduction: Imaginative Literature and the Geographer," in *Humanistic Geography and Literature: Essays on the Experience of Place,* ed. Douglas C. D. Pocock (London: Croom Helm, 1981), 9–19; Nigel Thrift, "Literature, the Production of Culture and the Politics of Place," *Antipode* 15, no. 1 (1983): 12–24; D. W. Meinig, "Geography as an Art," *Transactions of the Institute of British Geographers* 8, no. 3 (1983): 314–28; and J. Douglas Porteous, "Literature and Humanist Geography," *Area* 17, no. 2 (1985): 117–22.
17. Porteous, "Literature and Humanist Geography," 117.
18. Douglas C. D. Pocock, "Geography and Literature," *Progress in Human Geography* 12, no. 1 (1988): 89.
19. Film is ignored by Pocock, Porteous, Thrift ("Literature"), Meinig, Noble and Dhussa, and Brosseau, who explains that his review will focus solely on the novelistic form because "most geographers have focused on this type of literature" (335).
20. Stuart C. Aitken and Leo E. Zonn, eds., *Place, Power, Situation, and Spectacle: A Geography of Film* (Lanham, MD: Rowman and Littlefield, 1994), ix.

21. Joanne P. Sharp, "Towards a Critical Analysis of Fictive Geographies," *Area* 32, no. 3 (2000): 328. See also Pocock's influential 1981 essay, "Introduction," which testifies to the "universality" and "primacy" of literature.

22. Sharp, "Fictive Geographies," 328.

23. Brosseau, "Geography's Literature," 333–34.

24. Andrew Thacker, "The Idea of a Critical Literary Geography," *New Formations* 57 (2005): 56.

25. Fabio Lando, "Fact and Fiction: Geography and Literature," *GeoJournal* 38, no. 1 (1996): 5.

26. Thacker, "Idea," 57. David Harvey, *The Condition of Postmodernity: An Enquiry into the Origins of Cultural Change* (Cambridge: Blackwell, 1989).

27. Thacker, "Idea," 57–58.

28. Graham Huggan, "Decolonizing the Map: Post-Colonialism, Post-Structuralism and the Cartographic Connection," *Ariel* 20, no. 4 (1989): 115–31.

29. Graham Huggan, *Territorial Disputes: Maps and Mapping Strategies in Contemporary Canadian and Australian Fiction* (Toronto: University of Toronto Press, 1994), 149–50.

30. These spatial studies of literature notably include Christopher GoGwilt's *The Invention of the West: Joseph Conrad and the Double-Mapping of Europe and Empire* (Stanford, CA: Stanford University Press, 1995); Tom Conley's *The Self-Made Map: Cartographic Writing in Early Modern France* (Minneapolis: University of Minnesota Press, 1996); Franco Moretti's *Atlas of the European Novel, 1800–1900* (London: Verso, 1998); Eric Bulson's *Novels, Maps, Modernity: The Spatial Imagination, 1850–2000* (New York: Routledge, 2007); Peta Mitchell's *Cartographic Strategies of Postmodernity: The Figure of the Map in Contemporary Theory and Fiction* (New York: Routledge, 2008); and Robert T. Tally's *Melville, Mapping and Globalization: Literary Cartography in the American Baroque Writer* (New York: Continuum, 2009).

31. See Leo E. Zonn and Stuart C. Aitken's influential articles relating to Australian film: Leo E. Zonn, "Images of Place: A Geography of the Media," *Proceedings of the Royal Geographical Society of Australasia* 84 (1985): 34–45; and Leo E. Zonn and Stuart C. Aitken, "Of Pelicans and Men: Symbolic Landscapes, Gender, and Australia's *Storm Boy*," in *Place, Power, Situation and Spectacle: A Geography of Film*, ed. Stuart C. Aitken and Leo E. Zonn (Lanham, MD: Rowman and Littlefield, 1994).

32. See Christopher Lukinbeal and Stefan Zimmermann, "Film Geography: A New Subfield," *Erdkunde* 60, no. 4 (2006): 315–26. This subfield includes Zonn and Aitken's work in the early 1990s, as well as Tim Cresswell and Deborah Dixon's edited collection, *Engaging Film: Geographies of Mobility and Identity* (Lanham, MD: Rowman and Littlefield, 2002).

33. See Ben Goldsmith, Susan Ward, and Tom O'Regan's *Local Hollywood: Global Film Production and the Gold Coast* (Brisbane: University of Queensland Press, 2010) and Susan Beeton's *Film-Induced Tourism* (Clevedon: Channel View Publications, 2005).

34. See, for example, Catherine Simpson, Renata Murawska, and Anthony Lambert's *Diasporas of Australian Cinema* (Bristol: Intellect, 2009).

35. See, for instance, Stephen Carleton's "Cinema and the Australian North: Tracking and Troping Regionally Distinct Landscapes via Baz Luhrmann's *Australia,*" *Metro Magazine* 163 (2009): 50–55; and Allison Craven's "Paradise Post-National: Landscape, Location and Senses of Place in Films Set in Queensland," *Metro Magazine* 166 (2010): 108–13.

36. See, for instance, Peta Mitchell and Jane Stadler's "Imaginative Cinematic Geographies of Australia: The Mapped View in Charles Chauvel's *Jedda* and Baz Luhrmann's *Australia,*" *Historical Geography* 38 (2010): 26–51, and Jane Mills's "Mapping Australia: Cinematic Cartographies of (Dis)location," *Senses of Cinema* 55 (2010): http://www.sensesofcinema.com/2010/feature-articles/mapping-australia-cinematic-cartographies-of-dislocation.

37. Recent interest in this field is evident in a series of articles in three journal issues featuring landscape and location in Australian cinema (*Metro* Magazine Issues 163 (Dec. 2009), 165 (June 2010) and 166 (Sept. 2010) and in Graeme Harper and Jonathan Rayner, eds., *Cinema and Landscape* (Bristol: Intellect, 2010).

38. See Ross Gibson's *South of the West: Postcolonialism and the Narrative Construction of Australia* (Bloomington: Indiana University Press, 1992), 6–7.

39. Tom O'Regan, *Australian National Cinema* (New York: Routledge, 1996), 209.

40. See Felicity Collins and Therese Davis's *Australian Cinema after Mabo* (Cambridge: Cambridge University Press, 2004).

41. Geographers such as Nigel Thrift have, however, been interested in the concepts of performance and performativity. See Thrift, "Performance and Performativity: A Geography of Unknown Lands," in *A Companion to Cultural Geography*, ed. James S. Duncan, Nuala C. Johnson, and Richard H. Schein (Cambridge: Blackwell, 2004), 121–36.

42. See Una Chaudhuri, *Staging Place: The Geography of Modern Drama* (Ann Arbor: University of Michigan Press, 2002); Una Chaudhuri and Elinor Fuchs, eds., *Land/Scape/Theater* (Ann Arbor: University of Michigan Press, 2000); and Gay McAuley's *Space in Performance: Making Meaning in the Theatre* (Ann Arbor: University of Michigan Press, 1999).

43. See, for instance, Helen Gilbert and Joanne Tompkins, *Postcolonial Drama: Theory, Practice, Politics* (London: Routledge, 1996); and Helena Grehan, *Mapping Cultural Identity in Contemporary Australian Performance* (Brussels: Peter Lang, 2001).

44. Helen Gilbert, *Sightlines: Race, Gender, and Nation in Contemporary Australian Theatre* (Ann Arbor: University of Michigan Press, 1998).

45. Stephen Carleton, "Staging the North: Finding, Imagining and Performing an Australian 'Deep North'" (PhD diss., University of Queensland, 2008), 7.

46. Roslynn D. Haynes, *Seeking the Centre: The Australian Desert in Literature, Art and Film* (Cambridge: Cambridge University Press, 1998).

47. See, for instance, Ruth Barcan and Ian Buchanan, eds., *Imagining Australian Space: Cultural Studies and Spatial Inquiry* (Nedlands: University of Western Australia Press, 1999).

48. Turner, *National Fictions*, 14.

49. Bertrand Westphal, *La Géocritique: Réel, fiction, espace* (Paris: Minuit, 2007) and Robert T. Tally Jr., "Geocriticism and Classic American Literature" (English Department Faculty Publications, paper 14, Texas State University, 2008) http://ecommons.txstate.edu/englfacp/14.

50. Tally, "Geocriticism and Classic American Literature," 4.

51. Ibid.

52. Bertrand Westphal, *Geocriticism: Real and Fictional Spaces*, trans. Robert T. Tally Jr. (New York: Palgrave, 2011), 113.

53. Ibid., 113–14.

54. Ibid., 114.

55. Ibid., 121.

56. Tristan Thielmann, "Locative Media and Mediated Localities," *Aether: A Journal of Media Geography* 5a (2010): 5.

57. D. R. Fraser Taylor, *Cybercartography: Theory and Practice* (Amsterdam: Elsevier, 2006)

58. See, for instance, William Cartwright, Michael P. Peterson, and Georg Gartner, eds., *Multimedia Cartography* (Berlin: Springer-Verlag, 1999); Mark Monmonier, "Cartography: The Multidisciplinary Pluralism of Cartographic Art, Geospatial Technology, and Empirical Scholarship," *Progress in Human Geography* 31, no. 3 (2007): 371–79; and Jeremy W. Crampton, "Maps 2.0: Map Mashups and the New Spatial Media," in *Mapping: A Critical Introduction to Cartography and GIS* (Cambridge: Blackwell, 2010), 25–38.

59. William R. Buckingham and Samuel F. Dennis Jr., "Cartographies of Participation: How the Changing Nature of Cartography Has Opened Community and Cartographer Collaboration," *Cartographic Perspectives* 64 (2009): 55.

60. Ibid., 61.

61. Hurni directs the ETH's Institute of Cartography, while Piatti and other researchers are based in Literary Studies.

62. See project description at https://www.rdb.ethz.ch/projects/project.php?proj _id=17484&z_detailed=1&z_popular=1&z_keywords=1.

63. See Sébastien Caquard, "Foreshadowing Contemporary Digital Cartography: A Historical Review of Cinematic Maps in Films," *The Cartographic Journal* 46, no. 1 (2009): 46–55.

64. Barbara Piatti et al., "Mapping Literature: Towards a Geography of Fiction," in *Cartography and Art*, ed. William Cartwright, Georg Gartner, and Antje Lehn (Berlin: Springer, 2009): 182.

65. Ibid.

66. Tom Conley, *Cartographic Cinema* (Minneapolis: University of Minnesota Press, 2007), 20.

4

Textual Forests

The Representation of Landscape in Latin American Narratives

Maria Mercedes Ortiz Rodriguez

In Latin America, transnational and multicultural spaces like the Amazon rainforest have been portrayed by politicians, entrepreneurs, intellectuals, and writers as inner frontiers, as spaces of otherness. They constitute what Mary Louis Pratt has defined as "contact zones": places of colonial encounters in which people who were geographically and historically separated come into contact with each other and establish among themselves relations based on coercion, radical inequality, and intractable conflict.[1] Rainforests have been seen in the dominant imaginaries on the one hand as the wilderness, and on the other hand as economic and symbolic repositories that offer wealth and hope to the nation. According to the central powers and the economic and political elites, these inner frontiers should be conquered and "civilized," totally ignoring the lives and rights of their Amerindian populations in order to extract from them their "unlimited" riches that should redeem Latin America from its poverty.

In this article, I will analyze the depiction of the rainforest in some Latin American narratives written in the first decades of the twentieth century as a socially constructed space, intertwined by race, ethnicity, social class, and gender and linked to the history of the so-called rubber boom (1879–1912). In addition, I will show how these representations emphasize the singularity of the places, the relation of people to them, and the bond between history and space.

A Wealth Repository

During the rubber boom, remote areas of the Amazon basin were intensively exploited in order to supply the demand for rubber in international markets, causing serious damage to the ecosystem and to numerous indigenous groups. With the boom, the Amazon region considered before as the wilderness and the periphery of the nation became an economic center and also received attention in cultural and intellectual life. Thousands of poor migrants from the Andean regions and the Brazilian *nordeste* (northeast) flooded the rainforest in pursuit of an ultimately illusory dream of richness, and their epic lives in the jungle, as well as the deeds of their rich bosses, "the rubber barons," occupied the pages of novels, poems, essays, memoirs, and travel narratives. Two of these texts are *A través de la América del Sur: Exploraciones de los hermanos Reyes* (or, in English, *Through South America: Explorations of the Reyes Brothers*), written in 1902, and *Memorias* (or *Memoirs*), written around 1911 by the entrepreneur, explorer, politician, and ex-president of Colombia General Rafael Reyes (1850–1921).

Reyes and his brothers made a fortune exporting quinine. Their business was located in Popayan, a town in the southwest of Colombia in the Cauca state. In 1874, Reyes explored the rainforests of the southeast of Colombia, which belong to the Amazon basin, looking for a cheaper alternative route to enable them to export quinine over the Atlantic Ocean via the Amazon River instead of over the Pacific, as his company had been doing. According to his biographer, Lemaitre, he was also interested in colonizing this region, which was expected to have a great future. In 1875, thanks to a treaty with Brazil, Reyes inaugurated steam navigation on the Putumayo River, an important tributary of the Amazon, and began to export quinine successfully over the Atlantic. He also began to exploit rubber and worked in the Colombian rainforests until 1884, when the quinine price went down on the world market and the company that belonged to Reyes and his brothers went bankrupt.

Reyes experiences in the rainforests are narrated from different perspectives in the two mentioned texts. *A través de la América del Sur* is the written version of the conference that Reyes gave in 1902 in the second Pan American conference in Mexico City. It is a narration of accomplished facts in which Reyes manipulates the text to triumphantly present to international opinion a monolithic image of his brothers and himself as heroes of progress and civilization. He compares himself to travelers of the stature of Stanley and Livingston, arguing that he had opened up for the progress of humankind a richer area than the one surveyed in Africa by these two famous explorers: "If some years ago, the territories of which I am talking about had a only a local and relative importance, is not the same today, because the development of navigation and commerce and the growing needs of humankind demand that they don't remain ignored and unproductive. In the extensive forests *in which the savage cannibals wandered when we did these explorations,* an important business of tens of millions is now maintained there and towns of thousands have also arisen."[2] There is almost no gap left in this text that allows a critical reading of the destructive repercussions of "progress" and "civilization" over the Amerindian populations—we don't know why they don't wander any more—the rubber tappers and the rainforest itself, after Reyes and others explored and exploited the Putumayo region.

On the contrary, *Memorias,* a combination of travel narrative and autobiography, is a work in which Reyes articulates more freely his whole experience in the rainforest. The book, based on memory and elaborated as an evocation of events that happened twenty-seven years ago, vividly describes the day-by-day activities of Reyes's enterprise. In the book, the ex-president is the subject as well as the object of his own narration, continuously unfolding in order to be able to talk about himself as well as about the rainforest and the Indians, turning his sensations, feelings, and ideas over this strange and unknown world that did not seem to change him much at all.

There are some similarities between *Memorias* and the sentimental travel narratives analyzed by Mary Louise Pratt like *Travels in the Interior Districts of Africa* (1799) by Mungo Park, a Scottish traveler who explored the Niger River in Africa. As Reyes did more than hundred years later, Park constructs himself as the protagonist and central figure of his own narration, which assumes the form of an epic serial of processes, challenges, and encounters with the unpredictable.[3] Pratt emphasizes that in Park's narration, as opposed to the narrations of the scientific travelers, social interactions are very important, as happens in *Memorias* in Reyes's interactions with Indians and workers.

One of the most remarkable features of *Memorias* is the changing portrayals of the rainforest that are depicted in connection with the process of rubber extraction. These portrayals appeal to metaphors in which the rainforest is alternatively described as the garden of Eden or the curse of God, according to man's success or failure in extracting its richness. As Hayden White explains in *Tropics of Discourse,* tropes play a fundamental role in the discourses of the humanities.[4] By examining these metaphors, I will show the kind of discourses that Reyes implements about the rainforest and its Amerindian populations in relation to the progress and development of the nation.

A Virgin at First Glance

Reyes saw and described the rainforest for the first time around 1870 from a tree in the heights of the eastern Andes mountain range in Colombia. His description strategy is, according to Nancy Stepan, characteristic of the one used by Humboldt, who customarily organized for the spectator his description of the landscape from the perspective of height or distance as if it were a painting.[5] In this first description, Reyes used the conventional metaphor of the virgin lands to legitimize from the very beginning of his endeavor the future conquest of these regions. We can also read in his text the dispute between old and new discourses about the rainforest:

> I climbed to the top of these [trees] to explore the horizon, in front of me, to the East, an unending and immense ocean of verdure expanded itself, not a mountain rose there, not a hill, it was plain as the sea, where it goes to die on the Atlantic shores, eight thousand kilometers away from where I was. Those virgin and strange rainforests, those vast places captivated and attracted me in order to explore them, traverse them, reach the sea and open roads for the progress and well-being of my patria (homeland); they [the rainforests] were totally unknown to the people who lived in the mountain range and the idea of penetrating them caused me fear and popular imagination populated them with wild beasts, with monsters, besides the numerous tribes of savages cannibals who were there. The popular fear for these rainforests was so huge that after ten days of walk my companions or hands manifested that they would not continue because we were reaching the region of the forests, of the savage cannibals and the infernal spirits of these rainforests.[6]

In this "incantation" of progress in which the forest is seen as the promise of wealth for the nation, Reyes cannot avoid the colonial fear of the other, depicted as savage and cannibal, a fear that traverses the imagination of postcolonial Colombia until the present. The entrepreneur and politician simultaneously feels attraction and repulsion for this rainforest that he wants so much to conquer; let us explain here that in Spanish *conquistar*, "conquer," also means to seduce a woman.[7] In fact, Reyes initially feminizes the landscape, constructing the rainforest as a passive other of which he takes possession first with his gaze and further on with his deeds. As Andrea Blair explains, quoting Gillian Rose in *Feminism and Geography*, this is the way in which landscape is constructed in a variety of different discourses: "Landscape implies a specific way of looking, 'a visual ideology' that privileges the masculine gaze. Rose writes that in popular and academic discourses, landscape is the passive, objectified Other that awaits the gaze for signification—plays the role of the feminine."[8] The feminization of the landscape implies a hierarchy between men and nature and a relation of subordination that equals the existing one between men and women. In Reyes's text, the location of viewer and viewed reinforces this hierarchy, namely the man looks from the heights upon the rainforest beneath him, extended to his feet. Next, once he has begun to exploit this region, Reyes presents his economic endeavor as the seduction of a virgin. Virgins, be they women or rainforests, invite possession because they do not belong to any man. Reyes assumes this conquest-seduction and opens the way for others in the future to do the same. In 1952, when Lemaitre published his biography of Reyes, these images, as well as the patriarchal system that nourished them, still remained strong: "Reyes loved nature, even more when it is wild and virginal as this of his homeland which offers to him, besides its treasures the almost sensual joy of receiving him as a bridegroom."[9]

The metaphor of the virgin lands has equated nature with women, according to Blair. Feminist ecocriticism has worked to dismantle this equation, showing how it constitutes a strategy of domination and subjugation of both women and nature: "Land is seen as the inviting concubine, waiting to be despoiled; as the chaste virgin, needing protection from rape; or as the all forgiving, long-suffering Mother Earth, who patiently tolerates abuse from her human children."[10] Even feminist critique is not enough to unveil the ethnic dimensions of the situation that this metaphor camouflages. In contact zones, where places of very different cultures clash together, the invaders dominate not only nature but entire ethnic groups that always lived there, both men and women. The rights of these people to their ancestral territories are precisely denied when their lands are considered virgin—that is, never touched by anyone. Evidently, the "savage cannibals" that according to Reyes and popular imagination populated the forests of southeastern Colombia were not fully considered to be human beings, and it was quite clear that their territorial rights would be totally ignored.

The trope of the virgin forest was also successfully used in more northern latitudes, namely in the United States, to dispossess Amerindian groups from their lands, ironically enough by declaring them "wild" areas in order to create natural parks, as William Cronon explains, "The myth of the wilderness as 'virgin,' uninhabited land had always been especially cruel when seen from the perspective of the Indians who had once called that land home. Now they were forced to move elsewhere, with the result that tourists could safely enjoy the illusion that they were seeing their nation in its pristine, original state, in the new morning of God's own creation."[11] Reyes's narrative and Cronon's example clarify how the notion of "wilderness" is a social construction and how the metaphor of the virgin forests favors some social sectors to the detriment of others, in both cases, the Indians.

The Garden of Eden

Once Reyes goes deep into the rainforest, he expresses his ideas about the landscape through the trope of the garden of Eden or paradise, depicting it as a newly created land, located in the origin of the world. This image of biblical origin has played an important role in moments of discovery and rediscovery of the Americas; it was used by Columbus, later on by Humboldt and other European travelers in the nineteenth century, and again in the internal conquests in postcolonial Latin America of regions seen as the wilderness, like the *Llanos* from Colombia and Venezuela, the Amazon region, and the Argentinean *Pampas*.[12] According to White, the figure of Eden corresponds to a stage on which the universe is envisioned as perfectly ordered and harmonious in its parts.[13] It allows Reyes to invest the trope of the virgin lands with a more transcendent and religious dimension and to reinforce it by presenting to the reader the image of a pristine rainforest: "We thought of our dearly loved, in our absent ones from this life as well as from the other, in the communion of the souls, which is taught to us with so much poetry and charity by Jesus Christ's religion. I felt in communication with the mines, it seemed to me that they were present, accompanying me in these immense solitudes to sense the intensity of the forces of a primitive nature which made me think that it should have been like this on the seventh day of creation, when the sovereigns Adam and Eve emerged there."[14]

By locating the rainforest in the origin of the world, Reyes divests it from natural as well as human history, because the history of humankind began after the expulsion of Adam and Eve from paradise, caused by the original sin. Thus the millenary Amerindian history in this region is completely erased with this trope. These same effects are pointed out by Mary Louise Pratt in her analysis of anticonquest narratives, in which the naturalist is presented as Adam in paradise and the landscape is depicted as an empty space, with nobody living there, not even the traveler himself.[15] The difference is that in *Memorias* there is no naturalist and that Reyes, the explorer, doesn't vanish from the narrative; on the contrary, he assumes the role of the Adam analyzed by Pratt, telling us that he is the first human being to put his feet in this unknown paradise. He poses as a new Columbus in the contemporary world of progress, science, work, and war, who uses the epic dimensions that have been conferred to the "discovery" and conquest of the Americas to magnify and make legitimate his entrepreneurial adventures.

When Reyes and his men began the exploitation of rubber, the figure of Eden is reversed in the narrative, and the rainforest is depicted as a hostile place, adverse to man, similar to the place where Adam and Eve fell after the expulsion from paradise.

The Curse of God

Reyes established a rubber camp called *La Concepción* (Conception) with hundreds of men by the *Incuisilla* river, close to a group of indigenous people with the same name. In this place, they began to experience the difficulties caused by the need to adapt to a complex and unknown environment: three workers were bitten by snakes, two by scorpions, and Reyes himself by a spider; worst of all they were hit by yellow fever. Of the hundreds of mainly Afro-Colombian workers, an anonymous mass without names or faces, only fifty survived the epidemic.[16]

The harmonious relation between man and nature, characteristic of the narrative of Eden has been transformed into a struggle without end. The rainforest is now depicted in *Memorias* as a desert, plunged into a state of "barbarism and savagery." The word desert, as Hayden White explains, besides meaning "uninhabited" also means "wildness" and had for the ancient Hebrews a symbolic value connected to a specific relationship to God:

> Wildness is a peculiarly moral condition, a manifestation of a specific relationship to God, a cause and at the same time a consequence of being under God's curse. But it is also—or rather it is indiscriminately—a *place*, that is to say, it is not only the *what* of the sin, but the *where* as well. For example, the biblical concordances tell us that the Hebrew word for "wilderness" (sh mâmâh), used in the sense of "desolation" appears in 2 Sam, 13:20 to characterize the condition of the violated woman Tamar; but the *place* of the curse (the desert, the void; the wasteland) is also described as a wilderness.[17]

In a sense, Reyes and his men had been also cursed by God, and their sins can be related to the disruption of the sublime in the rainforest. As Van Noy explains, "The sublime presented nature as omnipotent perfection, a sign of God's presence. To disturb or know that nature was to violate that sublimity and cause it to disappear."[18] Under this perspective, the work of the rubber tappers constitutes a violation of a sacred space and is kind of a sacrilege. This idea contains to a certain degree a moral and religious condemnation of the extractive economy that will be explicitly articulated more than a decade later in *La vorágine* (*The Vortex*; 1924), the foundational fiction of the *llanos* and the rainforest in Latin American literature written by the Colombian José Eustasio Rivera.

The whole episode of the rubber camp *La Concepción* reveals the costs of an extractive economy in terms of human lives and darkens the progress that Reyes had exalted so optimistically. It is not so easy to extract the riches of the rainforest, and Reyes argues that Virgin Nature seems to be defending herself from man's domination. The rainforest is not behaving itself as it should according to Rose (i.e., as a suffering mother who patiently tolerates the abuses of her human children); on the contrary, it is reacting violently against them. This idea is also further developed in *La vorágine*, though in the novel the responsibility is attributed to the perversions produced by modernization in the so-called peripheral countries.

In *Memorias*, Reyes describes part of the Amerindian populations who lived in this desert as "savage cannibals." As White explains, the notion of savage has been associated from biblical times to the present with the idea of wilderness—"those parts of the physical world like desert, forest, jungle and mountains that had not yet been domesticated or marked out for domestication in any significant way."[19] Thus people and cultures became merely extensions of the places.

In his description of the Indians, Reyes combines evolutionary discourses with the recycling of colonial imaginaries about Amerindians that became very useful to legitimize their dispossession in these modern enterprises of conquest.

The Colonial Montage of Indianness

In the Colombia of the nineteenth century, the association between wilderness and savagery could still work perfectly because rainforest regions had not yet been "domesticated" by the white man. Reyes began to "tame" the Putumayo region and he needed to disseminate information about the geography and the inhabitants of the Colombian forests for the development of extractive economy and for future expeditions and new settlers. So he presents in *Memorias* a rudimentary ethnography with some descriptions of Amerindian cultures and the adequate way to relate to them in order to guarantee their very necessary collaboration to the white man in the present as well as in the future.

He classifies the different groups in a descendent order that reflects the schemas of linear evolutionism and is based on certain cultural characteristics like the presence or absence of agriculture, sedentary life, chieftainship, rules, cannibalism, and distance or vicinity to "civilized" centers of white population. The Kamtsa and Inga of Sibundoy, a valley located in the eastern Andes of Colombia, are considered semisavages, the groups of the upper Putumayo are seen as savages, and the ones of the lower Putumayo are presented as savage cannibals and nomads and as the most inferior of all. Though Reyes considers cultural traits in his classification, he linked, as others did before him, the Andes with civilization and the rainforest with savagery, a connection that has dominated Colombian imaginaries about landscape until the present, creating in Michel Taussig's words "a moral topography."[20]

Reyes states that he got to know a variety of groups in the Upper Putumayo, which are depicted in *Memorias* as savages; as the Kamtsa and the Ingas from Sibundoy they practiced agriculture and were evangelized by the Jesuits in colonial times, but they lived far away from civilized centers. This people were very amicable and hospitable to Reyes; a relationship that turned to be lethal to them as shown in the case of the Cosacunti, who were infected with a disease by the entrepreneur and his men, leaving only one woman and one child alive. Reyes laments their extinction but doesn't assume any responsibility for it.

The groups of the lower Putumayo are portrayed as savage cannibals. According to Roger Barta, the association between savagery and cannibalism is an ancient one and was already established by the Greeks, who widely disseminated in Europe through their popular Dionysian rituals the myth of the wild men and their main characteristics, like lasciviousness, cannibalism, animal-like behavior, bestial traits (nakedness, hairy skin, tails, equine legs, etc.), an uncontrollable lust for wine, and a rejection of "normal" sociability. The figure of the savage cannibal was brought by the Europeans to the New World and was applied to different groups and used to justify their enslavement. The cannibalism of the Amazonian Indians was assumed as a truth very early, as Augusto Gómez states, even when many groups of the lower and middle Putumayo were not really known in the seventeenth century.[21] Reyes describes the people of the lower Putumayo as people who constantly fight among themselves and practice cannibalism on their war prisoners, even if he never saw a case. In 1902, in the second Pan American conference, he affirmed that his brother Nestór, who disappeared in the rainforest, had been devoured by the Uitoto. These powerful images, which were propagated in public, perfectly suited the interests of the rubber entrepreneurs, who presented the extermination and brutal exploitation of the Indians as a civilizing mission that rescued them from their shocking habits.

The supposedly nomadic group that Reyes encountered on a riverbank is described in coarse, racist terms as the most degenerate species of man, similar to the black nomad pigmies that Stanley encountered during his trip to Africa.[22] The entrepreneur compares them to monkeys and compares their language to the unarticulated sounds of animals. These kinds of images made their way throughout Latin American literature until the present, being used in novels like the famous *La casa verde* (1965) by Mario Vargas Llosa. The encounter reveals the constant obsession of whites with cannibalism because Reyes immediately assumes that the Indians want to engulf him and his men. He terrifies the Indians by shooting his gun, tidying them up afterward, and leaving the place forever.

The episode uncovers the intercultural tensions in the Amazonian contact zone in which the whites' obsession with cannibalism constituted kind of a metaphor of their fear of the unknown and of other cultures. On the other side, the Indians had reasons enough to consider, as they did, the whites, too, as cannibals, with their arsenal of tortures, murders, epidemics, and mutilations. Roberto Pineda Camacho, who has analyzed this situation, considers that in the space of terror and death created by the rubber tappers, cannibalism as practice and as representation erased the borders between cultures, being assumed by whites and Indians, each one having different cannibal actors equipped with their respective paraphernalia and symbols of violence.[23]

Living Images

Memorias constitutes a rich repertoire of ideas and tropes about the rainforest and the Indians that was already popular in Colombia and other Amazonian countries toward the end of the nineteenth century and the beginning of the twentieth. The genealogy of some of these ideas and images can be traced to the Old Testament, ancient Greece, and colonial times in Latin America; others reflect more modern discourses on fashion in Reyes epoch-like evolutionism and the ideal of progress. Through the use of different tropes, a specific landscape, the Amazon rainforest, is represented as a gendered and dynamic space that undergoes changes according to the process of rubber extraction, being alternatively shown as virgin land, the garden of Eden, and God's curse. Indigenous people are mostly seen as an appendix of landscape, even though is impossible to avoid some reference to their cultural traits, which are interpreted by Reyes following a rough and linear evolutionary schema.

The analysis of the social and cultural construction of the rainforest in *Memorias* reveals the interplay of interests that lie behind the different tropes employed in the text that are ultimately used to legitimize the conquest of the rainforest and the dispossession and even extermination of its Amerindian population for the sake of the progress of the Colombian nation. Some of them, like the figure of the savage cannibal, also constitute metaphors for the deep feelings of fear that characterized the conflictive intercultural encounters in the Amazonian contact zone.

The process of conquest of the rainforest has persisted until the present; if rubber and quinine are no longer the riches to be extracted, the current constant search for gold, oil, timber, and other materials continues damaging the environment and the people, though many voices in international scenarios, including the ones of indigenous organizations, strongly oppose this destruction. The metaphors so vividly used by Reyes in his depiction of the rainforest haven't lost their power: they appear over and over again in Latin American literature and in hegemonic imaginaries updating the messages transmitted by him. They constitute a rich symbolic repository that can be used at any moment to support and justify the new conquests of Amerindian territories in our time and will continue to live in people's minds until these can be stopped.

Notes

1. Mary Louise Pratt, *Imperial Eyes: Travel Writing and Transculturation* (London: Routledge, 1992), 6.
2. Rafael Reyes, *A través de la América del Sur: Exploraciones de los hermanos Reyes* (Barcelona: Ramón de S. N. Araluce, 1902), 13, my emphasis.
3. Pratt, *Imperial Eyes*, 75.
4. Hayden White, *Tropics of Discourse: Essays in Cultural Criticism* (Baltimore: Johns Hopkins University Press, 1978), 5.
5. Nancy Leys Stepan, *Picturing Tropical Nature* (London: Reaktion Books, 2001), 37.
6. Rafael Reyes, *Memorias, 1850–1885* (Bogotá: Fondo Cultural Cafetero, 1986), 81. All the translations from Reyes and Lemaitre's quotes are mine.
7. These feelings express to a certain extent the crossroad in which Colombia was situated at that moment between traditional economic structures and imaginaries and an incipient modernization.
8. Andrea Blair, "Landscape in Drag: The Paradox of Feminine Space in Susan Warner's *The Wide, Wide World*," in *The Greening of Literary Scholarship: Literature, Theory and the Environment*, ed. Steven Rosedale (Iowa City: University of Iowa Press, 2001), 116.
9. Eduardo Lemaitre, *Rafael Reyes: Biografía de un Gran Colombiano* (Bogotá: Banco de la Republica, 1981), 66.
10. Blair, "Landscape in Drag," 112.
11. Cronon, "The Trouble with Wilderness, or Getting Back to the Wrong Nature," in *Uncommon Ground: Toward Reinventing Nature* (New York: W. W. Norton, 1995), 79.
12. As Ileana Rodríguez indicates, on the 21st of February, 1493, Columbus located the Paradise in the Caribbean; see Rodríguez, *Transatlantic Topographies: Islands, Highlands, Jungles* (Minneapolis: University of Minnesota Press, 2004).

13. White, *Tropics of Discourse*, 158.

14. Reyes, *Memorias*, 127.

15. Pratt, *Imperial Eyes*, 51.

16. Reyes only mentioned their places of origin, mainly the Caribbean coast and the Pacific coast of Colombia, both of which were populated by people of African descent who were supposed to be able to support the difficult conditions of the tropical rainforest.

17. White, *Tropics of Discourse*, 159.

18. Rick Van Noy, "Surveying the Sublime: Literary Cartographers and the Spirit of Place," in *The Greening of Literary Scholarship: Literature, Theory and the Environment*, ed. Steven Rosedale (Iowa City: University of Iowa Press, 2002), 182.

19. White, *Tropics of Discourse*, 53.

20. See Taussig, *Shamanism, Colonialism and the Wild Man* (Chicago: University of Chicago Press, 1987).

21. Gómez, "Raza, 'salvajismo,' esclavitud y 'civilización': fragmentos para una historia del racismo y de la resistencia indígena en la Amazonia," in *Imani Mundo: Estudios en la Amazonia colombiana*, ed. Carlos E. Franky (Bogotá: Unibiblos, 2001), 205.

22. See Reyes, *Memorias*, 137.

23. Roberto Pineda Camacho, *Holocausto en el Amazonas: Una historia social de La Casa Arana* (Bogotá: Planeta Colombiana Editorial S.A., 2000), 34.

5

Land of Racial Confluence and Spatial Accessibility

Claude McKay's Sense of Mediterranean Place

Michael K. Walonen

He too was touched by the magic of the Mediterranean, sprayed by its foamy fascination.

—Claude McKay, *Banjo*

Critics have for some time rightly insisted on the integral role of place in pioneering black modernist Claude McKay's body of work,[1] situating it vis-à-vis the intellectual and cultural fomentation of the Harlem Renaissance and incisively considering McKay's role as an expatriate Caribbean intellectual. But scant attention has been accorded to one of the regions most significantly encountered and represented by McKay, a set of places that arguably influenced McKay's thinking on race and the possibilities of belonging just as much as Harlem and Jamaica: the Mediterranean locales he experienced during his extended sojourn in the south of France, in Spain, and in Morocco from 1924 to 1934. Some critics have recognized the importance of these places to McKay's oeuvre, but their analyses have moved in directions other than providing a thorough examination of McKay's conceptualization of the Mediterranean. William J. Maxwell, for instance, insists on the importance of grasping the transatlantic valence of McKay's *Banjo* (1929) as part of the overall project understanding the international scope of the Harlem Renaissance.[2] In "Rereading *Banjo*: Claude McKay and the French Connection," Robert P. Smith Jr. stresses the importance of France's role in McKay's career and work but limits himself largely to asserting the role of McKay in Paulette Nardal's black Parisian literary salon and his influence upon Aimé Cesaire and Léopold Sedar Senghor, while in *Claude McKay: The Literary Identity from Jamaica to Harlem and Beyond*, Kotti Sree Ramesh and Kandula Nirupa Rani note that McKay's physical and literary peregrinations between Europe, Africa, and the Caribbean/North America replicated the slave trade triangle, losing sight of the fact that McKay personally and creatively explored North Africa rather than sub-Saharan East Africa, the locus of the slave trade.[3]

Outside of these exceptions, there has been a definite lack of critical attention accorded McKay's Mediterranean writings. One reason for this might be that the places and times McKay chose for his sojourns of expatriation were not shared by other major writers and hence are not particularly familiar to literary scholars. McKay lived in and wrote of France during the 1920s, but he quickly turned away from the Paris beloved of the Lost Generation and a succession of African American visitors and expatriates stretching from Langston Hughes to Richard Wright to James Baldwin, finding it less interesting and vital than the Marseilles and French Riviera that he came to embrace.[4] He was enamored of Spain but last left its soil in 1934, two years before the outbreak of the Spanish Civil War made it a bloody battleground for international ideological conflict and a common destination for progressive Western intellectuals such as Ernest Hemingway, John Dos Passos, George Orwell, Langston Hughes, and André Malraux. And McKay sojourned in Africa but in Mediterranean "Arab" Africa rather than the "black Africa" flocked to by later generations in search of their roots.

Another reason for this general lack of critical interest might be the difficulty of finding a copy of McKay's second, unfinished Marseilles novel, *Romance in Marseilles* (written between 1929 and 1933). Unpublished during McKay's lifetime, the novel was scheduled to be printed in 2001 by the University of Exeter Press, but it has not yet appeared as of this writing of this article.[5] Whatever the reason for this critical silence, this article will sound out the imaginative dynamics of Claude McKay's Mediterranean— the manner in which it is conceptualized as a place of racial and cultural convergence whose overriding multifariousness made for an openness to various forms of difference far in excess of that of any place encountered by McKay in northern Europe or North America.

Before turning to McKay's Mediterranean writings, it is crucial to note that the idea of a unified Mediterranean identity has come under considerable warranted criticism during the recent era of antiessentialist identity politics. Gilles Boetsch and Jean-Noel Ferrié, for example, argue that broad generalizations regarding an overall Mediterranean character ignore the performative localized aspect of identity, emphasize sameness at the expense of difference, conceive of culture as something static and atemporal, and ignore the plethora of diverse social contexts found across the Mediterranean basin.[6] Mauro Peressini and Ratiba Hadj-Moussa note that the concept of Mediterranean regional identity is highly problematized by its utter absence in the culture of Muslim North Africa, which instead identifies geographically with Mecca and the rest of the Muslim world, and they further posit that in recent history the Mediterranean has served chiefly "as the Other of Nordic modernity."[7] This variety of critique has served as a corrective to the excessively totalizing and stereotyped popular and scholarly vision of the Mediterranean that had prevailed for some time, but there are at the same time within the region a number of similarities (of architecture, diet, and other social practices) brought on by disparate people's responses to a common mountainous environment bordered by a large sea, as well as an undeniable common history of Greek, Phoenician, Roman, Arab, and Ottoman cultural influences. So while the Mediterranean is a politically problematic and excessively homogenized "imaginary community" (in the sense of the term proposed by Benedict Anderson) unevenly subscribed to by the different groups living within the region, the concept of the Mediterranean still holds a powerful allure for observers of southern Europe, northern Africa, and the western Middle East. This allure was even stronger in McKay's day and received its penultimate expression in Annales School historian Fernand Braudel's three-volume work *The Mediterranean and the Mediterranean World in the Age of Philip II* (1949).[8]

McKay tended to conceive of races and peoples, Mediterranean or otherwise, in somewhat essentialist terms as embodying a set of transnational traits. For example, as David Nicholls points out, the representation of Jamaica in McKay's novel *Banana Bottom* (1933) hinges on a vision of "the timeless values and collective identity of Afro-Jamaican peasant life" that provides "the solace of essentialism."[9] McKay's vision of a shared black identity was highly influential—the representation of bonds of common blackness uniting disparate members of the African diaspora from West Africa, the Caribbean, and North America in *Banjo* served as one of the chief inspirations for the *Négritude* movement of Aimé Césaire, Léopold Sedar Senghor, and others, which in turn profoundly informed the American Black Power Movement of the 1960s.[10] In the words of Césaire, who was deeply influenced by the translation of the novel he encountered as a student in early thirties Paris, "Claude McKay can be considered [...] as the veritable inventor of *Négritude* [...] not of the word [...] but of the values of *Négritude*."[11]

Along similar lines, the text of *Banjo* refers in generalizing fashion to "Provencals and Corsicans and others of *the Mediterranean breed*" (212, my emphasis) and enumerates these "Mediterranean peoples, Greek, Jugo-Slav, Neapolitan, Arab, Corsican, and [interestingly enough] Armenian, Czech and Russian" (10). While these peoples are multiple and distinctive, there is, for McKay, enough commonality between them to distinguish a common type, the product of thousands of years of mixing, due to which no amount of parsing could ever separate into "pure" constituent strains, as Predrag Matvejevitch points out.[12] Repeatedly in his autobiography, *A Long Way from Home* (1937), McKay uses the French term *métèque*—a foreigner of Mediterranean European ancestry residing in France—to reference this type (263, 318). "Mediterranean" individuals in McKay's oeuvre are physiologically similar enough for natives of one nation to be confounded with those of another, as in the case of the Provencal prostitute in *Banjo* with "features [...] brown as an Arab's" (171). But "Mediterranean" does not just denote a common physiological type for McKay; it also refers to a common cultural heritage. For instance, in *A Long Way from Home* McKay uses the term "Mediterranean" to refer to the everyday cultural practices of Morocco (336). In this sense, McKay's Mediterranean, awash with these practices, is as much a "possessed and possessive ambiance" as it is a "totalizing milieu," to use terms drawn from Daniel Madelenat's analysis of French poetry of the Mediterranean (282).

But while McKay envisions a common Mediterranean "type," he also sees the region as a kind of geographic crossroads, a place of convergence for different culturally distinctive peoples. This is only natural, given that from its origins Marseilles has been a meeting place of incongruous vectors, as Martine Agathe Coste observes, a place of "harmonious encounter between fresh water and the sea, between Greece and the barbarian world, between masculinity and femininity, between Europe and Africa."[13] "Yellow, brown, white, black" come into contact in Marseilles, according to McKay's short story "Nigger Lover" (1932), "Far Orient, Occident, African, and broad-based Mediterranean between drawing, uniting, and holding all like a magnet" (*Gingertown*, 248). In other words, the Mediterranean, as a geographic location and a people, serves as a center that attracts and binds together the different races of the world. This is evident in the port of Marseilles, setting of both "Nigger Lover" and *Banjo*. In the latter, the port and adjacent beach are described as the refuge of "Finns, Poles, Italians, Slavs, Maltese, Indians, Negroids, African Negroes, West Indian Negroes—deportées from America for violation of the United States immigration laws—afraid and ashamed to go back to their own lands, all dumped down in the great Provençal port, bumming a day's work, a meal, a drink, existing from hand to mouth, anyhow any way, between box car, tramp ship, bistro, and bordel" (6).[14]

While Marseilles is a "dumping ground" that attracts the dispossessed and footloose of the races of the world, Spain is seen as a "bridge" between Africa and Europe (*Long Way from Home*, 309). In the poems "Barcelona" and "Cadiz," McKay lauds the beauty and kinetic energy of Spain, but he became particularly captivated by the country's residual "Moorish"[15] cultural attributes during his summer 1928 sojourn in Barcelona.[16] It is this cultural influence, "the strong African streak in its character" (*Long Way from Home*, 296)—manifested in the Spanish language, architecture, cuisine, and so forth—not just the fact that Spain constitutes the closest point of European geographical proximity to Africa, which makes the country a "bridge" in McKay's eyes. It is a zone of Afro-European cultural overlap, a land that offers a gradual segue rather than a stringent dividing line between the two conceptually opposed continents and their cultures.

McKay also uses this bridge image in his poem "Tangier," an evocation of the city where he dwelled during the early thirties and felt more at home than he had at any time since leaving Jamaica due to Morocco's "cultural and ethnic pluralism."[17] "Tangier" describes this city on the southern end of the Straits of Gibraltar as the "bridgehead of the broken span," which is to say that this historical bridge between Europe and Africa has been destroyed by antagonisms McKay goes on to pinpoint as being religious and colonialist in nature. After describing Tangier's change from Barbary pirate haven to tourist destination, the poem depicts the city in its final stanza as a locus of conflict and confluence across time:

Oh, I have felt the breaking wave on wave
Of ages washing up against your base,
From warm Sahara, heart of dark Soudan,
The clash and clamor of time, the human race
Within the cradle Mediterranean
Round yon high symbol of the Berber brave! (*Complete Poems*, 226)

Tangier thus is envisioned as a place of encounter and struggle for groups from across the Sahara to the south and throughout the Mediterranean just as much as it is part of a bygone "bridge" or zone of *meztiso* border culture drawing from European and Arab/African sources.

It is this latter attribute that McKay also sees as defining Tetuan, the city forty miles to the southeast of Tangier, to which many Moors fled following their expulsion from Spain at the end of the Reconquista. In *A Long Way from Home* McKay describes Tetuan as embodying a synthesis, or "perfect miscegenation" of Moroccan and European cultures (308), while in the poem "Tetuan" he evokes the city as a product of Andalusian Moorish culture, stylistically "Arabian," but animated by a Spanish vitality ("sparkling with flamenco laughter"; *Complete Poems*, 327). Furthermore, "Tetuan" presents its titular city as both an "homage" to the lost era of Moorish Spain and, by virtue of its continuance, a testament or memorial to this era.

Further south in Morocco, McKay observes the traces of a different confluence of peoples and culture—"black Africa" and the Arab-Islamic world. *Romance in Marseilles* describes Marrakesh, birthplace of the protagonist's love interest, the biracial Arab-Sudanese Aslima, as "that city of the plain where savagery emerging naked from the jungle meets civilization" (44). This convergence of North and sub-Saharan Africa is not always represented in such conventional stereotypical terms of "savage" and "jungle," however. The city of Fez—described in the short story "Little Sheik" (1932) as home to an "Afroriental" culture (*Gingertown*, 268)—is evoked in the poem "Fez" as a "Baghdad/In Africa" (*Complete Poems*, 226). The poem foregrounds the Arab character of the city through the Orientalist character of the descriptions of its physical contours:[18] "labyrinthine lanes and crooked souks[19] [. . .] dim passages and nooks" (226). Western representations of Arab cities tend to dwell on the space of the souk for the reason that Arab urbanism is oriented around the public space in and around a city's central souk and mosque.[20] References to "labyrinthine" streets and shadowy "passages and nooks" such as those of McKay draw on and affirm the stock Western concept of the "mysterious Orient." But regardless of whether McKay's depictions of Morocco slide at times into caricature, the Arabness of his Fez is not unalloyed. The final two lines of "Fez" impute to the city an "African [. . .] shape and form" animated, like McKay's Tetuan, by the "glowing fire of Andalusian eyes" (226). So the Fez represented by McKay derives its richness from being simultaneously Arab, African, and Moorish Spanish.

Being deeply pluralistic and situated at the intersection of so many cultural vectors, the Mediterranean that McKay experienced and documented bore a considerable amount of openness to and acceptance of various forms of difference. Places with a history of sea traffic tend to have a greater exposure to a variety of practices, ideas, and ways of living, and thus tend to be more tolerant and liberal minded than inland locales. This is particularly the case of large ports on the Mediterranean Sea, and it is this, coupled with the proletarian earthiness of the city, that attracted him to "the cosmopolitan shore of Marseilles" (31), the "piquant variety" (68) of whose street life he celebrates so richly in *Banjo*. Though the text labels the rest of the city staid and bourgeois, the port area of Marseilles is lovingly portrayed as permissive and nonexclusionary: "There was a barbarous international romance in the ways of Marseilles that was vividly significant of the great modern movement of life. [...] Europe's best back door, discharging and receiving its traffic to the Orient and Africa [...] the town seemed to proclaim to the world that the grandest thing about modern life was that it was bawdy" (69).

When he moved on from the south of France, it was this same sort of openness that made Morocco so attractive to McKay as a new place of residence. In *Romance in Marseilles* the character of Aslima is an embodiment and, for the protagonist, Lafala, a personification of Africa. As previously noted, Aslima incarnates the heterogenous nature of Africa—her ancestry is a mix of Arab North Africa on her father's side and black sub-Saharan Africa on her mother's (44). Lafala sees her as "one native thing by which he would begin finding his way back [to Africa] [...] she was an alien like himself" in Marseilles, "an admirable piece of Africa abroad" (4). Aslima spent her formative years in Moulay Abdullah, the prostitutes' quarter of Fez, where she learned a cultivated and refined approach to the world's oldest trade that is for McKay evidence of a more sophisticated understanding of human sexual need than is to be found in the West (45). She brings this comprehension to bear on Lafala, who, though she has previously exploited him materially, she comes to love despite the loss of his legs. If, as the text encourages, the Moroccan Aslima is to be fundamentally equated with Africa, her ability to authentically love one whose status in Western society is defined by his handicap represents the capacity of Africa and Morocco as places to be open to individuals regardless of differences that would stigmatize them in the West.

In the same vein, McKay's poem "Morocco" (1937) gives voice to the sense of attachment, belonging, and enthrallment that McKay felt toward the country even after his departure from it. Addressing the people of Morocco as his "friends," McKay writes of the occasion of Ramadan as a means of expressing the affective connection that he, a nonnative, felt to the land and its people. He addresses Morocco as holding him "willingly [...] captive" by "a magnetic force" and proclaims that when the sounds and practices of Ramadan break out, his thoughts and "hungry spirit" will "fly" there while calling on its people to recall him in their memories and by making for him "One melody, / Of love" (*Complete Poems*, 234). In that festivals are one of the most profound means of performing and affirming a sense of collectivity and common identity among a people, and given that Ramadan is the cardinal holiday of the Muslim world, McKay's sense of being linked to Morocco through and at the time of Ramadan testifies to the extent to which he felt that he was accepted and hence belonged there.

One of the main reasons for this, which McKay expresses in *A Long Way from Home*, is that in Morocco "for the first time in [his] life [he] felt [himself] singularly free of color consciousness" (300). The country's long history of racial mixing between Berbers, Arabs, black Africans, and Europeans made for a relative lack of racial prejudice, a less racialized mode of perceiving others; in the absence of daily interpellation as a black man, he experienced for a time a mode of living "instinctively and by sensations only" (300). This is not to say that McKay claims that Moroccans are blind to race but rather that he sees skin color as less of a primary determinant of identity for them. When Carmina, a former girlfriend, starts a rumor that McKay is racist toward whites, McKay reflects that

> the natives were puzzled about that, because large numbers of them are as white as some Spanish and French. In the Rif[21] and other mountain regions there are blue-eyed and blond-haired types resembling Nordics, except that they are rather bronzed. But they are all remarkably free of any color obsessions or ideas of discrimination. They are Africans. The others are *roumi* or Europeans.[22] So they thought that Carmina meant that I did not like the *roumi* or Europeans. And that did not displease them. They opened their doors wider for me. And I did not mind the report, for I was not particularly interested in European society in North Africa [in the following paragraph he goes on to qualify this statement, noting that he did have white European and American friends in Morocco]. (334)

This description stands in contrast to the criticism McKay provides earlier of European conceptions of race in Morocco: "When I was going to Morocco, some Europeans on the boat had remarked facetiously that Morocco was not a Negro country. Themselves divided into jealous cut-throat groups, the Europeans have used their science to make such fine distinctions among people that it is hard to ascertain what white is a true white and when a Negro is really a Negro. I found more than three-quarters of Marrakesh Negroid" (304). So McKay casts doubt upon the European system of racially characterizing place by both pointing to physiological variation within regional populations and contrasting this mode of seeing with the more color-blind Moroccan mode of conceptualizing difference.[23]

Because he was not marginalized within this latter mode of seeing, McKay could access the different spaces of Morocco, native and colonial European, freely and without attracting disapprobation and hostility from the local population. This mobility contrasted sharply with his experience of more rigidly racially zoned places such as New York City, with its stark divide between black Harlem and white Manhattan, and London, where McKay could not find anyone in close proximity to the British Museum willing to rent a room to a black man (*Long Way from Home*, 304). But the sense of tranquility, racial harmony, and freedom of circulation that suffused McKay's early Moroccan days was eventually ruptured by the colonialist embodiment of "the white hound of Civilization," "the white terror always pursuing the black" (304). Harassed by the British Consul of Tangier as a potential Bolshevik agitator straying from his proper place in frequenting the spaces of the city's native Moroccan population and increasingly aware of the fragmenting social divisions instituted by the Spanish and French protectorates running the country, McKay grew increasingly disillusioned with the southwestern shores of the Mediterranean (*Long Way from Home*, 301–4).

But nonetheless, the spatial accessibility he experienced in Morocco continued to attract McKay. Another reason for the comfort and acceptance McKay felt was that which drew many later (more celebrated expatriate artists such as Paul Bowles, William Burroughs, and Tennessee Williams to Tangier): its tolerance or tacit acceptance of homosexual behavior. Much recent scholarship, including Gary E. Holcomb's "Diaspora Cruises: Queer Black Proletarianism in Claude McKay's *A Long Way from Home*," has considered the role of homoerotic desire in McKay's oeuvre and how his bisexuality contributed to the political commitment so prominent in his work.[24] There is a long tradition of "looking the other way" in Morocco where homosexual sex, officially condemned by Islam, is concerned. Iain Finlayson, in his *Tangier: City of the Dream*, attributes this to the strong valuation of female virginity as a prerequisite of marriageability in Morocco's Islamic society—that is, with young women sexually unavailable, male adolescents and young men often have to turn to each other as sex partners.[25] McKay offers another common rationale for Morocco's traditional acceptance of homosexuality in an elliptic reference to Fez keeping "the cup of Eros containing a little of the perfume of the flower of the passion of ancient Greece" (*Long Way from Home*, 299). In other words, McKay attributes the acceptance of homosexual behavior he encountered in Moroccan society—but never treats directly in his writing, given the conventions of his era—to the residual cultural influence of ancient Greek Eros (or love between men). This idea that the Mediterranean was a bastion of access to gay sex whose practice was rooted in classical culture had become increasingly prevalent during the nineteenth century, particularly following the publication of Sir Richard Burton's 1885 "Terminal Essay" appendix to his translation of *The Arabian Nights*, in which he outlined an imaginary geographical "sotadic zone" running through the Mediterranean in which homosexual "vice" was "not just prevalent but endemic."[26]

Whatever the actual complex historical reasons, this ostensible regional absence of condemnation of homosexual behavior was another key aspect of the openness that endeared Morocco to McKay. He celebrates Morocco's sensuality across his body of Moroccan writings in such poems as "Morocco," "Two Songs of Morocco," and "Xauen," and this sensuality takes on particular homoerotic overtones in the sonnet "Marrakesh."[27] The octet of "Marrakesh" sketches the topography and architecture of the former imperial city of Morocco, glowingly juxtaposes the "ruins of austere monuments" with "gazelle-like [...] Salome-sensual dance of jeweled boys" (*Collected Poems*, 227). The sexual allure of these "Berber youngsters" is both animal (gazelle-like) and lacking in the hard, rugged attributes that McKay attributes to the desirous adult male body in *Home to Harlem* (1928) and elsewhere in his oeuvre.[28] One of the particular allures that Morocco held for the expatriate homosexuals that increasingly flocked there in the years after McKay's departure was the availability of younger male sex partners, who, as Greg Mullins points out in his *Colonial Affairs: Bowles, Burroughs, and Chester Write Tangier*, were prized as bisexual or "sexually undifferentiated" rather than gay and hence seen as men "whose masculinity is uncompromised."[29] So in Morocco, as far as his sexuality was concerned, McKay found a place outside of social prohibitions both regarding the age and gender of viable partners and delimiting categories of identity.

But at the same time that McKay celebrated the greater degree of acceptance of difference he experienced in the Mediterranean locales he inhabited, he was by no means blind to the forms of oppression that also prevailed within the spatial fabric of these places. The teeming port life of Marseilles was exciting to McKay, but it was also "sinister" (*Long Way from Home*, 230), a place whose rampant prostitution testified to "the naked exploitation of man's sexual needs [that] epitomized for him the corrupt greed at the heart of Western materialist society."[30] McKay was a committed socialist who had used autographed copies of his collection *Harlem Shadows* (1922) to solicit enough donations to attend the Fourth Congress of the Communist International in 1922.[31] While the text of *Banjo* appreciated the lively bustle of Marseilles's port and the profusion of goods it teems with, the description of these goods quickly elides into an erotically tinged praise of the "black" and "brown" workers that enables their production: "Sweat-dripping bodies of black men naked under the equatorial sun. [...] Brown men half-clothed, with baskets on their backs, bending low down to the ancient tilled fields under the tropical sun" (67). The exploitation of overseas labor that makes the prosperity and liveliness of Marseilles possible, then, is registered quite clearly, and so is the crushing effect that the economic system has upon the proletariat of the city. *Romance in Marseilles* reveals the existential dynamic of the wage slavery shared by the prostitutes and other workers of the port: "Here [...] was no space, no air. Nothing but the suffocating grinding present" (70). Unlike in Africa, a prostitute could not save up enough to buy her way into a respectable life with a husband due to the ineffaceably stigmatizing mark of prostitution in the West (70). The life available to Marseilles's port denizens did not offer any hope of release or betterment; one was trapped within the socioeconomic system. The unfinished text of *Romance in Marseilles* ends abruptly after the introduction of a radical reformist public speaker and other members of a proletariat meeting hall. While the communist dogma Lafala encounters there is dismissively referred to as a "[r]eligion offering a social millennium" (86), it would been interesting to see what possibilities of social reform and escape from the oppressive circumstances of daily life in working class spaces a completed text might have offered.

But regardless, just as McKay's Marseilles writings critique capitalist forms of oppression, his Tangier writings evince an awareness of the oppressive nature of European colonial possession of Morocco. During the period in question, Morocco, following considerable dispute, was divided into French and Spanish protectorates, with Tangier separately governed by an international administration made up of representatives of the United States and most European states. McKay graphically describes Morocco under this order of colonial control as a grisly plaything of Europe, knocked about in the jockeying for the expansion of colonial empires—"Morocco's severed head is Europe's ball / Kicked from goal to goal and all around— / In the African game of the European" (*Collected Poems*, 225). Tangier itself is portrayed as chained in heavy iron manacles, its formerly anarchic and proud spirit subdued, at least externally, as it is reduced to a tourist destination:

> The tourists stop to gaze at you in chains
> And purchase from the souks a souvenir,
> Thinking your soul breathes in a servile guide.
> But in the bled[32] the rugged mountaineer,
> Invoking God in fierce fanatic pride,
> Lives by the shattered glory that still remains. (*Collected Poems*, 225)

In *A Long Way from Home* McKay also reflects at times on colonialism's more immediate impact on the spaces and practices of daily life. At one point he is persecuted by the authorities of Tangier for stepping outside of the spaces reserved for Westerners under the colonial order by spending the night in a native dwelling (301–2). Later, he is forced to leave Fez under the suspicion of being a communist agent (327–28). McKay insists in *A Long Way from Home* that he was too absorbed by "the purely physical happiness" he experienced in Morocco to "plunge deep enough down into the native ways" or get "too deeply involved" in the religious and political life of its people (332–33), but the incidents noted previously and his earlier remarks regarding the divides in Moroccan social and legal life brought on by the international administrative partitioning of the country show that on some level he registered the forms of oppression going on around him under the colonial regime. Politicized as McKay was—a recent study of his work is entitled *A Fierce Hatred of Injustice: Claude McKay's Jamaican Poetry of Rebellion*—one would not expect otherwise, living as he did roughly halfway between the 1921–1926 war of Abd el-Krim's Riffian guerilla army against the Spanish and French colonial armies and the 1944 founding of the Istiqlal Party,[33] which would eventually agitate successfully for Moroccan independence in 1956.[34] It could be that his avowal of having not been "too deeply involved" is a rhetorical gesture geared, for a change, toward justifying a period of his life spent pursuing sensual enjoyment rather than social justice. It could also be that resistance to the colonial regime around him was muted and nascent enough that it did largely escape his notice. But either way, McKay's Moroccan writings manifest at least a passing awareness of the oppressive nature of colonial governance of Morocco and the presence of native resentment against the "roumis."

* * *

In *Ride Out the Wilderness: Geography and Identity in Afro-American Literature* Melvin Dixon posits that for African American writers the experience of alternative spaces is a means of exploring the sorts of "behavior or performance" endemic to or permitted there and that this exploration is "one step toward the recovery of [a] wholeness" that is missing in these writers' racism-inflected spaces of origin.[35] A major contribution of McKay, the self-professed "troubadour wanderer," "to Afro-American letters has been his consistent search for a home where art and identity can flourish," Dixon further argues. Dixon highlights McKay's embrace of Marseilles as a place geographically and symbolically "squarely between Europe and Africa," where one can find "an exchange of cultural values and a chance to discover hidden racial attributes,"[36] but this was just one localized manifestation of McKay's larger attachment to, and affirmation of, the Mediterranean as kind of "third place" between the white and black regions of the world. The Mediterranean that he conceptualized offered an alternative to the limitations that he as a black man experienced in North America and Europe and to the limited opportunities of the underdeveloped Jamaica of his birth. All told, McKay's Mediterranean is a place of refuge and fellowship, one that, tainted as it was at times by the specter of imperialism, offers glimpses of the closest he was to come in his life and work to finding an ideal spatio-racial order, a privileged place from which he could gain the necessary perspective to interrogate race as a social phenomenon during one of the most intensely creative periods of his life.

Notes

1. The following works by Claude McKay will be hereafter cited by page parenthetically in the text: *Banjo* (San Diego: Harcourt Brace Jovanovich, 1957), *Complete Poems* (Urbana: University of Illinois Press, 2004), *Gingertown* (New York: Harper & Brothers, 1991), *A Long Way from Home* (New York: Arno Press, 1969), and *Romance in Marseilles* (Claude McKay Collection, Yale Collection of American Literature, Beinecke Rare Book and Manuscript Library).

2. William J. Maxwell, "Banjo Meets the Dark Princess: Claude McKay, W. E. B. Dubois, and the Transnational Novel of the Harlem Renaissance," in *The Cambridge Companion to the Harlem Renaissance*, ed. George Hutchinson (Cambridge: Cambridge University Press, 2007).

3. See Robert P. Smith Jr., "Rereading Banjo: Claude McKay and the French Connection." *CLA Journal* 30, no. 1 (September 1986): 46–58; see also Kotti Sree Ramesh and Kandula Nirupa Rani, *Claude McKay: The Literary Identity from Jamaica to Harlem and Beyond* (Jefferson, NC: McFarland, 2006).

4. See McKay, *Long Way from Home*, 230. As Ray, the writer character of McKay's *Home to Harlem* (1928) and *Banjo* flippantly puts it, in class-based terms, when asked why he occupies himself with the vagabond blacks of Marseilles rather than the successful "race men and women" of Paris, "I'm not a reporter for the Negro press. Besides, I can't afford to keep up with the Negroes of Paris. And as they are society folk, they might prefer to have a society writer do them" (*Banjo* 116).

5. The manuscript copy of *Romance in Marseilles* consulted in the writing of this article was provided by Yale's Beincke Library.

6. Gilles Boetsch and Jean-Noel Ferrié, "Ancient Survivals, Comparatism, and Diffusion: Remarks on the Formation of the Mediterranean Cultural Area," in *The Mediterranean Reconsidered: Representations, Emergences, Recompositions*, ed. Mauro Pernissi and Ratiba Hadj-Moussa (Gatineau: Canadian Museum of Civilization, 2005), 9–11.

7. Mauro Pernissi and Ratiba Hadj-Moussa, "Introduction," in *The Mediterranean Reconsidered: Representations, Emergences, Recompositions*, ed. Mauro Pernissi and Ratiba Hadj-Moussa (Gatineau: Canadian Museum of Civilization, 2005), 1.

8. Fernand Braudel, *The Mediterranean and the Mediterranean World in the Age of Philip II*, trans. Sian Reynolds (New York: Harper and Row, 1972).

9. David Nicholls, "The Folk as Alternative Modernity: Claude McKay's *Banana Bottom* and the Romance of Nature," *Journal of Modern Literature* 23, no. 1 (Fall 1999): 80, 94.

10. Wayne F. Cooper, *Claude McKay: Rebel Sojourner in the Harlem Renaissance* (Baton Rouge: LSU Press, 1987), 259, 290.

11. Ibid., 259.
12. Predrag Matvejevitch, "Avant-propos," in *Le rivage des mythes: Une géocritiqe méditerranéenne, Le lieu et son mythe*, ed. Bertrand Westphal (Limoges: Presses Universitaires de Limoges, 2001), 14.
13. Martine Agathe Coste, "Marseilles, ombres portées e ville solaire," in *Le rivage des mythes: Une géocritiqe méditerranéenne, Le lieu et son mythe*, ed. Bertrand Westphal (Limoges: Presses Universitaires de Limoges, 2001), 293, my translation.
14. McKay was far from the only commentator of the time to observe this radical heterogeneity of the city. In his 1930 work of racial theory, *The Myth of the Twentieth Century*, Nazi theorist and future minister Alfred Rosenberg accused Marseilles of being a breeding ground and broadcasting center of "bastardization" (Coste, "Marseilles," 298).
15. The term "Moorish" has a long history of pejorative usage, but no ready English language alternative exists to describe the successive Umayyad, Almoravid, Almohad, and Nasrid dynasties of Muslim Berbers and Arabs that ruled parts of the Iberian peninsula for over seven centuries.
16. See Cooper, *Claude McKay*, 249.
17. Ibid. 252, 271.
18. "Orientalist" in the sense of the term initially proposed by Edward Said in *Orientalism* (New York: Vintage, 1978): "a style of thought based on an ontological and epistemological distinction made between 'the Orient' and (most of the time) 'the Occident,'" a form of discourse that serves "as a Western style for dominating, restructuring, and having authority over the Orient" that operates via (here Said quotes Nietzsche) "a mobile army of metaphors, metonyms, and anthropomorphisms—in short, a sum of human relations, which have been enhanced, transposed, and embellished poetically and rhetorically, and which after long use seem firm, canonical, and obligatory to a people" (2–3, 203). Interestingly, McKay likely appeared as an extra in the 1927 desert romance film *The Garden of Allah* (Cooper, *Claude McKay*, 226) that helped to popularize an exotic and alluring mainstream American conception of North Africa.
19. Arabic for "markets."
20. André Raymond, *Arab Cities in the Ottoman Period: Cairo, Syria, and the Maghreb* (Burlington: Ashgate Publishing, 2002), 10–13, 35–36.
21. A region of northern Morocco.
22. Other commentators on Morocco, such as the artist Brion Gysin, posit that this is rather a roumi/Muslim conceptual dichotomy, with selfhood versus Otherness conceived of in terms of religious affiliation.
23. Though, as noted earlier, McKay often falls into ascribing shared basic defining traits to different racial groups.
24. See Gary E. Holcomb, "Diaspora Cruises: Queer Black Proletarianism in Claude McKay's *A Long Way from Home*," *Modern Fiction Studies* 49, no. 4 (2003): 714–45.
25. See Iain Finlayson, *Tangier: City of the Dream* (London: Harper Collins, 1993).

26. Gordon Waitt and Kevin Markwell, "The Lure of the Sotadic Zone." *Gay and Lesbian Review Worldwide* 15, no. 2 (April 2008): 21.

27. Homosexuality, or more precisely lesbianism, is present in *Romance in Marseilles* as well, but there it is depicted among the déclassé prostitute class.

28. See Patti Capel Swartz, "Claude McKay," *Gay & Lesbian Literature, Vol. 2*, eds., Tom and Sarah Pendergast (Detroit: St. James, 1997): 251–53.

29. Greg A. Mullins, *Colonial Affairs: Bowles, Burroughs, and Chester Write Tangier* (Madison: University of Wisconsin Press, 2002), 126.

30. Cooper, *Claude McKay,* 235.

31. Ibid., 168.

32. Darija (North African Arabic) for "countryside" or "small agrarian community."

33. Arabic for "independence."

34. See Harold D. Nelson, *Morocco: A Country Study* (Washington, DC: American University Press, 1986), 56–57.

35. Melvin Dixon, *Ride Out the Wilderness: Geography and Identity in Afro-American Literature* (Urbana: University of Illinois Press, 1987), 5.

36. Ibid., 45, 50.

6

The Shores of
Aphrodite's Island

Cyprus and European Travel Memory,
1600–1700

Antoine Eche

Cyprus's mythical aspect is well-established. Its praises as cradle of the goddess of love have been sung from Homer to Lawrence Durrell (at least), making clear Bertrand Westphal's statement that, if "few human spaces are left untouched by literature, no Mediterranean place is so."[1] On the maritime road to Jerusalem, its very position on the articulation of Occident and Orient (where, as Voltaire put it, "Europe ends and Asia begins") activates *un imaginaire du lieu*, reminding us of the Greek eschatological idea of the limits of the known world. History came to reinforce this idea, as the island was lost to the Ottomans in 1572, after the Battle of Lepanto saw the victory of the Holy League over the Ottoman Empire. With fewer pilgrims going east and not being one of the most economically attractive places of the eastern Mediterranean, the island of Cyprus did not attract many travelers. It was seen as a contingent stop on the road to the Middle East and the East. In this particular context, it seems crucial to examine the views of Western travelers about the island as its various representations turn it into an ideological space in a time when a new conception of space slowly permeates our mentality thanks to the development of travel writing.[2]

Travel Writing and Geocriticism

Our corpus being exclusively European, we clearly steer away from the idea that the geocritical approach relies on *multifocalization*, understood as the intersection between three types of different cultural points of view. Indeed, in his attempt to distinguish geocriticism from *imagologie*, Westphal asserts that geocriticism relies on the compared study of the exterior (*exogène*), the in-between (*allogène*), and the interior (*endogène*) points of view at work in different texts.[3] In this respect, the study of travel narratives written by Europeans falls into the first category. This is what Westphal calls the "egocentered" approach, the *ego* standing for an individual or a cultural group. This approach is generally chosen in imagological studies as they focus not so much on the representation of the Other but on what this representation tells of the representing culture. This reflexive movement shows that the "I" negates the "he" and in doing so develops an egocentered discourse. As Daniel-Henri Pageaux puts it, the image is "a culture fact and an anthropological usage to express both identity and otherness."[4] However, I would like to assert that it is possible to maintain a geocentered approach through the study of varied media such as poetry, travel writing, and cartography as long as they belong to different and identified cultural subbodies. If our travelers belong to the same cultural area and have in common a similar historical development, it is difficult to assert that they perceive the world (and space) in the same way. Visually speaking, for instance, it is evident that seventeenth-century Dutch painting style differs from the French style of the same period. The question of the referent, among many other things (including the historical development of painting and of its techniques), is crucial here, as those painters would be used to a certain way of looking at space (to avoid the word "landscape" here), a certain light, a different architecture, a certain use of space, and so on. If we had two of these painters to represent the same scene, the result would certainly be different, not just for egotistical reasons but also for cultural ones. This shows that the seventeenth-century European point of view cannot be reduced to a simple entity but is rather a mere retrospective construction.

This is precisely where Paul Hazard's seminal study, *La Crise de la conscience européenne*, focused on the period between 1685 and 1715, shows its limits as it assumes the existence of a single entity. Europeans certainly have many things in common, but they are culturally shaped by their country of residence. With Westphal, in order to distinguish geocriticism from imagology, it seems necessary to focus on the representation of the space of the Other (*l'Ailleurs*) rather than on the representing culture. The use of other perspectives (whether interior or in between, depending on the one already secured) is indeed necessary as long as they are available and historically coherent. It seems impossible to follow such a geocritical approach on a human space that is deprived of local literary expression for various reasons.

In the case of Cyprus, and at the period chosen for this study, there is no literary production from the Greek local population. Writings of philosophers such as Clearchus of Soli, Zeno of Citium, or Epiphanius of Salamis cannot be considered here for two reasons; first, they do not apply to Cyprus, and second, they span from fourth century BC to fourth century AD. Works such as Leontius Machairas's *The Sweet Land of Cyprus* or George Boustronios's *Chronicle*, both written in Cypriot dialect, belong to the beginning and to the end of the fourteenth century. Apart from Etienne de Lusignan's *Description de toute l'isle de Chypre*, published in 1588, there is no evidence of a local literary production until 1788 and the publication by Archimandrite Kyprianos of his *Chronological History of Cyprus*. Leaving aside the fact that the four last texts mentioned belong to history writing rather than fiction, it seems difficult to balance our travelers' observations with contemporary local writings. And considering intertextual references to expand the time frame does not prove useful as they are only available through writings belonging to the exterior point of view and referring to ancient authorities. There are indeed stories—legends—but they are transmitted (if at all) through the representing group. And it is very difficult to identify the origin of a story told by travelers in their narrative as they rarely pinpoint their sources. Moreover, the Other is rarely represented in a communicative interaction with the traveler, and when he is, it rarely concerns the local literary production.[5] As for the Turkish occupants presently on the island, none of them has been known for their writing about the Cypriot space. It is therefore an impossibility to conduct such an approach unless using writings from different periods, which would then imply comparing different objects. For us it is necessary, when possible, to first study texts belonging to the same temporal context and then compare the various periods in order to understand the inevitable fluctuations, novelties, and resurgences of these representations. These two steps seem essential to follow the dynamic movement of spatial representation. Therefore, if some period-centered studies prove unbalanced, it is important to bear this disequilibrium in mind during the second step of the geocritical process. Now, to reflect on Westphal's useful taxonomy, what works with the *exogène* point of view can very well be said of the *endogène* perspective, as Robert T. Tally Jr. shows when he applies geocriticism to classic American literature, where no other point of view seems needed.[6]

All critical points of view converge when considering that the aim of geocriticism is to explore real and imagined geographies. In this sense, there is no contradiction in considering the geography of the imagination in relation to such factual writings as travel narratives, in spite of their referential ambition. Imagined geography appears in two main instances that need to be distinguished here before going any further. First, and before setting sail, the traveler had to question the very notion of "elsewhere" in thinking (or imagining) an unknown space. This is why travel can be seen as a "*mise en intrigue du monde*," as Jean-Didier Urbain puts it.[7] Also, this *rêverie* is bound to its historical and social context. Hence as a person of his time and place, the seventeenth-century traveler can only imagine the island of Cyprus through the collective representations of the place, brought to him through various texts, images, and discourses submitted to the *principe de véridiction*.[8] It has therefore been proven necessary to distinguish between two moments in the spatial apprehension (the imaginary geography) of Cyprus. In medieval times, travelers and men of letters referred to the island in terms of the Christian marvelous.[9] Later, and despite the fact that the connection between the island and Aphrodite had been made centuries ago, it is during the Renaissance that this connection was poetically celebrated following the rediscovery of antique culture (discussed later on in this chapter). This filter affects the representation of the Cypriot space itself in its own shape. For instance, and to focus on the modern period, references to ancient myths are mixed with direct observations or actualized data. A recurrent trait is found in the shared concern for the etymological origin of the name of the island. Many authors evoke ancient historical assertions where Cyprus's sharp and rocky capes are compared with the horns of the Cerastae described in Ovid's *Metamorphoses*, therefore turning a piece of land into a mythical creature. In his *Description de toute l'île de Chypre* (1580), Etienne de Lusignan devotes the first chapter to such etymological concerns and lists fourteen definitions, the thirteenth one mentioning the Cerastae. In 1615, the anonymous author of *Le Pèlerin véritable de la Terre Saincte* quotes Xenagoras and his treaty on the islands where this etymology is to be found.[10] In 1621, the author of *Le Voyage au Levant* mentions this one among three others.[11] What is striking here is to see how ancient knowledge has to fit in modern observations to the point where it seems that "the travel narrative's role is to prove that the world corresponds to the knowledge that we have of it. Travel is no more discovery but confirmation of 'sources.'"[12] Elsewhere, it is the overall shape of the island itself that is said to be like that of a tortoise without any further explanations but that of the authority of the Ancients.[13] These examples show how persistent the memory of old imaginative geographies can be. Their persistence could very well be explained with the development of a well-known encyclopedic attitude that would make these reminiscences almost unavoidable for a conscientious traveler. But they have also become part of its reality, as it seems now almost impossible to evoke this island (not to mention the rest of the Mediterranean area, as Westphal observed) without its mythical dimension.[14]

The second instance to consider is the nature of factual writing itself. Westphal already posed the necessity of questioning the generic nature of the literature used in geocriticism. He eventually argued that fable-weaving was coextensive to travel writing and that because space was product of perception, it transited through *l'imaginaire* as soon as it was represented. This needs to be refined a little in order to understand the cartography of a travel narrative. There is no opposition in the construction of an imaginary geography and the referential ambition of a travel narrative, as it is well established that the separation between fiction and factual writing is purely theoretical, both depending on the subjective process of *mise en intrigue*.[15] There is no pure factual writing just as there is no pure fictional writing. There are indeed zones where fiction appears to be a salient feature of travel writing. The perceived emptiness of maritime space can then be filled with real or fictitious anecdotes, providing the reader with a feeling of duration and pleasure.[16] Also, imaginary geography can appear when the referential ambition has been said to fail in achieving its aim—the wording of the world. Christine Montalbetti has thus shown that writers would resort to the mediation of intertextuality in order to produce the narrative of their travels. This filtering device would ultimately deform the object and reveal the impossibilities of the referential ambition.[17] In our sense, the use of intertextuality in travel writing is not a sign of a failure but rather the mark of the genre itself. As Jean-Michel Racault puts it, "The traveler's look inevitably relies on a preconceived imaginary, and his discourse inscribes itself within an intertextual network. This explains the persistence of geographical or anthropological myths that experience should have demented, as with the giant Patagonians that even the most serious travelers described not as tall as it has been said without questioning their existence."[18]

The tribute paid to prior authoritative knowledge shows that setting an arbitrary borderline between referential writing and fiction is erroneous. In fact, travel writing usually exemplifies conditioning by cultural filters, three aspects of which are the perpetuation of myths, plagiarism, and inspirational readings. Such elements are precisely inherent parts of the genre, understood as a montage of genres and nonhomogenized types of discourses.[19] To expand on Pasquali, it is rather its integrative capacity that stands out, rather than its failure to express reality. A fine example of this is to be found in Awnsham Churchill and John Churchill's *Collection of Voyages and Travels*. In the preface, the editors introduce the narratives chosen for their collection in brief notices and legitimate not only their authenticity but the truth of their content. The public figure of the author, the presence of witnesses, the nature of the facts and the plainness of the style are elements used here to authenticate the narratives. But for one of them, this critical approach is unexpectedly abandoned: "The adventures of M. T. S., an English merchant, taken prisoner by the Turks of Argier, and carried into the inland country of Africk, 12°. Containing a short account of Argier in the year 1648 of the country about it, and more particularly of the city Tremizen, where the author resided three years, going abroad with several parties which his master commanded, and relates some love intrigues he had with Moorish women, as also very strange metamorphoses of men and other creatures turned into stone. The relation is plain and without artifice."[20] The contrast between the last two sentences is a remarkable paradox founded on the constraints brought by the developing, critical attitude of the Enlightenment and the imaginary potential of a place, and here, not the least of all when considering the history of the Oriental taste.

Taking what can be considered as an extreme example of an imaginary perception of Cyprus is the depiction made in 1615 by Henry de Beauveau, who has seen the island from afar but has never set foot on the shore. Beauveau is on his way to Jerusalem and follows the traditional route to the Holy Land. Sailing along the coast from Paphos to Famagousta, his description is mainly an indirect one, as it sums up historical and mythical data, displayed as a veil over the very brief allusions on the natural and agricultural resources of the island. Contemporary Cyprus is only evoked in one tiny sentence to point out how few inhabitants are left on the island and how heavily taxed they are by the local Pasha.[21] This description is therefore a montage of various texts, where ancient and Christian mythologies are not questioned but rather are sustained by each other. Indeed, in mentioning the former presence of the first temple dedicated to Aphrodite on the island, Beauveau does not forget to recall that one prayer done by Saint Barnabas, the local patron saint, was enough to put down both the temple and the idol. The road is therefore open to promote Christian authority over the Cypriot space with a second mythical anecdote as he recalls the legend of Saint Helena transporting the holy cross through Cyprus. Her unexpected stay eventually led to the renaming of the highest mountain of the island as the Mount of the Cross, as opposed to Mount Olympus.[22]

Memories of Aphrodite

As part of the Christianized Greek cultural heritage, Cyprus is perceived as a part of a territorial and spiritual entity. The traveler is well aware of this particular situation, especially for the period chosen for this study. The dual character and the use of the past of an area that founded the occidental cultural identity are inscribed in the practice of cultural memory as defined by Jan Assman. For Assman, cultural memory is "a collective concept for all knowledge that directs behavior and experience in the interactive framework of a society and in that obtains through generations in repeated societal practice and initiation."[23] This memory is based on the horizon of "fixed points [that] are fateful events of the past, whose memory is maintained through cultural formation (texts, rites, monuments) and institutional communication (recitation, practice, observance). We call these 'figures of memory.'"[24] Both Christian and Pagan mythological references constitute the figures of Cypriot memory, and both of them will be celebrated through their textual perpetuation. It is of course the figure of Aphrodite that will reemerge from the sixteenth century onward, paralleling Christian myths and both resulting in the mapping of an ideological space delimiting the ultimate border between the West and the East.[25] This is a blatant feature of both literary and geographical writings of the 1570s. At the historical point of the passing of the island from the Venetians to the Ottomans, the description of Cyprus in *Theatre of the World* by Abraham Ortelius is based on ancient references stressing Aphrodite in particular (1573). Following the change of ruling power, the French poet Pierre de Ronsard devotes a sonnet to the island, *Vœu à Vénus pour garder Cypre de l'armée du Turc*, which concentrates the attributes associated to the goddess; the strength of Aphrodite will free the island from its invaders.

> Belle Déesse, amoureuse Cyprine,
> Mere du Jeu, des Graces et d'Amour,
> Qui fais sortir tout ce qui vit, au jour,
> Comme du Tout le germe et la racine:
> Idalienne, Amathonte, Erycine,
> Garde du ciel Cypre ton beau sejour:
> Baise ton Mars, et tes bras à l'entour
> De son col plie, et serre sa poitrine.
> Ne permets point qu'un barbare Seigneur
> Perde ton isle et souille ton honneur:
> De ton berceau chasse autre-part la guerre.
> Tu le feras, car d'un trait de tes yeux
> Tu peux flechir les hommes et les Dieux,
> Le Ciel, la Mer, les Enfers et la Terre (*Amours diverses*, IL, 1578)

From the end of the sixteenth to the end of the seventeenth century, this figure of memory will usually be used to explain the island's etymology and to evoke its abounding natural resources. Thus Aphrodite appears in Etienne de Lusignan's *Description* (3) as well as in Corneille Le Brun's narrative (381). It is however absent from the anonymous narratives of *Le Pèlerin véritable* and *Le Voyage au Levant*. However, in both cases, the etymology is clearly addressed in mythological terms. This etymological concern has a dual function, both explicative and memorial. Through textual repetition and the creation of a literary *topos*, it acquires the social function of a ritual, where the sharing of cultural references induces the acknowledgment of this culture and of its identity. It is not surprising to see under Lusignan's pen an etymology that does not appear anywhere else. For personal reasons described in sad and violently anti-Islamic terms (preface, nonpaginated), Lusignan asserts that the first name of the island derives from the name Cetin, son of Japheth. His historical description is therefore subordinated to this primal Christian origin and defies the actual occupation of the island by the Ottomans. What can be seen as a personal act of revenge is conditioned by Lusignan's cultural background and therefore magnifies the practice of cultural memory though the constitution of an ideological space.

As an object of etymology, Aphrodite is definitely associated with the land itself in terms of fertility and sensuality, alluding to her mythical birth. As she touched the ground, Hesiod wrote, the land became green and profligate with natural resources.[26] Fertility was associated with sensuality in an always active connotative network. If Ortelius, while detailing the resources of the island, recalls the legendary Cypriot times of debauchery, Ariosto furnishes a poetical evocation of these two traits in a different light, escaping the judgment of morals. In this section, the poet describes the arrival of a boat around Paphos, "a country of love and pleasure," where the navigator finds himself surrounded by sweet smells of laurel, cedar, orange tree, saffron, rose, lily, and rosemary. This very fragrant approach is followed by the allusion to fertile waters and is ended by the characterization of the female inhabitants who are always in love, even to their death. Not only parts of a poem by itself, these verses form the epigraph of Lusignan's narrative. In Beauveau's text, previously evoked, the fertility of the Paphos area is mentioned without any precision (86), and the whole island is described as fertile in fruits and vegetables (88). Cornelius von Bruyn celebrates its wines as well as its cereal production and the profusion of game, outclassing the rest of the world (385). However, if fiction sets the emphasis on agreeable fragrances, factual writing tends to eradicate such a representation, as with von Bruyn. He reports that the air is unbreathable three to four months a year during the summer and is the known cause of a sometimes lethal sickness. In fact, von Bruyn left before the hot season and could not verify the effects of the Cypriot summer air (386). What is interesting, however, is that in spite of the travelers' observation of the deprived aspects of the island in terms of population, the island remains fertile, even for resources necessitating the help of man. Thus von Bruyn asserts that there are only two fortified towns left, Nicosia, the capital, and Famagousta, as opposed to the thirteen described by ancient authors. The other villages are usually portrayed as ruined boroughs (382). Beauveau states that after Catherine Cornaro's departure, the number of inhabitants fell (89). In both cases, the fertility of the island remained intact.

Aphrodite on the Map

Completing the traveler's material for memory, maps appear as a mixed object that provides more to see and read than the contour of a determined territory.[27] Following Christian Jacob we "prefer to consider the materialisation and the construction of an image instead of the representation of the earth [...]. A materialization and construction of an image of space: above all in the minds of the cartographer and of the society to which he or she belongs."[28] As a vision of space and the summary of various pieces of knowledge, the map is one of the many expressions of the rapport between man and space, whether near or far. This is where notions such as situation (and orientation), knowledge, understanding, and exploration (and therefore power and identity) interconnect to create symbolic figurations and ideological representations. While constructing a space, the map also creates an identity, both individual and collective, that goes through the adherence to a proposed organization of an heterogeneous world.[29] Drawn by Europeans belonging to different cultural subbodies, these maps constitute valuable material for our geocritical approach. It is essential to take into consideration the repetitive appearances of Aphrodite on the maps of Cyprus edited during the seventeenth century and even later on. Indeed, Aphrodite and the island are found on the same edited page in what constitutes a cartographical topos that needs to be focused upon through salient examples.

After Aphrodite set foot on the shore, she was then led to the Immortals to be dressed, as Homer put it.[30] The goddess is therefore associated with the idea of guidance, of orientation. This could explain why an illustrated Aphrodite is to be found on various maps of the island in a cartouche, usually set in the lower right corner. Her image stands out as the overall outline of these maps is based on the same pattern, with the island set in the middle of a maritime space, sketched with a few waves and ships. This is the case in Willem Blaeu's map, *Cyprus insula*, which first appeared in 1635.[31] In this colorful copper engraving, Aphrodite is presented facing the viewer, half-naked and sprawled on a blue and gold drape over a shell-shaped vessel pulled by two white swans over a blue and brown sea. She is holding the reins in a careless way with a right hand while holding roses with her left hand. A cherub is poking her with an arrow above her right breast. Her face does not show any pain and she looks somewhat detached from what is happening. In the background of this scene, two crooning doves are resting on an engraved stone, where the title of the map is displayed. It must be said that this scene really stands out, first because of its ungeographical character but also because of the dual representation of the sea. The island should be surrounded by water, but, of course, that is not the case as the interest lies in the first space, the land itself. The vacuum around it is a representation *in absentia* of the sea, only made explicit by the depiction of three small vessels sailing in various directions. Now the bluish zone, as a representation *in praesentia*, creates a third space that adds realism. However, it is connected to the second one, which isolates it from the rest of the map. Aphrodite is therefore obliquely associated with the island: she is part of the map and belongs to a figurative space that conveys paradoxically more realism than the "scientific contour" of the island itself. Is the viewer to understand that the myth is linked to the reality of Cyprus?

However, considering the rationalizing context of the period, it could be surprising to have such a mythological reference on a geographical figure chosen since 1573 for its renowned accuracy and its scientific authoritative presence in Ortelius's *Theatre of the Universe*. But there is apparently no direct reference to the fiction of the myth and its supernatural reality if one agrees that classicism and the Enlightenment will eventually evacuate the marvelous from the myth.[32] What appears rather significant is that this little and sometimes colorful vignette appears in the seventeenth century, precisely in Willem Blaeu's *Atlas Novus* in 1635—that is to say, in a booming baroque period.[33] The little icon would only be granted an illustrative role corresponding to the baroque aesthetics. It must be noted here that if the presentation of the map varies over the seventeenth century, its figure (*tracé*) will not evolve from 1573 until 1750, coinciding with the beginning of the Ottomans' reign. The added image would then help to distinguish the map it belongs to from other maps using the same island figure. This illustrative dynamic, however, is antagonistic to the scientific correctness of the map. Indeed, the recurrence of the same figure indicates some stagnation in the ongoing cartographic impulse of the period that is known to spread over exclusive geographic concerns to major philosophical questioning, as with Pascal for instance. The only acceptable reason seems to be due to the lack of direct observation during the Ottoman period.[34] The relative obsolescence of the map needs to be dissimulated under ornamental vignettes in a rather commercial way, as illustrated books become more and more fashionable and sought after. In an aesthetic context globally based on Horace's notions of instruction and pleasure, the map of Cyprus, while offering average instruction, compensates with the explicit assertion of aesthetic pleasure of looking at the whole image and also with the reassertion of the island's sensually pleasurable character, mixed with abundance (with the icon). Finally, if toponyms are the same, evocative names referring to traditionally accepted places of cult such as Paphos or Amathonthus can play a double role here because they not only denote actual places but also constitute fragments of a mythological code that speaks for itself. As part of the traveler's equipment, maps appear essential in their *magasin de la mémoire*, to use Saint Augustine's words, and interconnect with other published material.

This opposition is echoed by the nature of the space these images inscribe themselves: one is terrestrial and constitutes itself into an iconic object; the other is maritime and is the one where Aphrodite is set, but it also contains the terrestrial space. Introducing a world that can be qualified as *"métoyen"* ("in between") in its composition, in order to use an expression often used to qualify travel literature in the seventeenth century,[35] the figure of the island only makes sense thanks to its surrounding and yet antagonistic element. Therefore the island belongs to the sea and the one that dominates the sea dominates the island. The Cypriot space is almost always seen through and for its mythical dimension, as the constant evocations of the travelers show. Otherwise, how can we interpret the orientation of Aphrodite's face turned toward the viewer but as a game of power where the myth looks at the person looking at the map? The off-center position of the goddess is not fortuitous; it is used as a *"délégué de l'énonciation cartographique"* as long as it is accepted that the map signifies and shows that it does so.[36]

This seems to be confirmed by the double-stereotyping effect produced by the copying of the island figure and the icon. Referring to the essence of things, the stereotype gives an eidetic character to the relation between these two instances and therefore poses the question of identity. The little vignette is not only illustrative but re-presents the indefeasible link between the island and the goddess, as they cannot be thought otherwise by the cartographers. Part of the same representative text, symbol, and icon produce two discourses that are transcended through their interaction. The stereotype not only becomes the sign of the blocking of a thought, partly due to an unfavorable context for exploratory travel and partly due to a lack of interest, but also becomes the sign of the denial of a contemporary Cypriot space other than Hellenic. The question of the Other, under the figure of the Ottoman and of the space of the Other, the Orient, is therefore posed *in absentia*.

The second map I have in mind explicitly confirms this reading. Drawn in Holland by the cartographer Jacques Peters, it stands out from the rest of the production by its regressive figure borrowed from the deformed map used by Beauveau earlier in the century. The map notably adds Oriental motifs inside the cartouche, such as a palm tree, a camel, and characters with their ethnic costumes. All these characters (including the camel) are drawn facing the viewer. They all are looking to their left—that is to say, to the East—and the character closest to the island points to it. On a different scale and below the Oriental man's hand, a basic representation of Aphrodite on her seashell-shaped cart looks up in direction of this group. Considering the size and the layout of all these figures, this situation clearly interrogates the representation of the Orient and that of the island's identity. The island is no longer predominantly Hellenic and its identity needs to be apprehended through the fluctuations of its history. As a symbol for change, the sketching of maritime battles all around the island recalls its violent history and its consequences. That the discourse that will be developed for this already appears blocked is another story. What matters are the perception and the representation of the dynamic nature of space. It is not the only occurrence where such a dichotomy is presented in a map concerning this area. In a larger vision of the area (from Italy to Syria), *Orientalor districtus Maris Mediterranei* by Frederick de Wit, originally published in 1675 and republished in 1745, a cartouche placed at the top of the map opposes a group of three Europeans to one of three Orientals.[37] What is noteworthy is that while the three Orientals all carry weapons in a nonthreatening way, only one European is raising a sword at them, while the second one seems to be talking to them and the third is playing music. The balance clearly swings in favor of the occidental world since force, eloquence, and arts are opposed to force alone. The cartouche clearly transcends its ornamental and baroque grandeur and can be seen as an ideological key to the map itself.

Conclusion

The diachronic perspective appears essential to conduct a geocentered approach when dealing with a shortage of both *endogène* and *exogène* text material that is explained by the history of the place. As Alain Corbin put it, the study of the "imaginaire" should be conducted within a historically contextualized framework.[38] The resurgence of Aphrodite in the Renaissance and her role as a figure of memory clearly meets ideological expectations after the Battle of Lepanto. Therefore the imaginary geography of Cyprus is to be considered not only through the tidal rhythms of its history but also from an angle differentiating subcultural bodies within the European point of view, as well as a means of representation. Dutch maps and travel writing and French travel writing and poetry evoke the island and "construct an image," to use Christian Jacob's words, of the Cypriot space that is not uniform. If the French Beauveau does not set foot on the shore, the Dutch Corneille Le Brun visits places that have not been described by Europeans before and probably writes the most detailed travel narrative on Cyprus of his time. However, and in spite of his actual and direct observations, he resorts to intertextuality and therefore a preconceived imaginary as the traditional generic rules of travel writing "advise" to do. Intertextuality is due not only to the sensual apprehension of space but also to the genre itself. If the quality of direct observation may vary and produce an uneven image, the eschatological idea of limits, applied here to the division between Orient and Occident, appears consistent. This binary system is also echoed in the French attitude toward the Ottomans. To obtain cultural supremacy, it is necessary to develop the terrifying idea of an Oriental despotic regime. Etienne de Lusignan's egocentered point of view falls therefore into a more global process, and his own imaginary geography lights up one of the facets of Cyprus's figurative dimension, as with Miguel Cervantes in the opening lines of one of his exemplary novels, *The Generous Lover*. At the same time, it has been observed that the depiction of such a despotic power offers a mirrored image of France's own political system from Louis XIII to Louis XIV.[39] This situation is not shown in our Cyprus-focused approach, but this would probably happen for more popular Oriental destinations. The shores of Aphrodite's island still need to be overstepped.

Notes

1. Bertrand Westphal, *Le Rivage des mythes: Une géocritique méditerranéenne* (Limoges: PULIM, 2001), 9.
2. See Sylvie Requemora, "L'espace dans la littérature de voyages," *Etudes littéraires* 34, no. 1–2 (2002): 249–76.
3. Bertrand Westphal, *La Géocritique: Réel, fiction, espace* (Paris: Minuit, 2007), 208–9.
4. Daniel-Henri Pageaux, *La Littérature générale et comparée* (Paris: Armand Colin, 1994), 61.
5. I discuss Cyprus in particular in my as yet unpublished "Représentations de la communication dans les récits de voyages à Chypre aux XVIIe et XVIIIe siècles."
6. See Robert T. Tally Jr., "Geocriticism and Classic American Literature" (English Department Faculty Publications, paper 14, Texas State University, 2008) http://ecommons.txstate.edu/englfacp/14.
7. Jean-Didier Urbain, *Secrets de voyages: menteurs, imposteurs et autres voyageurs invisibles* (Paris: Payot, 1998), 31.
8. Michel Foucault, *La naissance de la biopolitique* (Paris: Seuil/Gallimard, 2004), 37.

9. See Gilles Grivaud, ed., *Excerpta Cypria Nova, Vol I: Voyageurs occidentaux à Chypre au XVème siècle* (Nicosia: Sources et études de l'histoire de Chypre, 1990), 15.

10. Anonymous, *Le pèlerin véritable de la Terre Saincte* (Paris: Louis Feburier, 1615), 447.

11. D. C., *Voyage au Levant* (Paris: Adrian Taupinar, 1621), 325–326.

12. François Moureau, "Imaginaire vrai," in *Métamorphoses du récit de voyage*, ed. François Moureau (Paris/Genève: Librairie Honoré Champion/Slatkine, 1986), 165–67.

13. Anonymous, *Le Pèlerin*, 446.

14. See Fabienne Baider, *La communication touristique: approches discursives de l'identité et de l'altérité* (Paris: L'Harmattan, 2004).

15. Gérard Genette, *Fiction et diction* (Paris: Seuil, 1997), 53.

16. Requemora, "L'espace," 261.

17. Christine Montalbetti, *Le Voyage, le monde et la bibliothèque* (Paris: PUF, 1997), 5, 41.

18. Jean-Michel Racault, "Voyages et utopie," in *Histoire de la France littéraire, Classicismes. XVIIe-XVIIIe siècles*, ed. Jean-Charles Darmon and Michel Delon (Paris: PUF, 2006), 293.

19. Adrien Pasquali, *Le Tour des horizons. Critique et récits de voyages* (Paris: Klincksieck, 1994), 131–32.

20. Awnsham Churchill and John Churchill, *A Collection of Voyages and Travels* (London: 1732), xciii.

21. Henry de Beauveau, *Relation journalière du voyage du Levant* (Nancy: Jacob Garnich, 1615), 86–92.

22. Ibid., 91.

23. Jan Assman, "Collective Memory and Cultural Identity," *New German Critique* 65 (Spring–Summer 1995): 126.

24. Ibid., 129.

25. Following Louis Althusser's definition of ideology in *Pour Marx* (Paris: Maspéro, 1975), 238.

26. See Hésiode, *Théogonie et autres poèmes*, suivi des *Hymnes homériques,* ed. Jean-Louis Backès (Paris: Folio, 2001), 102–202.

27. Louis Marin, "La ville dans la carte et son portrait," in *De la représentation*, ed. Daniel Arasse (Paris: Gallimard/Le Seuil, 2000), 207.

28. Christian Jacob, *The Sovereign Map* (Chicago: University of Chicago Press, 2006), 99.

29. See Deleuze and Guattari, *Milles Plateaux* (Paris: Minuit, 1980); see also Jacob, *Sovereign Map*, 100.

30. See Homère, *Hymne à Aphrodite* in *Théogonie et autres poèmes*, suivi des *Hymnes homériques*, ed. Jean-Louis Backès (Paris: Folio, 2001), vol. 2, 1–18.

31. A fine reproduction can be found in Leonora Navari, *Maps of Cyprus* (Nicosia: Bank of Cyprus Cultural Foundation, 2003), 165.

32. See Pierre Albouy, *Mythes et mythologies dans la littérature française* (Paris: Armand Colin, 1998).

33. See Leonora Navari, *Maps of Cyprus*, 164–165.

34. Andreas Hadjipaschalis, "Cyprus: 2,500 Years of Cartography," in *Maps of Cyprus*, ed. Leonora Navari (Nicosia: Bank of Cyprus Cultural Foundation, 2003), 27.

35. See François Bertaud, *Journal du voyage d'Espagne* (Paris: Denys Thierry, 1699), vol. 4.

36. Marin, "La ville," 212, 206.

37. See Navari, *Maps of Cyprus*, 203.

38. Alain Corbin, *Le Territoire du vide: L'occident et le désir du rivage, 1750–1840* (Paris: Champs Flammarion, 1990), 321–322.

39. Requemora, "L'espace," 269.

7

Jefferson's Ecologies of Exception

Geography, Race, and American Empire in the Age of Globalization

Christine M. Battista

One of the essential characteristics of modern biopolitics (which will continue to increase in our century) is its constant need to redefine the threshold in life that distinguishes and separates what is inside from what is outside. Once it crosses over the walls of the *oikos* and penetrates more and more deeply into the city, the foundation of sovereignty—nonpolitical life—is immediately transformed into a line that must be constantly redrawn.

—Georgio Agamben, *Homo Sacer: Sovereign Power and Bare Life*[1]

The earth is in effect one world, in which empty, uninhabited spaces virtually do not exist. Just as none of us is outside or beyond geography, none of us is completely free from the struggle over geography.

—Edward Said, *Culture and Imperialism*[2]

Conceiving of the planet as "a lump of minerals," instead of as "a complex web of life," capitalism relies on colossal technical "gimmicks" to simplify and homogenize life on earth, thereby "undoing the work of organic evolution" and leading to biospheric breakdown. Capitalism is "the absolute incarnation of social evil," because of its competitiveness, its egoism, its commitment to endless growth, and its arrogant view that humans can remake the natural world. [. . .] If current trends go unchecked, we are told, the future holds two grim scenarios: either nature will take "revenge" on our profligate behavior, or capitalists will replace faltering biological systems with synthetic substitutes.

—Michael E. Zimmerman, *Contesting Earth's Future: Radical Ecology and Postmodernity*[3]

In the age of our current world picture, the momentum of globalization has vastly redefined our geopolitical constitution through an aggressively reductionist ethos that has mediated the ways in which humans relate to the nonhuman world. We find ourselves in the midst of an ecologically precarious moment in which borders are increasingly redefined and threatened by environmental disasters. Despite the ways in which we have sought to implement order and space both nationally and globally, the environment, it seems, cannot be contained or defined. So if we are to think about geocriticism and what it means to examine geocritical practices in literary scholarship, I suggest that we should more carefully consider the relationship between *geocriticism* and *ecocriticism*, articulating and examining the myriad ways in which theories of space and geography conjoin with theories of ecology. In this respect, I illustrate the sociopolitical importance of developing an ecocritical geoontology—an ecologically centered examination of geography. I define *geoontology* as a critical examination of how Being has been defined and coded spatially according to the hegemonic truth discourse of Western modernity. I derive my definition of "Western modernity" from William V. Spanos, who describes it as a "truth discourse whose origins lay in a totalizing metaphysical interpretation of being that spatialized, structuralized and, more precisely, territorialized temporality (the difference it always already disseminates) in the name of a transcendental principle of identity—an order tethered to an absolute Origin, the anthropologos."[4] I argue that this truth discourse has permeated and mediated how we inhabit the earth and has likewise led to the destruction of the environment, reducing and annulling the "living" nature of the earth itself into mere material matter for the developmental and global flows of capitalism. By imagining the relationship between theories of ecology and geocriticism, we can begin to envision an alternative relationship with the earth, one that unfolds into a more ethical, humane form of dwelling with both the human and nonhuman world.

I ground the origins of my discussion within one of America's earliest cultural archives, beginning with the taxonomic model Thomas Jefferson implemented within *Notes on the State of Virginia.*[5] Composed in 1781, *Notes* served as a spatialized foundation through which Americans were expected to learn and interpret their environment. By neatly arranging each of his chapters into orderly, comprehensible categories, this book would later provide a tremendous influence for how Americans would learn to inhabit the land. Jefferson established this ordering in *Notes*, for his intentions were to inform Americans how to properly arrange space and how to code, control, and orient the land according to the imperial interests of the American republic. *Notes* was one of the first archival documents to incorporate nature into the state apparatus by presupposing that lines, boundaries, and borders preceded the radical alterity of the land itself, thus systematically concealing alternative ways of relating to the land: more equitable, humane, ethical, nonimperial, ecologically sustainable methods that could potentially threaten to disrupt America's careful management of its human and nonhuman organization. As Krista Comer articulates, "natural spaces themselves, when mapped by human minds, not only reflect human social organization but, as representational systems, participate in both the construction and maintenance of every kind of racial, gender, class, sexual, regional, and nationalist relationship imaginable."[6] *Notes* serves as an integral example of the ways in which the American imperial imaginary was distinctly defined in and through its organization of its human and nonhuman landscape.

Mapping Precedes Ecology: The Jeffersonian Vision

When Thomas Jefferson composed *Notes on the State of Virginia* in 1781, he was particularly concerned with establishing a universal American national identity that was distinctly separate from, and superior to, its European counterpart. Bewildered and discomforted by the vast expanses of uncultivated land that lay before him, Jefferson needed to compose an imperial doctrine that established an eco-exceptionalist frame of reference through which the American body politic could code the land.[7] An inheritor of post–Revolutionary War American idealism, Jefferson's vision culminated within the yeoman farmer—the dutiful, industrious American male who could achieve order over the land through his cultivation of the soil. The yeoman farmer was, for Jefferson, the key to achieving this kind of order across the American continent. In this respect, *Notes* served as an interpretive grid through which Americans were intended to learn their environment.[8] By neatly arranging each of his chapters into orderly, comprehensible categories, the book was, in Jeffrey Myers's words, a "continental-wide vision of ecological and racial hegemony, whereby all elements of the natural world—land, watersheds, climate, trees, beaver, bison, and people—would be under the control and exploitation of an expanding, increasingly Anglo-American society."[9] This book would later provide a tremendous influence for how Americans would learn to interpret space and nature—and would learn a form of inhabitancy that neglected the actual "living" portion of nature in exchange for an imperial, developmental land ethics. What follows throughout the course of the nineteenth century is a manufactured "ordering of space" that constituted, in Giorgio Agamben's words, "not only a taking of land—the determination of a juridical and territorial ordering—but above all a taking of the outside, an exception."[10]

The beginning of Jefferson's *Notes on the State of Virginia* embodies this element of spatial coding. By opening his book with the mathematical parameters of Virginia's state boundaries, Jefferson implies that, first and foremost, spatial order precedes ecology—and that, in order for Jefferson to establish any frame of reference with American land, he needed first to territorialize and enclose the landscape. The first passage in the book reads as follows: "Virginia is bounded on the East by the Atlantic: on the North by a line of latitude, crossing the Eastern shore through Watkin's Point, being about 37° · 57' · North latitude; from thence by a streight line to Cinquac, near the mouth of Patowmac; thence by the Patowmac, which is common to Virginia and Maryland, to the first fountain of its northern branch; thence by a meridian line, passing through that fountain till it intersects a line running East and West, in latitude 39° · 43' · 42.4" which divides Maryland from Pennsylvania" (3). Beginning with the parameters of Virginia, or, perhaps more poignantly, establishing Virginia's boundaries as *central* to *Notes*—and to how the rest of the text would unfold—reveals Jefferson's desire to orient and produce an American national narrative predicated distinctly on its exceptional ability to control and police the landscape. In this respect, Jefferson implemented what I describe as an "ecological state of exception." As Agamben defines it, "through the state of exception, the sovereign creates and guarantees the situation that the law needs for its own validity."[11] Jefferson, who represents the sovereign American authorial voice, composed a spatialized code of ethics, a code that revealed America's burgeoning anxiety over open, unenclosed landscapes. America's imperial development was predicated on its ability to continually refract these anxieties through the management of punitive landscapes and a patriarchal biopolitics of identity formation. *Notes on the State of Virginia* is a treatise as to how America's state of nature was to be incorporated into the state apparatus.

I place such emphasis on Jefferson's inaugural discussion of Virginia's boundaries because I believe it is symptomatic of a more global phenomenon that has permeated the twenty-first century, a phenomenon that Mary Louise Pratt terms the "global classificatory project." This "project" is initially exemplified through Jefferson's systematic drawing and policing

of geopolitical boundaries alongside his taxonomic "observing and cata-
loguing of nature"—a modality through which nature itself became "nar-
ratable" and thus controllable.[12] And it is at this particular moment that
America begins to define its "ecologies of exception": American land, as
open space, as *terra nullius*, was always on-call for dominion, management,
and exploitation. Trees were clear-cut on a massive scale; masses of animals were willfully exterminated; landscapes, rivers, and other watersheds
were decimated and polluted. America became "exceptional" because it
could willfully disavow the violence it continually perpetuated on its living environment. As Jeffrey Myers accurately assesses, America's imperial
dominion was dependent "on imagining the essential otherness of the
physical world [because] any recognition that the 'self' was ecologically
interconnected threatened to erase individual identity as it is defined in
European metaphysics, an identity 'whose sole essence or nature consists
in thinking.'"[13] Ecology—nature—could only make sense in the American
imagination if it were capable of scientific examination. In this respect,
Jefferson's geoimperial ethics were inherently environmentally destructive
because they produced an exceptional principle of presence through which
the radical ecological alterity of the land was denied and annulled.

Elements of Jefferson's geoimperial ethics are redolent throughout *Notes*.
Each section is organized into neatly ordered and definable categories. The
table of contents, for instance, begins with "Boundaries of Virginia," followed by "Rivers"; "Sea-Ports"; "Mountains"; "Cascades"; "Productions of
Mineral, Vegetable, and Animal"; and "Climate" and continues with this
Linnaean classification from "Aborigines" to "Religion" to "Subjects of
Commerce." Jefferson's categorization of the American natural archive is
arranged according to each section's potential commodity value. Rivers, for
example, only make sense to Jefferson as potential ports of transportation
that can accelerate the continental momentum of westward expansion.[14]
Similarly, Virginian soil is unthinkable to Jefferson unless it generates some
kind of use value.[15] The potential of the land to exist in its own right is simply eliminated from the Jeffersonian imagination. Jefferson's ontological
authority *depends* on his ability to subordinate the landscape, a phenomenon that is symptomatic of the Cartesian mind-body dualism that "views
'nature' as everything that is 'not-me,' which leads to a radical splitting off
of the mind from the human body and the body of earth in which the latter
becomes subaltern."[16] By giving form to an inherently subaltern, shapeless
body of land, Jefferson becomes the American Adamic patriarch who has
the distinct power to name, arrange, and develop an orderly landscape.

A number of recent essays treat Jefferson's *Notes* as a rigorous work of
natural environmental history and represent him as a painstaking conserva-
tionist, naturalist, and emancipatory intellectual.[17] And although Jefferson

certainly had a vision for an ecologically responsible republic, his "vision" was nevertheless contingent on an ethos that actually *denied* the land as having any kind of living agency.[18] Jefferson's reading of the American landscape enabled, in William Spanos's words, an anthropocentric "binary logic" that empowered the position of the surveyor while representing the land as "some kind of arbitrary threat" that needed to be "subdued and appropriated."[19] In order for the land to have any kind of meaning to Jefferson, it needed to become *Americanized*—which meant transforming the open wilderness into cultivated, settled spaces that could be carefully monitored and controlled. Jefferson's insistence on a spatialized and compartmentalized landscape paralleled a dramatic shift in spatial awareness and human relations that were coming to full fruition during his historical juncture. As I emphasize in the next section, this spatialized ethics was deeply mired within a patriarchal, racialized paradigm that severely annulled the agency of women and people of color, including Native Americans.

Racial Ecologies and the Formation of a Fractured Body Politic

It is common knowledge that nomads fare miserably under our kinds of regime. We would to any length in order to settle them. [. . .] But the nomad is not necessarily one who moves; some voyages take place *in situ*, are trips in intensity. Even historically, nomads are not those who move about like migrants. On the contrary, they do not move; nomads, they nevertheless stay in the same place and continually evade the codes of settled peoples.

—Gilles Deleuze, "Nomad Thought"[20]

On January 10, 1806, Thomas Jefferson wrote the following letter to the chiefs of the Cherokee Nation:

My friends and children, chiefly of the Cherokee Nation,—Having now finished our business and finished it I hope to mutual satisfaction, I cannot take leave of you without expressing the satisfaction I have received from your visit. I see with my own eyes that the endeavors we have been making to encourage and lead you in the way of improving your situation have not been unsuccessful; it has been like grain sown in good ground, producing abundantly. You are becoming farmers, learning the use of the plough and the hoe, enclosing your grounds and employing that labor in their cultivation which you formerly employed in hunting and war; and I see handsome specimens of cotton cloth raised, spun and wove by yourselves. You are also raising cattle and hogs for your food, and horses to assist your labors. Go on, my children, in the same way and be assured the further you advance in it the happier and more respectable you will be. (561)

Jefferson addresses the Cherokee Nation from the vantage point of a lawful patriarch who is aiding this otherwise primitive tribe of native "children" toward the development of a more "civilized" mode of existence. Living as vagrant wanderers without any legitimate rights to American soil and, consequently, any legitimate claim to an American national identity, Jefferson enacts the role of the benevolent democratic benefactor who can help this tribe usher in a new way of relating to the land that may secure their inclusion into the American republic. Like "grain sown in good ground," these individuals express the capability of developing into a more refined, domesticated people. But the Cherokees' development hinges on their ability to be tamed and managed—a momentum that informs Jefferson's vision of an American agrarian ethos.

One can see how this "vision" is developed throughout Jefferson's *Notes on the State of Virginia*, as his writings emphasize the need to produce an orderly and manageable American continental landscape. Through his articulation of an imperial agrarian ethic, Jefferson deploys, in Michel Foucault's terms, a form of "governmentality" that would saturate the American populace "to govern a state will therefore mean to apply economy, to set up an economy at the level of the entire state, which means exercising towards its inhabitants, and the wealth and behaviour of each and all, a form of surveillance and control as attentive as that of the head of a family over his household and goods."[21] With the nation and its inhabitants functioning as an American "family" over which Jefferson is the dutiful patriarch, Jefferson's *Notes on the State of Virginia* functions as a geopolitical treatise on how to craft a governable and controllable populace through the systematic arrangement of the land itself.[22] In this respect, *Notes* was admittedly one of the first published documents that inaugurated American eco-exceptionalism.[23] Producing a systematically organized Linnaean text, Jefferson ambitiously demonstrated his capacity to work within an American expansionist ethos.[24]

Jefferson's masculinist, imperial orientation toward American land created a new problematic that formed a nexus between the domestication of the landscape, the growing American imperial order, and the distribution of geographical space into racialized, biopolitical settlements.[25] Only certain populations gained inclusion into the American exceptionalist paradigm, while others were excluded. Jefferson's Query XIV on "Laws," for instance, distinctly orders the population into a hierarchical structure that systematically denies blacks and Native Americans commensurate inclusion into the republic. As the following passage reveals, Jefferson's imperial orientation is predicated on a panoptic principle of presence that codes the populace into racially specific geopolitical categories: "I advance it therefore as a suspicion only, that the blacks, whether originally a distinct race or made distinct by time and circumstances, are inferior to the whites in the endowments of body and mind. [. . .] Will not a lover of natural history then, one who views the gradations in all the races of animals with the eye of philosophy, excuse an effort to keep those in the department of man as distinct as nature has formed them? This unfortunate difference of colour, and perhaps of faculty, is a powerful obstacle to the emancipation of these people" (143).

This passage is symptomatic of Jefferson's own propensity to overcode the populace into essentialist, racially specific categories. Emphasizing that "cultivators of the earth are the most virtuous and independent of citizens" (175), Jefferson denies blacks inclusion into the agrarian republic because they have no lawful claim to the land itself. Similarly, Native Americans posed a more complicated obstacle to America's agrarian-expansionist narrative because, in Jefferson's eyes, they were governed by an unwieldy nomadic impulse that needed to be subdued and domesticated. Living as landless wanderers, Native Americans were unable to claim any lawful right to American soil. In order to be recognized as "individuals," Native Americans needed to be indoctrinated within the American eco-imperialist imagination. In the following passage, Jefferson codes the settlement of land and American identity under the discourse of "land laws":

> [The land surveyors] therefore thought it better to establish general rules, according to which all grants should be made, and to leave to the governor the execution of them, under these rules. This they did by what have been usually called the land laws, amending them from time to time, as their defects were developed. According to these laws, when an individual wished a portion of unappropriated land, he was to locate and survey it by a public officer, appointed for that purpose: its breadth was to bear a certain proportion to its length: the grant was to be executed by the governor: and the lands were to be improved in a certain manner, within a given time. *From these regulations there resulted to the state a sole and exclusive power of taking conveyances of the Indian right of soil: since, according to them, an Indian conveyance alone could give no right to an individual, which the laws would acknowledge.* (136, emphasis added)

Jefferson tacitly assumes that the Native American population does not merit legitimate inclusion in America for "an Indian conveyance alone could give no right to an individual, which the laws would acknowledge." The American imperial imagination recoils from recognizing anything outside of its domesticated structure of representation. In this respect, the potential for the Native American population to exist *in its own right* is simply eliminated. Jeffersonian scholar Robert J. Miller argues a similar point in that "Jefferson was eager to expand America's borders, power, and influence, and he utilized almost every strategy he could devise to promote those aims. He knew, as did almost every other American of his time, that American territorial expansion could come only at the expense of Indian Nations and tribal property rights."[26] Jefferson's utter abdication of Native American individuality precipitated the violent appropriation of Indian lands: "[Jefferson] actually resisted any real assimilation by Indians. The form of 'assimilation' that Jefferson was really interested in imposing on Indians was to transform their entire way of life by encouraging them to sell their lands to the United States and to bend them to America's desires."[27] What complicated this issue further is the fact that Jefferson "ignored [...] that most Native Americans were *already* 'yeoman farmers.' Almost all the Indian Nations in the eastern United States actively practiced agriculture and had been doing so long before Europeans arrived on this continent."[28] But even *these* indigenous agriculturalists were denied inclusion because they were not originally members of the American imperial imagination. Their expulsion was necessitated as part of America's civilizing mission, its perpetual errand into the wilderness. America, as a nation predicated and developed through the grace of "divine providence," had duties to perform—duties that were often violent, contradictory, and unethical—but were nevertheless disavowed and necessitated under the aegis of American expansionism.

Geographical Hegemony: A Vision of the Future

If *Notes* is a doctrine of how Americans were intended to interpret and inhabit the land, it is also a doctrine of how land and identity are inseparable.[29] In this respect, the shaping of the American social body politic into a unitary, homogenous collective that was loyal to the Jeffersonian agrarian vision was crucial. Consequently, having young Americans learn geography was the key to producing such a population. As literary historian Martin Brückner articulates, "the discourse of geography provided Jefferson and his American audience with a strategic tool through which to prescribe and control the nation's literary basis."[30] As Jefferson himself writes, the young boys "of the best genius" are those who should be chosen for forms of higher education, with concentrations in "Greek, Latin, *geography*, and the higher branches of numerical arithmetic" (146, my emphasis). The learning of geography enforced, in Foucault's terms, a degree of "normality" that produces a "homogenous social body" not only at the "level of consciousness" but also "at the level of what makes possible the knowledge that is transformed into political investment."[31] By internalizing geography from this reductionist orientation, students were dissuaded from actually *encountering* the land on its own terms; instead, they learn to interpret the land through a disinterested lens, a lens that "*redefines* human involvement with the land and its occupants" by imposing a metaphysical principle of presence that privileges "landed property" over ecosystemic space.[32] The Jeffersonian model of education is predicated on a geopolitical apparatus of production that produces, manages, and *sustains* a useful population that is commensurate with the shaping of a "spatial, instead of a temporal, everyday consciousness."[33] This spatialized geoconsciousness would become *the* national frame of reference for how Americans would learn to inhabit the land for many years to come.[34]

Conclusion: Notes toward a Global Eco-Imperial Empire

Jefferson's *Notes on the State of Virginia* serves as a point of reference for examining, critiquing, and exploring the ways in which America was learning to refine its ability to control, mediate and manipulate both its natural environment as well as its body politic through its separation of the "subjective self" from "the natural world," a separation that was contingent on America's burgeoning hegemonic dominion over both its land and its people. No less, Jefferson's geoontological interpretation of the land and the American body politic was predicated on a metaphysical orientation that privileged a spatialized, orderly consciousness over and against the nonhuman and human world. Redolent of a scientific ethos, Jefferson's vision was exemplary of what Hannah Arendt describes in *The Life of the Mind* as the Western scientific enterprise: "Thinking, no doubt, plays an enormous role in every scientific enterprise, but it is the role of a means to an end; the end is determined by a decision about what is worthwhile knowing and this decision cannot be scientific. Moreover, the end is cognition or knowledge, which, having been obtained, clearly belongs to the world of appearances; once established as truth, it becomes part and parcel of the world."[35] *Notes on the State of Virginia* reveals how nature was truly coming to be understood and interpreted within the American imagination as a "means to an end," the fulfillment of what Michael Zimmerman describes as a "growing technical mastery over nature."[36] And although Jefferson seemed viably concerned with developing an agrarian, ecologically sensible land ethic, he nevertheless privileged spatial boundaries over and against the natural world, thus (perhaps somewhat unwittingly) providing justification for what has become a global environmental crisis through this disinterested, imperial orientation over and against nature.

As many globalization theorists have argued, the trajectory of globalization has created environmentally racist and misogynistic geopolitical "zones" that divide the population into racialized and gendered hierarchies. For instance, David Harvey emphasizes that "not only do the rich occupy privileged niches in the habitat while the poor tend to work and live in the more toxic and hazardous zones, but the very design of the transformed ecosystem is redolent of its social relations."[37] Harvey's depiction of our environmental world order is the precipitation of an imperial geoontology that has historically privileged mapping, boundaries, and spatial separation over and against the natural world—a separation that has not only adversely impacted the environment but has also produced a racialized global biopolitics. It seems, because of our global condition, we cannot ignore or deny the intersections between geocriticism and ecocriticism because it has been through the very nature of mapping itself that land and ecology have been radically transformed and reproduced and the design and ordering of ecosystems alongside poor, minority populations have been gravely impacted. Reconsidering how we have established a frame of reference with the land, while keeping the question of ecology generative, open, and alive, would be an integral step for challenging our global environmental crisis.

Notes

1. Georgio Agamben, *Homo Sacer: Sovereign Power and Bare Life*, trans. Daniel Heller-Roazen (Palo Alto: Stanford University Press, 1998), 131.
2. Edward Said, *Culture and Imperialism* (New York: Vintage, 1994), 7.
3. Michael E. Zimmerman, *Contesting Earth's Future: Radical Ecology and Postmodernity* (Berkeley: University of California Press, 1994), 153.
4. William V. Spanos, *American Exceptionalism in the Age of Globalization: The Specter of Vietnam* (Albany: SUNY Press, 2008), 5.
5. See Thomas Jefferson, *Notes on the State of Virginia*, ed. William Peden (Chapel Hill: University of North Carolina Press, 1955); hereafter cited parenthetically in the text.
6. Comer, *Landscapes of the New West: Gender and Geography in Contemporary Women's Writing* (Chapel Hill: University of North Carolina Press, 1999), 12.
7. I am revising the term *American exceptionalism* as defined by many New Americanist scholars. In particular, I have in mind Richard Slotkin's definition from *The Fatal Environment: The Myth of the Frontier in the Age of Industrialization, 1800–1890* (New York: Athenaeum, 1985), in which he asserts, "the Myth of the Frontier" operated as a "rationalizer of the processes of capitalist development in America," which was predicated on an American exceptionalist ideology that resided within an "American society originated in a set of colonies, abstracted and selected out of the nations of Europe, and

established in a 'wilderness' far removed from the home countries" (34). I am also influenced by Myra Jehlen's claim, in *American Incarnation: The Individual, the Nation, and the Continent* (Cambridge: Harvard University Press, 1986), that America's "originating ideas were neither original nor exceptional; they derived from the essential principles of the European Reformation and Enlightenment. These principles—notions of individual autonomy defended by natural, inalienable rights, of the sanctity of private property as it fulfills individual self-possession, and of representative government as an ideal social order implied by such non-possessive individualism—bespoke another liberal nation, not a new world" (3). By inserting the term *eco-*, I intend to argue that American empire was realized through its distinct ability to overcode the land according to an imperialist ethos that reconstellates the "living land" into disposable material—an ethos predicated on Enlightenment rationalism, reason, and order.

8. I adopt the term "interpretive grid" from Martin Brückner and Hsuan L. Hsu's discussion of this term in *American Literary Geographies: Spatial Practice and Cultural Production, 1500–1900* (Wilmington, DE: University of Delaware Press, 2007), 11–12.

9. Myers, *Converging Stories: Race, Ecology and Environmental Justice in American Literature* (Athens: University of Georgia Press, 2005), 20–21.

10. Agamben, *Homo Sacer*, 19.

11. Ibid., 34.

12. Pratt, *Imperial Eyes: Travel Writing and Transculturation* (London: Routledge, 1992), 26.

13. Myers, *Converging Stories*, 15.

14. Other scholars have remarked on the significance of Jefferson's preoccupation with mapping. For instance, as Matthew Cordora Frankel argues in "Nature's Nation Revisited: Citizenship and the Sublime in Thomas Jefferson's *Notes on the State of Virginia*" (*American Literature* 73, no. 4 [2001]), "Within the representational system of *Notes*, Jefferson incorporates the map here as a concrete substitute for Virginia's natural boundaries as well as a conceptual paradigm directing his own literary project. This is to say, *Notes* ventures to represent a construction, and in so doing foregrounds the constructedness of the country itself" (704). In other terms, Jefferson's map serves as a model for what later becomes a "fixed" geographical entity with measured and enforced boundaries.

15. In *Converging Stories*, Myers notes that, "For Jefferson, the composition of the earth's layers below the surface was uninteresting" if there were no useful metals or commodities to be found (35).

16. Myers, *Converging Stories*, 13.

17. There is significant scholarship concerning Jefferson's propensity toward developing an agrarian and ecologically conscious republic, including Michael P. Zuckert's *The Natural Rights Republic* (Notre Dame, IN: University of Notre Dame Press, 1996), Donald Jackson's *Thomas Jefferson and the Stony Mountains* (Chicago: University of Illinois Press, 1981), Lawrence S. Kaplan's *Thomas*

Jefferson: Westward the Course of Empire (Wilmington, DE: Scholarly Resources, 1999), Thomas S. Engeman's *Thomas Jefferson and the Politics of Nature* (Notre Dame: University of Notre Dame Press, 2000), Alan Pell Crawford's *Twilight at Monticello: The Final Years of Thomas Jefferson* (New York: Random House, 2008), and Charles A. Miller's *Jefferson and Nature: An Interpretation* (Baltimore: Johns Hopkins University Press, 1988).

18. In *Converging Stories*, Myers explores how Jefferson couples his "agrarian philosophy of conservation and the laborer's closeness of the land with a baldly commercial overtone that sanctions industrial overexploitation of natural resources" and paradoxically "extends a radically democratic vision of social equality to a working class of yeomen farmers—and then sharply delimits that vision to whites" (24).

19. Spanos, *American Exceptionalism*, 12.

20. Gilles Deleuze, "Nomad Thought," in *The New Nietzsche*, trans. and ed. David B. Allison (Cambridge: MIT Press, 1985), 149.

21. Michel Foucault, "On Governmentality," in *The Foucault Effect: Studies in Governmentality*, ed. Graham Burchell (Chicago: University of Chicago Press, 1991), 92.

22. Deborah Allen meticulously catalogues Jefferson's relationship with Lewis and Clark and argues that Jefferson used *science* in order to gain control of the continent: "Jefferson understood that acquiring accurate knowledge of little-known rivers and regions such as the Missouri and the trans-Mississippi region was crucial to his expanding nation's commercial dominance of the continent, and he shrewdly presented Lewis and Clark's pioneering efforts to explore North America's geographical unknown as a 'merely literary' enterprise" (Allen, "Acquiring 'Knowledge of Our Own Continent': Geopolitics, Science, and Jeffersonian Geography, 1783–1803," *Journal of American Studies* 40, no.2 [2006], 232).

23. As many historians have articulated, Jefferson wrote *Notes* as a response to Buffon's insinuation that America was an inherently inferior nation to that of Europe, especially in respect to the size of its animals, the variety of its plants, and the general climate of the region. See Alan Bewell, "Jefferson's Thermometer: Colonial Biogeographical Constructions of the Climate of America," in *Romantic Science: The Literary Forms of Natural History*, ed. Noah Heringman (Albany: University of Albany Press, 2003); see also David Hurst Thomas, "Thomas Jefferson's Conflicted Legacy in American Archaeology," in *Across the Continent: Jefferson, Lewis and Clark, and the Making of America*, ed. Douglas Seedfeldt et al. (Charlottesville: University of Virginia Press, 2005).

24. Jefferson himself was particularly interested in the Linnaean classification system. For a more detailed analysis, see David Hurst Thomas, Donald Jackson, and James P. Ronda, *Thomas Jefferson and the Changing West: From Conquest to Conservation* (Albuquerque: University of New Mexico Press, 1997).

25. I am using the term *biopower* in Foucault's sense. See his *The History of Sexuality: Volume I*, trans. Robert Hurley (New York: Vintage, 1978); see also Matthew G. Hannah, *Governmentality and the Mastery of Territory in the*

Nineteenth Century (Cambridge: Cambridge University Press, 2000), 20–25, for a cogent explanation of the relationship between biopower and territorial distribution.

26. Robert J. Miller, *Native America, Discovered and Conquered: Thomas Jefferson, Lewis and Clark, and Manifest Destiny* (Lincoln: Bison Books, 2008), 77.
27. Ibid., 91.
28. Ibid., 92.
29. See Jehlen, particularly where she discusses the relationship between Jefferson, "physical landscape," and "national identity," Jehlen, *American Incarnation*, 32.
30. Brückner, *The Geographic Revolution in Early America: Maps, Literacy and National Identity* (Chapel Hill: University of North Carolina Press, 2007), 210.
31. Foucault, *Discipline and Punish: The Birth of the Prison*, trans. Alan Sheridan (New York: Vintage, 1977), 184–85.
32. Brückner, *Geographic Revolution*, 48–49; emphasis added.
33. Ibid., 37.
34. In *American Literary Geographies*, Brückner and Hsu further examine the sociopolitical importance of "geography" in their introduction: "During periods of increased political stress, such as the late colonial and early national decades or the antebellum and reconstruction eras, the discipline of geography enjoyed a more prestigious place in school curricula than history" (13).
35. Hannah Arendt, *The Life of the Mind* (New York: Harcourt, 1971), 54.
36. Zimmerman, *Contesting Earth's Future*, 60.
37. Harvey, "What's Green and Makes the Environment Go Round?" in *The Cultures of Globalization*, ed. Fredric Jameson and Masao Miyoshi (Durham, NC: Duke University Press, 1998), 335.

Part III

Transgressions, Movements, and Border Crossings

8

Geopolitics, Landscape, and Guilt in Nineteenth-Century Colonial Literature

Rebecca Weaver-Hightower

In the second volume of the Australian novel of settlement, *The Recollec-tions of Geoffrey Hamlyn* (1876), a good-natured debate about colonization occurs between two Australian settlers. One of the debaters, Doctor Mul-haus, has just been presenting a history of the continent's geological develop-ment when he shifts into forecasting the continent's colonization: "The spirit of prophecy is upon me, and I can see far into the future, and all the desolate landscape becomes peopled with busy figures."[1] He continues to describe the glory that the Australian colonies by the 1850s—the setting of the novel— would achieve: "I see [...] a vision of a nation, the colony of the great-est race on the earth."[2] He follows this rosy pronouncement, however, with warning of how, if the colonists go astray, the colony could fail: "I see a vision of a people surfeited with prosperity and freedom grown factious [...]. I see a bankrupt exchequer, a drunken Governor, an Irish ministry, a—."[3] The doctor is interrupted in his pessimistic prognostication by the scene's other debater, Major Buckley, who offers a more positive vision of the future:

> "I see," began the Major, "the Anglo-Saxon race—"
> "Don't forget the Irish, Jews, Germans, Chinese, and other barbarians," interrupted the Doctor.
> "Asserting," continued the Major, scornfully, "as they always do, their right to all the unoccupied territories of the earth—"
> ("Blackfellow's claims being ignored," interpolated the Doctor.)[4]

The debate continues, with the Major forecasting busy Australian harbors and a brisk business in the mining of coal and gold, predictions that the Doctor continues to subvert with his commentary.

What makes this scene remarkable is that the Doctor's explication amends the positive narrative of Australian colonization first presented by himself (he interrupts his own optimistic forecast by recognizing potential disaster) and then by the Major (the Doctor interrupts the Major's glorious prognosis by reminding of indigenous land claims), as if the book itself were correcting the claims brought into existence through its own and other narratives. This brief debate marks the only moment interrupting the narrative of colonial progress. Otherwise, the novel could be read as a fairly straightforward colonial fantasy: a community of English friends immigrates to Australia, overcoming hardship to find a happier and more prosperous life.[5] This chapter will argue that hiding beneath that story of successful settlement, however, are expressions of doubts, which sometimes erupt in brief scenes like the debate just narrated but that more often can be detected through the textual labor to paste over cracks in the colonial fantasy. That is, close attention reveals that underneath the hype lies suspicion of the colonial mission and even guilt over the dispossession of indigenous people.

A common objection to this argument is that colonial guilt is a twentieth-century phenomenon. Yet historians have documented doubt about the legitimacy of land ownership and guilt over aggression toward indigenous people in social movements like the campaign to abolish slavery and debates like that over the treatment of colonized people.[6] Historians like Henry Reynolds have even archived examples of ordinary people expressing their reservations about the morality of settlement, such as when a Port Philip settler wrote in the 1840s, "this right to Australia is a sore subject with many of the British settlers [...] and they strive to satisfy their consciences in various ways."[7] Based on literacy rates of the day, one can only speculate about how many more people experienced such pangs of conscience than those who had the skills and time to write about them, yet that writing is all the evidence contemporary scholars have to explore complicated responses to colonization. In that vein, this chapter will examine texts about settlement for how they betray hidden feelings of colonial guilt; moreover, I will explore how such guilty feelings are linked to the settler's relationship with the land.

To return to the debate in *Geoffrey Hamlyn* with which I began, another remarkable characteristic of that scene is that it grows out of meditation on the landscape. The characters are at a picnic, sitting in a meadow formed by the crater of an ancient volcano, and it is this natural setting that inspires the Doctor's lengthy exposition on Australian geology, culminating in his meditation on colonization. Colonization, we must remember, involves the transformation of *land* into *landscape*, by which I mean the natural land being transformed by man-made structures, adaptations, uses, and perceptions.[8] *Geoffrey Hamlyn* is not the only settler novel to associate reflection on the landscape with musing on the morality of colonization, an occurrence that might be partially explained by the sheer amount of time and space devoted to the landscape: passage after passage describes in rich language what the new landscape looks like to the settlers—the first sight of land followed by the trip inland, followed by the first look at the future homestead site; and once settlement begins, the books detail the colonist surviving natural disasters, struggling to transform the land into something farmable, and toiling to build houses, fences, forts, and other structures. Because so much of the text concerns landscape, one could argue that thoughts questioning colonization would logically correlate with thoughts about the land, but I want to argue that there is something more fundamental at work. Physical and psychological land possession is at the heart of struggles for colonization, and the settler's relationship with the land is key to the identity shift from colonist to settler. Thus it makes sense that the settler's relationship with the landscape provides a site where uneasiness can seep into a narrative that otherwise presents a predictable fantasy of settler heroism.

Moreover, the settler's interaction with the landscape forms a key site not only for expressions of ambivalence but also for the processing of guilt. This chapter will argue that one of the means to, as Reynolds's Port Philip settler puts it, "satisfy the conscience" was through literature, through repeated stories that functioned like the accounts that we all tell ourselves to lessen uncomfortable feelings.[9] Psychologists say that it is part of the human condition to use narratives as defense mechanisms—that in order to relieve anxiety we deny an event (denial), cast ourselves as the real victim in dramas of our own making (identification), attribute our own uncomfortable thoughts as those of another (projection), and explain away uncomfortable actions and feelings (intellectualization).[10] A close reading of these settler narratives suggests that they perform this very work, helping individuals deal with their own guilt and—because these stories were widely read and copied—helping the larger culture to manage a sense of *collective* guilt.

For this analysis, I have chosen three works of nineteenth-century literature that tell stories of settlers: Henry Kingley's The *Recollections of Geoffrey Hamlyn*; Catherine Parr Traill's account of the Canadian frontier, *The Backwoods of Canada*; and John Robinson's tale of South African settlers, *George Linton: Or the First Years of An English Colony*.[11] Each comes from a *settler colony*, meaning a colony where European immigrants established permanent settlements and took on new identities, sometimes in greater numbers than the indigenous inhabitants.[12] The three countries these texts represent were colonized at different times and in different ways, yet in the twentieth century each has seen cultural movements to apologize for the harms of colonization and make reparations (like Australia's Sorry movement, Canada's official apology and work with treaty renegotiations, and South Africa's Truth and Reconciliation Commission responding to apartheid, itself a legacy of colonialism). Also, all three countries have produced twentieth-century literature that directly explores issues of colonial guilt and reparation.[13] In looking back at nineteenth-century literature, written before debates over guilt and apology became front page news, we can see the origins of the sentiments so clearly explored in the twentieth century, unpack more covert expressions of doubt, and better understand how stories about the landscape especially participated in managing guilt.

To that end, this chapter first examines the settler's relationship with the land immediately surrounding him in order to show how the books portray the settler legitimately earning ownership through hard work. Next, I examine the settler's relationship with the landscape on the macro level of community and nation in order to analyze how the texts, through description of the landscape as always/already settled, create a narrative of the inevitability of colonization that mitigates guilt. Finally, I investigate consistent portrayals of the landscape as enclosed in order to unpack how texts create a narrative not of the settler as invader of another's land but as defender of his own land. All these narratives, I will explain, can lessen the discomfort of guilt by forwarding alternative versions of reality where there is nothing to feel guilty about.

The Settler Victim on His Homestead

Many stories of the settler's interaction with the landscape occur on the micro level, where the settler toils ceaselessly on his privately owned plot of land. Constant references to sacrifice and work legitimize land ownership, since settlers have not, this intellectualization goes, taken the land; they have earned it. And in the process the land has equally transformed the people, a shift recognized by a change in self-designation from "colonist" to "settler" or "Canadian," "Australian," or "South African" instead of "British." In this way, the settlers' heroic efforts better both themselves and the land.

The Backwoods of Canada, for instance, contains many such scenes of the hardworking settler, but one especially telling example comes in conversation with "a civil landlady, at whose tavern [Traill and her husband] stopped to change horses."[14] In remarking on the work taken to produce homespun cloth from homegrown wool, the woman explains the relationship between the settler and the land: "Many of these very farms you now see in so thriving a condition were wild land thirty years ago, nothing but Indian hunting grounds. The industry of men, and many of them poor men, that had not a rood of land of their own in their own country, has effected this change."[15] Two important ideas emerge in this short passage, one being this distinction between "wild land" and "thriving farm," which negates claims of land ownership through prior occupation and use. Indian hunting and settlement are perceived as *lack* of use, to be naturally replaced by the farm, a proper use of the land resulting in real ownership. A second important idea in this passage is that it paints the settler as heroic victim. Settlers are not invaders taking someone else's land: they are victims who deserve the land—each a "poor man that had not a rood of land in his own country"—who has earned ownership through industry. Such depictions of the settler as victim also direct attention from other victims of colonization, the indigenous Canadians/Australians/South Africans, in another textual move assuaging the uncomfortable guilt of colonization, which psychologists would call *identification*.

Significantly, the remark by this landlady leads Traill to reflect on her own relationship with the land: "I was much gratified by the reflection to which this good woman's information gave rise. 'We also are going to purchase wild land, and why may not we see our farm in process of time,' thought I, 'equal to these fertile spots.'"[16] Traill here identifies with the narrative of victimhood. Even though her family could not be described as poor and even though landowners in England, by transforming the land from frontier to farm, they become the industrious farmer/victim earning ownership.[17]

Similarly John Robinson's tale of South African colonization, *George Linton: or The First Years of an English Colony* similarly paints the settler as the heroic victim who legitimately earns his rights to the land. One especially telling scene contains two characters—one a settler from the fictional community of Benvale and the other the newly elected magistrate—ruminating on the hardworking settler's lot during a dinner honoring the new magistrate. The settler, Mr. Joffins, during what was to have been a toast, airs complaints about how he and his fellow settlers have been victimized: "We emigrant settlers at Benvale have been chiseled and cheated in such a way as I would never have believed had I been told it before we came to this blessed place, which what with savages, droughts, wild beasts, vermin, and plagues is—is—is enough to scare away a man's wits."[18] The other settlers in the moment are embarrassed by Mr. Joffins's directness (and breach of protocol), yet a number of characters had already made the same observation, making the complaint about settler victimhood one of the novel's dominant themes.

In answer to Mr. Joffins, the magistrate makes his own speech, which verifies Joffins's account of the settler's hardships while retooling Joffins's complaints into a compliment:

> [I]f the privations of an early settler's career are, as they must necessarily be, severe, the duties and responsibilities of the position are both high and ennobling. You, gentlemen, are laying now, as deep and firm as may be, the foundations of a state that may outrival old England in the future. You are the vanguard of a civilization that may be to Africa what that of Greece was to Europe—what Britain has already been to America. Your toils and struggles are but the travail of a birth from which another nationality shall proceed, and you may well be cheered amidst your pains by the reflection that a posterity, whose grandeur it would be folly to forecast, shall appreciate your sacrifices and revere your memories.[19]

As with Traill's examples, these references to settlers' transformative efforts legitimize land possession. Not only have they earned personal ownership, but their toil has earned the right to establish a new nation, thus superseding the many African nations (and prior Dutch settlers) already inhabiting that ground. The magistrate's question if this new nation might eventually "outrival old England" perhaps prefigures the first Boer war, fought only four years after the novel's publication, where Dutch South African settlers rebelled against British colonial rule. This creation of a new nation, of course, also concretizes the identity shift of the settler from colonist and cements the idea of the settler's toil and relationship with the land bringing about a change for the good, both of which could help to lessen a reader's sense of guilt and responsibility for the dispossession of indigenous people, since land ownership is earned and deserved.

The Inevitable Colony

Because settlers have a relationship to the landscape of the larger colony as well as to their own homesteads, it is important to examine how they perceive their community, and an important part of this perception involves comparison between the "new" land and the landscape at home. As J. M. Coetzee in *White Writing* has recognized, settlers brought with them to the new country a preconceived schema of what the landscape was meant to look like, which was to many like the English countryside.[20] So descriptions of the new land can betray a great deal of ambivalence over the settlement project as the settler makes mental comparison. The new landscape is sometimes described as superior to that of "home," with the excited settler expounding on the beauties of the perceived "untouched" landscape, while at others times, the new land is described as inferior. Traill's narrative, for instance, spends much space comparing the Canadian landscape before her to the English home she left, and when describing the forests of her new home, Traill admits, "I was disappointed in the forest trees, having pictured to myself hoary giants almost primeval with the country itself, as greatly exceeding in majesty of form the trees of my native isles, as the vast lakes and mighty rivers of Canada exceed the locks and streams of Britain. There is a want of picturesque beauty in the woods [. . .]. There is no appearance of venerable antiquity in the Canadian woods."[21] Wanting to be awed by the wildness of Canada, Traill is disappointed that the woods are *not* superior to those of England. Yet it is important to note that even while being disappointed, Traill perceives Canada in terms of this preconceived schema; England is the norm that Canada is supposed to conform to or vary from.

I want to add to the discussion of preexisting schemas an analysis of another common trope in these texts that also divulges the settler's mind-set: the description of the landscape in terms of what it will become, a figure of speech that in narrative theory is called *prolepsis*. As an example from the texts, Traill consistently describes the natural landscape she sees by layering onto it the towns and villages that she imagines will have tamed the land in one hundred years: "Some century hence how different will this spot appear! I can picture it to my imagination with fertile fields and groves of trees planted by the hand of taste;—all will be different; our present rude dwellings will have given place to others of a more elegant style of architecture, and comfort and grace will rule the scene which is now a forest wild."[22] Again, Traill is implying a comparison with English "taste" and "elegant architecture," but more importantly such moments in this text (and others) create a sense of the inevitability of colonization, which helps to justify current (nineteenth-century) settlement. Put simply, one way to assuage guilt about an action is to present it as inevitable (as in the phrase *manifest destiny* used to justify the United States' colonization of much of its continent), since one needn't feel responsible for an inevitability. This treatment of the landscape corresponds to the trope of the "disappearing Indian" as described by Patrick Brantlinger in *Dark Vanishings: Discourse on the Extinction of Primitive Races, 1800–1930*: "The belief that savagery was vanishing of its own accord from the world of progress and light mitigated guilt and sometimes excused or even encouraged violence toward those deemed savage."[23] This trope is also exemplified in Traill's letters: "The [Native American] race is slowly passing away from the face of the earth, or mingling by degrees with the colonists, till, a few centuries hence, even the names of their tribes will scarcely remain to tell them they once existed."[24] As with the inevitability of colonization, this forecasted decline of Native Americans involves a disturbing but also comforting fantasy of denial, one that takes away individual responsibility for the violence of colonization. If settlement and the extinction of indigenous people are inevitable, this rationalization goes, one should not feel guilty, since indigenous people were going to be slaughtered, robbed, displaced, and oppressed whether or not one participated.

A similar faulty logical syllogism can be found in descriptions of how settlement has progressed in the gaps between the story's temporal setting and the text's publication. So for instance, much of *Geoffrey Hamlyn* (which was actually published in 1876) occurs in the early part of the century, but the novel is framed by a story in 1857, as the characters who are now old men and women remember their lives. It is those memories—that act of looking back at a prophecy come true—that makes up the novel. Such a framing presents settlement as inevitable since it creates a linear path from the past when the success of colonization was in question to the novel's present and the book's later publication, when colonization has already been (as the book presents it) successfully accomplished.

We can find a good example of backward forecasting halfway through the novel, when an older Geoffrey Hamlyn comments on how Major Buckley's past dreams for Australian settlement have come true: "The Major has lived to see his words fulfilled—fulfilled in such marvelous sort, that bald bare statistics read like the wildest romance. At the time he spoke, twenty-two years ago from this present year 1858, the Yarra rolled its clear waters to the sea through the unbroken solitude of a primeval forest, as yet unseen by the eye of white man. Now there stands there a noble city, with crowded wharves, containing with its suburbs not less than 120,000 inhabitants."[25] The description continues to narrate how quickly Melbourne grew, how much its wharves bustled, how noble its architecture was, and how dense its population became. Through such hindsight the novel creates a sense of inevitable settlement. The major's forecast about the future of the fledgling Melbourne made in 1836 is substantiated by the narrator in 1858 and even further by the novel itself in 1876. Not only is the success of settlement confirmed by a parallax observation of Melbourne from three different points in time, such a description also confirms that the land was only waiting for the settler to arrive and release its destiny. If settlement was ordained, the violence that settlement equals and brings is taken out of the hands of individuals into the realm of God or the gods, who control destiny. Individual readers could breathe a sigh of relief over their own troubled consciences since they were fated to behave as they did and need not feel guilty.

The Defensive Posture

A third narrative of the settler and landscape justifying colonization involves the way settlers and the texts imagine the colonizable space. Considering the vast distances settlers travelled and the extensive open and "available" lands of the frontier and considering how other settler-era literature, as Coetzee remarks, is focused on the landscape as "expansive" and "all-embracing," it is remarkable how consistently settler narratives describe space as enclosed.[26] In his conclusion to *Literary History of Canada*, Northrop Frye refers to this trend in Canadian literature as a "garrison mentality" resulting from "small and isolated communities surrounded with a physical or psychological 'frontier,' separated from one another and from their American and British cultural sources."[27] I am interested in exploring Frye's "garrison mentality" as another form of deeply rooted psychological defense against guilt.

Like the other defense mechanisms this chapter discusses, the garrison mentality stems from a basic human instinct to protect the self, which we see expressed in settler narratives in response to specific psychological and physical threats. Just as we don a warm shawl to insulate our bodies from the cold or, in a more violent situation, curl into a ball to shield vital organs, enclosing the body in times of threat is a deeply rooted instinct. In settler literature this protective instinct becomes a psychological defense mechanism. In response to the threatening Other or frightening landscape, settlers build houses, fences, and other barriers, which mark their ownership and create a sense of protection but also exclude; that is, they define what is outside the enclosure as a threat. In settler literature, settlers—actually the invaders of the land—claim land and create enclosures, leading to psychologically imagining oneself as a victim—the person needing to defend against invaders, a role in reality belonging to the indigenous people whose land is being invaded. The defensive posture, then, can be a mechanism for projection—that is, of imagining the violence one is committing oneself as being the actions and intentions of another. The guilty awareness of "I have invaded his land" becomes projected into "he wants to invade my land, and I must defend it." In settler narratives the reality of the invading colonist becomes recast through descriptions of the landscape into stories of the defensive settler, with the indigenous person as attacker instead of defender and moreover as attackers without reason for aggression. One can see this configuration of space in old American western films, when the wagon train linearly penetrating Native American land becomes encircled into an entrenched posture while the "Indians" attack the innocent and defensive settlers for no good reason.

The Recollections of Geoffrey Hamlyn contains many examples of enclosed space and decontextualized assaults by indigenous people. The "attacks" are presented as senseless and unprovoked, not as the defensive actions of desperate people themselves under assault by waves of settlers. One settler, when hearing of a group of violent indigenous Australians, comments that the "Blacks [...] are mortal troublesome just now down the river. I thought we had quieted them, but they have been up to their old games lately, spearing cattle and so on. [...] I don't think they are Macquarrie blacks; I fancy they must have come up from Darling through the marshes."28 This comment contains several pertinent fantasies, the first being that troublesome "blacks" are invaders from elsewhere, not local men who have legitimate claims to the land, and that the men are "playing games," not justifiably resisting or are "spearing cattle," not hunting on communal land as their ancestors have for tens of thousands of years. This depiction shows settlers as men with the power to "quiet" the "troublesome blacks." Later in that scene, when the "blacks" attack, the settler is also shown as simply defending himself.

That scene also describes the landscape as enclosed. The books typically describe expansive and spacious settler homesteads as grouped together to form a circumscribed community, but in battle scenes, space becomes more tightly enclosed. For instance, after making the comment just described, the group of settlers, which is tracking escaped cattle, follows hoof prints into a valley. The narrator explains, "We were in the lower end of a precipitous mountain-gully, narrow where we were, and growing rapidly narrower as we advanced. In the fog we had followed the cattle-track right into it, passing, unobserved, two great heaps of tumbled rocks which walled the glen."29 This enclosed space provides the perfect setting for a trap, which the settlers fall into: "Before we could pull up we were against the cattle, and then all was confusion and disaster. Two hundred black fellows were on us at once, shouting like devils, and sending down their spears upon us like rain."30 Again, the battle is presented as an unprovoked and illogical "attack" by black "devils" against the confined settlers. Even though the enclosed space is a dangerous one the settlers have wandered into, it is still the ground they must defend from encroaching blacks; and by configuring settlers as defensive and not offensive, the book mitigates readers' guilt over the dispossession of indigenous people by psychically reconfiguring the entire colonial project from invasion to plantation.

The fact that the enclosure in this example is a trap, though, suggests another of those moments of ambivalence rupturing the colonial fantasy. The enclosure the settlers enter (the gully) is momentarily controlled by someone else, meaning that the settlers are simultaneously attacked and invading their Other's protected space. For that moment, the book seems unable to decide if the settlers are defenders or invaders and if enclosures are protective or threatening, just as the book at isolated points ponders whether colonization is a positive or negative force. We can see this discomfort with enclosed space—what I call "colonial claustrophobia"—in other settler narratives, too, which I argue provides further evidence of submerged ambivalence over the colonial project.

Similar to that scene in *Geoffrey Hamlyn* is the following description from *George Linton* of an attack on settlers by indigenous Africans. In exploring the perspective of "people at home, sitting by their own firesides, read[ing] of native massacres, it may be with a shrug of horror but with no real conception of all that such events portend" that the narrator explains how these readers could not understand the reality of the settler's omnipresent fear:

> They should see these people as I have seen them, dressed up in their war paint, brandishing their spears, and shaking their great shields, with their eyeballs gleaming, and their teeth shining; and they should stand as we did in a defenceless cottage shut in by precipices in a gorge as wild as the men that erst lived in it, and listening silently to the savage war-song of these barbarians, coming, it might be, to accomplish our destruction in the dead of night, rightly to estimate this the most terrible experience that a British colonist has to undergo.[31]

This passage raises several significant issues, the first being that space is configured so that, again, the offensive becomes recast as the defensive. Settlers who are in reality the aggressors are here defensive and defenseless, and the space that is being defended is tightly encompassed, though again not comfortingly so, invoking a claustrophobic doubt about the wisdom of colonization. Second, this passage is remarkable for the distinction it creates between the colonist's "reality" (which is in actuality the novel's fantasy of a colonist's reality) and the imagined reader's imagined fantasy of colonization. The reader is positioned as outside this "most terrible experience," only able to access it through the novel's description. This positioning creates an inside/outside space of the novel corresponding to the novel's use of circumscription elsewhere. The settler is inside the experience, which is horrifying because of what he describes but is also privileged in terms of insight, while the outside reader is presented as naïve. Again the text seems ambivalent about the benefits of enclosure.

As with space on the micro level, these texts often depict the larger community and settlement as engirdled, with the effect of presenting the colonial town as natural and rooted and the indigenous people as nomadic with transient settlements. *George Linton*, for instance, constructs the new settlement of Benvale as in a protected valley. When first surveyed, the narrator, Sydney Marsden, comes upon the valley "with a shout of astonishment" and describes Benvale as a "tremendous valley-basin [. . .] walled in by a precipice."[32] He continues, "Hundreds of feet below, almost from our feet, stretched the wave-like undulations, all clad with dark bush."[33] The surveyor with Marsden simply states, "There is Benvale," a remarkable statement since the naming of the space preceded its actual settlement, marking another moment of the inevitability of colonization. Marsden admits being "almost stunned by the abruptness of the disclosure" before remarking that "here at last was a glimpse of Savage Africa in all its barbarism and grandeur. It seemed impossible that raw English settlers could do anything in a region so desolate."[34] Benvale's valley location, of course, mirrors the reality that settlements were often enclosed to make them more easily defended, but the mindset that led to that reality is the same one that led to this fictional representation of space—the need to construct space so that one could more easily make the psychical shift to it being one's own.

Mary Louise Pratt discusses this correlation between enclosure, elevated viewing of space, and ownership in *Imperial Eyes* with her analysis of the "monarch of all he surveys" motif found in nonfictional travel literature. As Pratt explains, these narratives routinely contain moments where a traveler will come upon a space that he or she views from an elevated position and then claims and names because of the simple act of viewing it. Viewing the space provides a sense of ownership and power for the traveler.[35] We can see a similar psychological mechanism at work in *George Linton*, for Marsden and later the other settlers view Benvale from above and, though at first overawed by the sight, that act of gazing upon that circumscribed space initiates their sense of ownership of it.[36]

Also important in that scene is that everything about Marsden's description of Benvale depopulates the landscape, setting it up as both sublime and empty; so it is surprising when Marsden remarks without explanation, "That night they slept in a native kraal [village]."[37] Further, the narrator explains that they were given their own hut since they "were the first Europeans who had visited them [the indigenous Africans]."[38] That is, this passage acknowledges that the land called Benvale preexisted settlement and was named and claimed by others whose existence and rights the novel does not otherwise recognize, though the word "visited" implies awareness on some level of just whose home the settlers were in. This half admission that indigenous people already inhabited the land and had a settlement of their own is striking coming on the heels of the colonists' surveying of the settlement already claimed and named Benvale. It is as if the novel, even in the midst of one of the most paradigmatic moments in settlement, could not contain its own ambivalence.

Also striking is how that chapter ends. Soon after discussing how they and their rudimentary technology astonished the indigenous people, Marsden and the other travelers went to their hut and talked until past midnight. The section ends with Marsden commenting, "So I have found an anchorage ground at last."[39] What is striking here is that while enclosed in a space (a hut) that so clearly belongs to the Other, who has a prior claim to the land they call Benvale, Marsden expresses the belief that he has found his own home, which he expresses in terms of his relationship to the landscape as an "anchorage ground," a base where he can secure his own wandering self. The level of denial presented here is remarkable.

Conclusion

This chapter began by calling attention to moments of ambivalence about empire spilling over in texts that are otherwise seen as colonial apologists and traced how the settler's relationship with the landscape provides an especially fertile space for examining the colonial ambivalence extant in nineteenth century society. The question becomes then, how would readers have responded to reading texts that were at war with themselves? Did readers have their own acceptance of empire shaken by the presence of complicated passages like the debate between Doctor Mulhaus and Major Buckley in *The Recollections of Geoffrey Hamlyn*? Would readers have found their own doubts catalyzed or confirmed, or would they have ignored such moments? Did the texts instead, despite their internal contradictions, allow readers to assuage their guilt and explain away their doubt? The evidence we have of these texts' effects comes through history: people kept settling. Whatever they were reading, they kept claiming the land, and they justified pushing indigenous people into reservations. They created countries where indigenous people had no land ownership or eventually the right to move freely in space (in South Africa through the notorious pass laws and in Australia through the Ministry of Aboriginal Affairs). So it would seem that settler texts such as those examined here, despite moments of subversion, ultimately did propel settlement and colonization.

Yet still, I would argue, even if the texts did not ultimately change history, it is important to examine the ruptures in these texts, if not to remind ourselves of the complexity of colonial societies and of the fact that they were not so different from ourselves that they couldn't see the harm in their behavior, then to better understand the origin of twentieth century imperial devolution. Even though not the dominant discourse, it was the momentum building from nineteenth-century discord over colonialism that led to global decolonization in the twentieth century. And that momentum was surely advanced (as well as recorded) in literature. Finally, it is my hope that reexamination of nineteenth-century settler literature will teach contemporary readers about the twenty-first century as well, including the relationship between literature and politics. Investigations of minority stances in texts that are more complicated than they might first seem, such as the three under analysis in this chapter, remind us that persistence can eventually lead to real social change, even if not in the foreseeable future, and it is that idea that we must remember in our twenty-first century, neocolonial, and globally conservative world.

Notes

1. Henry Kingsley, *The Recollections of Geoffrey Hamlyn*, vol. 2 (New York: Charles Scribner's Sons, 1895), 152.
2. Kingsley, *Geoffrey Hamlyn*, 153–54.
3. Ibid.
4. Ibid, parentheses in original.
5. One can find this dismissal of *Geoffrey Hamlyn*, for instance, in J. P. Matthews's *Tradition in Exile* (Toronto, 1962). Such arguments see *Geoffrey Hamlyn* and other settler narratives as akin to the popular boys' colonial adventures of Ballantyne and Henty or the advice manuals so prevalent in the nineteenth century, which purport to give the would-be colonist accurate information with which to make the decision about whether to immigrate and to whence. One can understand why previous critics would read these settler sagas that way: they generally showed a successful example of colonization filled with hardship and toil but also joy and adventure. J. C. Horner's "*Geoffrey Hamlyn* and Its Australian Setting" offers a more complicated view of the novel as a romance, "not emigration propaganda disguised as romance" (4).
6. See, for instance, the work of the fifteenth-century priest, Bartolomé de las Casas, translator of the only surviving version of Christopher Columbus's diary and opponent of Spanish colonization, who argued for fair treatment of indigenous Caribbeans, like the Carib and Arawak peoples.
7. Henry Reynolds, *Frontier: Reports from the Edge of White Settlement* (St. Leonards: Australia, 1987), 162.
8. Simon Schama's etymology of "landscape" as a Dutch word originally designating a "unit of human occupation" proves useful here. Simon Schama, *Landscape and Memory* (New York: Vintage, 1996), 10.
9. Reynolds, *Frontier*, 162.
10. This language comes from Anna Freud's *The Ego and the Mechanisms of Defense*, trans. Cecil Baines (New York: International Universities Press, 1946).
11. Traill's account is ostensibly nonfictional since it is a collection of letters written while she was a settler. Yet I read it alongside these fictional texts because,

in providing one person's version of the settlement experience, the book does give access into the kind of personal fictions and defense mechanisms that are this chapter's subject.

12. Several recent books have examined the settler colony, including Annie Coombes's *Rethinking Settler Colonialism: History and Memory in Australia, Canada, Aotearoa New Zealand and South Africa* (Manchester: Manchester University Press, 2006) and Caroline Elkins and Susan Pedersen's *Settler Colonialism in the Twentieth Century* (New York: Routledge, 2005). Prior scholarship, though, has tended to come through collections of essays, with each essay focused on a different nationality and issue, and the comparison created by the volume itself. More intertwined comparative scholarship on settler colonies, like that of this chapter, is rare.

13. A few examples of these would be J. M. Coetzee's *Disgrace*, Kate Grenville's *The Secret River*, and Thomas King's *Green Grass, Running Water*.

14. Traill, *Backwoods of Canada (Toronto: Penguin Canada, 2006)*, 48

15. Ibid.

16. Ibid.

17. Biographies of Traill consistently remark on her family in England as middle-class. Charlotte Gray refers to the family (which also included Traill's noted settler-literary siblings, Susannah Moodie and Samuel Strickland) as living in "genteel poverty" (*Sisters in the Wilderness: The Lives of Susanna Moodie and Catherine Parr Traill*, x).

18. John Robinson, *George Linton: or the First Years of an English Colony* (London: Macmillan, 1876), 139.

19. Ibid.

20. J. M. Coetzee, *White Writing: On the Culture of Letters in South Africa* (New Haven, CT: Yale University Press, 1988).

21. Traill, *Backwoods*, 96.

22. Ibid., 251.

23. Patrick Brantlinger, *Dark Vanishings: Discourse on the Extinction of Primitive Races, 1800–1930* (Ithaca, NY: Cornell, 2003), 3.

24. Traill, *Backwoods*, 179.

25. Kingsley, *Geoffrey Hamlyn*, vol. 1, 289

26. Coetzee, *White Writing*, 61.

27. Northrop Frye, *The Bush Garden: Essays on the Canadian Imagination* (Toronto: Anansi, 1995), 227.

28. Kinglsey, *Geoffrey Hamlyn*, vol 1., 269–270.

29. Ibid., 276.

30. Ibid.

31. Robinson, *George Linton*, 85–86.

32. Ibid., 54.

33. Ibid.

34. Ibid.

35. Mary Louise Pratt, *Imperial Eyes: Travel Writing and Transculturation* (New York: Routledge, 1992).

36. See my *Empire Islands: Castaways, Cannibals and Fantasies of Conquest* (Minneapolis, MN: University of Minnesota Press, 2007) for an investigation of how the castaway island genre explicates connections between imagined ownership and literary constructions of space.
37. Robinson, *George Linton*, 55.
38. Ibid.
39. Ibid., 56.

9

"Amid all the maze, uproar, and novelty"

The Limits of Other-Space in *Sister Carrie*

Rachel Collins

A t the turn of the twentieth century, sociologists identified "*promiscuous spaces*, where people mingled with strangers, where boundaries were fluid, and traditional spatial segregation according to class, race, religion, sexuality, gender, or nationality held no purchase."[1] Such "promiscuous space" resonates with what historian Amy Richter has recently identified as the rise of "public domesticity" on rail cars in the latter half of the nineteenth century, which reshaped the social conventions of acceptable and respectable interaction between strangers, particularly for white, middle-class women.[2] Theodore Dreiser's 1900 novel, *Sister Carrie*, articulates his own understanding of changing spatial forms in the midst of both of these cultural formations and demonstrates the tensions between imagined and material spaces for many turn-of-the-century Americans.[3]

Sister Carrie recognizes that certain sites—like rail cars, theaters, and other such spaces—rely on alternative codes of social ordering that appear to diverge from everyday conventions. Indeed, these emergent spaces of leisure, luxury, and consumption take the form of the other-space that many geographers have called "heterotopia"—following Michel Foucault's formulation—particularly when they are considered against everyday spaces that continue to be characterized by dominant and residual valorizations of self-restraint and discipline. Seeming to work according to alternative codes of sociability and morality, these *other-spaces* primarily constitute sites of pleasure that inflame Carrie's desire to prolong her occupancy of such spaces. She acutely—if inarticulately—senses the difference between heterotopic and everyday spaces and spends the whole of the novel relentlessly searching out successive other-spaces to inhabit.[4] In fact, Carrie seeks out precisely the kind of spaces in which, as Rachel Bowlby has suggested, "responsibility is superseded by desire."[5] Carrie's desire to go to restaurants, to shop and adorn herself in high fashion, to visit theaters and various other pleasure palaces registers one aspect of what Kathy Peiss has identified as the "commercialization of leisure" that was transforming the nature of social relaxation, particularly among young, unmarried, working-class girls like Carrie Meeber.[6] These historical changes participate in the reshaping of urban landscapes, and Dreiser's novel demonstrates how emerging sites of leisure and consumption can seem to offer escape from everyday constraints. At the same time, however, *Sister Carrie* shows the limits of the seeming liberation offered by these alternative spaces, particularly insofar as these spaces are merely the flip side of the same social processes that govern the dominant order.

The Conventions of Rail Sociability

Carrie Meeber, eighteen years old, malleable and eager, first appears aboard a Chicago-bound train. As she steps onto the Pullman car, she enters a space ordered by social conventions distinct from those that order everyday spaces, and she quickly absorbs and establishes the conventions and paradoxes of rail sociability as her new manner. By 1889, when Carrie takes the train to Chicago, women traveling long distances on the rails were a relatively common sight, and they generally did not need to worry about damaging their respectability by traveling alone on a train. Over the preceding decades, the space of the rail car had developed an alternative sociability that defied older conventions of engagement, decorum, and modesty. Historian Amy Richter identifies this alternative sociability as a new form of public domesticity, explaining that "in the confined spaces of the railroad car, women and men renegotiated the boundary between private and public." In doing so, rail travelers "shaped public life to their will, reimagining it as a realm of moral and physical comfort" while simultaneously "transplanting the values and expectations of the private/feminine home onto the public/manly world on rails."[7]

Especially for white travelers in ornately decorated Pullman cars that literally resembled a host of familiar domestic interiors and yet were filled with strangers from a variety of backgrounds, rail cars presented spaces of alternate social ordering, very much like what Foucault would later term "heterotopias," which he characterizes as being "capable of juxtaposing in a single real place several spaces, several sites that are in themselves incompatible."[8] To the degree that rail cars were sites that combined the contradictions of masculinized public space and feminized domestic space into the single space of the railroad car, passengers "used the ambiguities of the experience to exert their own sense of control over social interactions" that did not resemble anything to which they were used.[9] Passengers used the rail cars as sites to pursue relationships and activities that would be unavailable to them in their everyday lives, including precisely the kind of acquaintance that Carrie strikes up with Drouet.[10]

Pullman cars, like the one Carrie travels on, were richly appointed and decorated to resemble the domestic spaces of parlors, libraries, dining rooms, and other typical domestic interiors. Rail car interiors constituted one way for ordinary people to experience luxury and "stirred up and temporarily fulfilled longings for domestic goods—even goods passengers could never dream of possessing in their own homes."[11] In the heterotopic space of the rail car, presumably surrounded by luxury and most definitely inspired by Drouet's flashy suit, Carrie gazes out the window, dreaming of Chicago and imagines, as Dreiser suggests, that the city is "for" her, even though she is journeying there to seek unskilled work, and she thrills to the rapturous belief that "the streets, the lamp, the lighted chamber set for dining are for me" and that her life will be rich and sumptuous (10).[12]

The rules of visibility and looking are different on the train than they are in everyday spaces, as well. Richter notes that "observing other passengers was one of the chief amusements of railroad travel" for men and women alike,[13] and that the train car offered an "opportunity for extended observation" of strangers, unlike the "fleeting encounters" that were available in the crowds of the ever-moving city streets.[14] But voyeurism was not the only attraction of the train: Richter notes that "some women entertained themselves by listening to the conversations around them."[15] Just as passengers watched and listened to their fellow travelers, they were aware of the ways in which they were being watched and heard themselves. Carrie, for example, is "conscious of a man behind" her, who she keenly feels "observing her mass of hair. He had been fidgeting, and with natural *intuition* she felt a certain interest growing in that quarter" (3–4). Although she is somewhat nervous under Drouet's eyes, being unaccustomed to such attention, she also enjoys the sensation of being watched with interest. While she understands being stared at on the street as vaguely disturbing, she also intuits that the same kind of attention might be admissible in the heterotopic space of the train.

In fact, the reshaping of social codes to yield new forms of "public domesticity" on nineteenth-century American trains allowed both men and women to flout everyday social conventions in the space of the rail car. Richter says that while "etiquette books warned women to avoid overfamiliarity with strange—especially male—passengers," respectable women routinely disregarded those conventions in order to engage in familiarities with strangers aboard trains.[16] In other words, by the end of the nineteenth century, rail cars constituted one cultural site where conventional behavioral norms were suspended in favor of a more promiscuous sociability, in which certain forms of verbal intimacy with strangers was freely admitted.

Charles Drouet, a drummer and regular rail traveler, is well aware of these altered conventions of train sociability and is able to identify Carrie as a likely recipient of his invitation to intimacy. In fact, his first appearance in the novel is one of remarkable proximity—and thereby implied intimacy. He first appears as "a voice in her ear" murmuring to her "that [. . .] is one of the prettiest little resorts in Wisconsin" as the train speeds away from Waukesha. Carrie responds politely but "nervously," for "her maidenly reserve and a certain sense of what was conventional under the circumstances called her to forestall and deny this familiarity" (4). She is vaguely aware that such conversations with strange men lie outside the norms of respectability. And even as she "turn[s] and look[s] upon him in full," the contradictory "instincts of self-protection and coquetry" mix "confusedly in her brain" as she slowly becomes aware that on the rail car she has the freedom to break with everyday social conventions (5). Indeed, what is "conventional under the circumstances" of the rail car is for young women to flout established conventions and speak to—even be entertained by—men they do not know.

Predictably, Drouet's "daring and magnetism" quickly win Carrie over, and she happily engages in intimate conversation with him (4). When she responds to his advances he "lean[s] forward to put his elbows on the back of her seat" while simultaneously endeavoring to "make himself volubly agreeable" (5), and "in a few minutes he had come about into her seat" to strike up an acquaintance with her and to talk "of sales, of clothing, his travels, Chicago and the amusements of the city" (7). Within a short time, the two are relating to each other intimately, for "already they felt that they were somehow associated." Indeed, "his words were easy. Her manner relaxed" as though they were long acquainted (9). Such quick intimacies were historically common in the altered sociability of rail cars, and Richter explains that "long-term confinement with strangers bred a peculiar kind of intimacy and encouraged self-revelation" between rail travelers.[17] Carrie experiences the rail car as a site of quick intimacy and personal pleasure through associating with a man she does not know, and though she is surely ignorant of many social niceties, she is also becoming aware of the altered conventions of rail sociability. That Carrie happily engages with Drouet on the train but also knows that she should avoid exiting with him suggests that she is aware of the train as a site of an alternate social ordering, for Dreiser suggests that she keenly registers a sociospatial shift as she steps off the car—above and beyond merely fearing her sister's disapproval.

Disembarking from the train in Chicago, Carrie is acutely aware that she is leaving a space of specialized social relations. She "realized the change of affectional atmosphere at once," and in her first few steps off the train she understands and experiences her reentrance into a space of more restrictive conventional social codes. Instead, "amid all the maze, uproar, and novelty she felt cold reality taking her by the hand. No world of light and merriment. No round of amusement." Carrie immediately senses that only "grimness and shift and toil" await her in her sister's flat, and she can do no more than make quick and furtive eye contact with Drouet as he leaves the station and she departs for her sister's home (11). The train's alternate social ordering with its pleasure of easy intimacy is gone, and as she walks alongside her sister into the streets of Chicago, Carrie feels herself to be "much alone, a lone figure in a thoughtless, tossing sea" (12).

What is most important about rail sociability is that once it is initially established in Carrie's mind as a baseline experience against which she can compare all her subsequent experiences, she spends the rest of the novel seeking out places that function according to the same alternate sociability. Driven by her desire to continually refind and remake the heterotopic space she first experiences on the train from Columbia City to Chicago, Carrie is repeatedly drawn to places where conventional sociabilities are dropped and neglected in favor of alternative ones that mimic her experience on the train. Upon arriving in Chicago she immediately recognizes that the streets are more likely to mimic the space of the train than is the Hanson flat, and thus she prefers standing in the apartment house's public entry-way to sitting in her sister's home. After securing work in Chicago, Carrie's first request is to see a play at H. R. Jacob's, which presages her subsequent interest in the stage. The stage itself ultimately functions for her as another space of rail sociability in which conventional rules are suspended in favor of new intimacies, new forms of engagement, and new transformations of the self.[18] In fact, the rest of the novel is largely an account of Carrie successively seeking out the theater, the parade of fashion on Broadway, Sherry's restaurant, and ultimately the luxury hotel where she takes up residence as potential sites of alternative sociability.

Theaters, Parades, and Restaurants

The novel's most obvious reiteration of rail sociability is the theater, to which Carrie is repeatedly drawn. The stage is clearly a space of alternate social ordering, and it seems to function for Carrie in the way that geographer Edward Soja has suggested his own version of other-space—which he calls "thirdspace"—functions. Soja asserts that "*everything* comes together in thirdspace: subjectivity and objectivity, the abstract and the concrete, the real and the imagined, the knowable and the unimaginable," and his emphasis is on a continual "cracking open" of space into an ever-expanding set of possibilities. Such seems to be one of the most literal functions of the theatrical stage: it is continually transformed into various places, which are, to borrow Soja's description of thirdspace, literally "filled with illusions and allusions."[19]

Carrie's first entrance onto the stage is, however, accidental. When Drouet's Elks lodge needs an actress to perform in a fund-raising production, Drouet volunteers Carrie for the part. Carrie has often longed to be on the stage, sensing that it represents a world apart from her own cares, wondering "how she would look, how delightful she would feel, if only she were" on the stage. Her desire to occupy the theater arises in part through her intuition that her presence on the stage might "compel acknowledgement of power" in a way that her everyday life in her tiny rented flat simply cannot (158).[20] It is, after all, the space of the theater that prompts Carrie's transformation from Carrie Meeber to Carrie Madenda and sets into motion her pathway to celebrity.

The feeling of importance that Carrie intuitively associates with the space of the stage begins to fill her as she prepares for her first ascent onto the brilliantly lit stage of Avery Hall. Backstage before her first performance, Carrie realizes that "this new atmosphere [is] more friendly" than much of what she had come to know in the city of Chicago and is "wholly unlike the great, brilliant mansions which waved her coldly away, permitting her only awe and distant wonder." The atmosphere of the theater, in contrast, takes "her by the hand kindly, as one who says, 'My dear, come in,'" and more importantly, the theater recognizes her as belonging, "open[ing] for her as if for its own" (176). Indeed, as she sits backstage Carrie does not understand herself to be in a space resembling the back freight entrance of the shoe factory where she once worked but instead sits behind the curtain amid an "atmosphere of carriages, flowers, [and] refinement," feeling herself to be "in the chamber of diamonds and delight." Not only does the theater apparently offer a space of alternative social ordering—a space of "diamonds and delight" in contrast to Carrie's everyday life as a vaguely bored woman posing as a housewife—but the theater also "admired, petted, raised to a state where all was applause, elegance, assumption of dignity" (177). Her strongest sensation is that the theater—in stark contrast to the recently quitted Hanson household—actively encourages her to imagine herself as she wishes to be for it functions, as Barbara Hochman has suggested, as "an arena for the flow of desire."[21] Such a feeling of unfolding desire is familiar to Carrie, who experiences a similar moment on the train to Chicago when she looks out the window and says to herself that the pleasures of the great new city "are for me," that they "are mine in the night" (10).[22]

The atmosphere of the theater certainly intoxicates Carrie with visions of grandeur, but what she feels in the theater is not merely personal fantasy. Instead, Dreiser marks it as a function of theater-space itself, which is, like Soja's thirdspace, simultaneously real and not real and which orders itself according to social rules outside the norm for both actors and audiences. Significantly, this novel figures the theater itself as a spatialized site of fantasy fulfillment: being on the stage is the equivalent of being in a world ordered by different—and better—conventions and possibilities. The theater becomes, then, other-space for both the audience and the actors who transform themselves on the stage, as well as a way of living the relation between real and imagined worlds that is constitutive of heterotopia itself.

But the other-space of the theater in Dreiser's novel is always of a particular sort, characterized by pleasure, comfort, and grandeur. The theater is always "above the common mass, above idleness, above want, above insignificance" and, in contrast to the everyday world of toil, the theater is a place of "finery and carriages" and most importantly, it is "ever a center of light and mirth" (389). The theater as other-space is decidedly a pleasure-space, for there seems to be no horror, no tragedy, upon the Dreiserian stage—and Carrie herself is, of course, a comic actress. Looking around the empty, shadowy auditorium in the Casino on the morning of her first rehearsal, Carrie exults that "if she could only remain, how happy would be her days," for the theater itself is continually articulated as a site of pleasure.[23] The novel's near-exclusive focus on pleasure, however, merely masks the disciplining and regulatory functions that other-spaces regularly perform, despite their destabilization of conventional social orderings. Dreiser's dramatization of other-space stages what neither Soja nor Foucault articulate as the limits of their own formulations: that these sites, though ordered by alternative codes of sociability, are not actually outside systems of power and control altogether. Other-spaces are merely regulated differently from everyday spaces. Difference from the dominant order does not necessarily indicate liberation from hegemony, for other-spaces can merely be sites where discipline is masked differently so that it doesn't resemble conventional forms of control.

The disciplining dynamic of other-space is clearest some months after Carrie arrives in New York. Carrie is simultaneously dismayed and delighted to find herself at Mrs. Vance's side, "in fashion's throng, on parade in a showplace" on Broadway. She quickly ascertains that the rules of conventional society do not apply in this new space, for here (as on the train and in the theater in similar forms), "to stare seemed the proper and natural thing." On Broadway Carrie finds herself "stared at and ogled" by spectators whose "glances were not modified by any rules of propriety" that would ordinarily require their gazes to be averted or at least directed at her more discretely (323–24). Instead, she discovers that Broadway is a city street that appears to operate according to codes that break the conventions of typical urban street engagement in which pedestrians anonymously flow past each other.[24]

The Broadway parade is a place where Carrie cannot lose herself in a crowd but instead finds herself to be a spectacle. In contrast to Chicago's business district, to blend in on Broadway is, paradoxically, to stand out as well groomed and well heeled. When Carrie finds herself "on parade in a show place" on Broadway, Dreiser notes that "the whole street bore the flavor of riches and show," which has spilled out onto the street from the "florist shops, furriers, haberdashers, confectioners" and jewelers that line the street interspersed with the theaters. "Pompous doormen in immense coats" control entrance to the shops, while liveried coachmen "waited obsequiously for the mistresses of carriages" and in the end, the "whole street bore the flavor of riches and show" and is characterized in terms that recall both the rail car and the theater: permissible gazing, luxury and sumptuous surroundings, the promise of pleasure, and a sense of marked difference from the everyday spaces she inhabits (324).

It is clear that "fashion's throng" operates according to a heightened visual scrutiny that lies outside everyday street conventions, and in this sense it is an other-space ordered by alternative codes. During the parade of finery, Broadway becomes a place where everyday codes of street etiquette are suspended while some of the primary heterotopic aspects of the theaters and other sites of luxurious consumption that line Broadway are extended into the street itself for a brief period. Despite the fact that fashion's throng takes place on an open street and is accessible to all passersby, it retains many of the features that Dreiser uses to demarcate other-spaces of pleasure and consumption, most particularly its dedication to visual pleasure and display, which Richard Lehan points out echoes what Carrie likes about the stage, saying "when Carrie walks down Broadway, she feels that she is part of a larger theater," for fashion's throng retains many traits of the other-space of the theater.[25]

However, Dreiser is careful to show the limits of other-space's plea-surability by demonstrating its self-disciplinary qualities and making clear that "fashion's throng" is also a highly regulated disciplinary space. Carrie can see that Mrs. Vance is an old hand at the scene. Familiar with its spectacular purpose, she goes not only "to see and be seen" but also with the self-disciplinary interest of "dispel[ling] any tendency to fall short in dressiness by contrasting herself with the beauty and fashion of the town." Carrie herself immediately internalizes the self-disciplinary purpose of the parade. She inwardly writhes under the spectators' stares, not because she dislikes being looked at (her experience on the train and the stage makes that clear) nor because she cringes at broken social conventions (she is, after all, continually breaking conventions herself), but instead because she fears being recognized as someone who does not "belong" on the streets of fashionable New York. She presumes she is easily recognized as "less handsomely dressed" than Mrs. Vance and the other women. True to the disciplinary function of the fashion parade, Carrie's consciousness of her inferior dress "cut her to the quick," and she immediately resolves that she will not return to the Broadway parade of finery—at least not until she can be sure of being among the best dressed present. She longs "to feel the delight of parading here as an equal" (323).

The Broadway parade is a particularly important instance of other-space. While the novel depicts the spaces of the train and the theater as having the liberatory qualities of Foucault's heterotopia and Soja's third-space, it also insistently represents other-spaces as sites of regulation and discipline. Foucault himself emphasizes that while heterotopias destabi-lize conventional social orderings they themselves are also highly con-structed and controlled environments: they are not (though they appear to be) public spaces for they are not "freely accessible" as a public space would be. Instead, as Foucault suggests, the movement from "regular" space to heterotopic space involves maneuvering through "a system of opening and closing that both isolates [heterotopias] and makes them penetrable" and that "to get in, one must have a certain permission and make certain gestures."[26] In the case of the train and theater, one must have the means to purchase tickets, and, in the case of the Broadway parade one must signal, through one's clothing, and carriage, that one ought to be welcomed in.

Carrie's dinner at Sherry's offers perhaps the clearest example of how heterotopias can merely reproduce existing forms and locations of power in new guises, for in the case of Sherry's restaurant, there are literal gate-keepers with whom to contend. Entrance into Sherry's is carefully regu-lated, as Carrie realizes when her party approaches the "imposing steps guarded by the large and portly doorman," who will determine who may enter and who will be excluded. Carrie peers into the restaurant's lobby, which she notes is "guarded also by another large and portly gentleman" (331). That Carrie sees the restaurant employees as "guards" of the place registers her lack of assurance about her own social position. However, unlike the imposing entrances to Chicago offices she had been afraid to approach several years earlier, these imposing guardians of sites of pleasure beckon to her and welcome her in, for these gatekeepers, these regulators of who may enter the space of Sherry's, show deference to Carrie's party. When the Vance carriage pulls up at the door, "an imposing doorman opened the coach door and helped them out" (330), and as Carrie's party enters the restaurant lobby, they are "waited upon by uniformed youths" who speedily take "care of canes, overcoats and the like." Dreiser makes clear that the most important gatekeeping is done invisibly: Carrie realizes that the sumptuous and "almost indescribable atmosphere" is a result of the fact that entrance to Sherry's is effectively restricted to the "monied or pleasure-loving class" for whom the matter of expense is trifling (331).

As with the Broadway parade, Sherry's exclusivity is also partly predicated on its own particular forms of visibility. The restaurant's prime location on Fifth Avenue makes it ever visible to theater-goers and wealthy residents, while its uniformed guards and closed doors ensure its shimmering interior is only visible to passersby in quick glimpses as its doors briefly swing open. Those passersby can instead gain access to the "gorgeousness and luxury of this wonderful temple of gastronomy" through reading the society page accounts of "dances, parties, balls, suppers," and the like. Indeed, Carrie herself recognizes the restaurant through her devotion to the society pages of the "Morning" and "Evening World," which she can "scarcely refrain from scanning each day" (331).[27] Indeed, it is precisely the contrast between a mundane, everyday world and the rarified spaces of places like the theater, Broadway, and Sherry's that signals the heterotopic for Foucault. He maintains that heterotopic sites "have the curious property of being in relation with the other [everyday] sites [. . .] in such a way as to suspend, neutralize, or invert the set of relations that they happen to designate, mirror, or reflect."[28]

Because the train, theater, Broadway, and Sherry's appear to be heightened and transformed versions of everyday society, they can all be classed as heterotopic other-spaces. Though each of these other-spaces differs in its specifics—the open-air publicity of the Broadway promenade is quite different from economically controlled access to the stage or Sherry's, for example—they all play on the promise that Carrie first feels on the rail car to Chicago and reactivate the "little ache in her fancy" brought on by contact with "the keener pleasures of life."

The Role of Discipline and Control

Both Foucault and Soja emphasize the pleasurable aspects of heterotopias to the near exclusion of the disciplining functions that heterotopias also perform. Foucault characterizes heterotopic sites as "effectively enacted utopias," while Soja calls thirdspace a "limitless composition of lifeworlds that are radically open and openly radicalizable," which work to promote "emancipatory change and freedom from domination."[29] Dreiser's novel illuminates, however, the numerous problems with such formulations. As I have already suggested, Dreiser is careful to make clear that such sites of difference do not necessarily function as liberatory spaces, and he gives special emphasis to the social controls and regulation in which these other-spaces engage.

While other-spaces often take on the appearance of pleasure, they do not actually exist outside discipline or dominant social relations altogether. At Sherry's, for example, not only is access controlled by gatekeepers, but its rarified interior space is continually reflected back upon its own patrons, who see themselves reflected "in every direction" by "tall, brilliant, bevel-edged mirrors" set around each room, which have the function of "reflecting and re-reflecting forms, faces and candelabra a score and a hundred times" (332). As Caren Town notes, Dreiser's novel "relentlessly" enumerates the "linens and lighting, mirrors and menus, clothing and costs" associated with the restaurant and the forms of display, acting, and performance that it requires of its patrons.[30] As the restaurant's mirrors and furnishings create an atmosphere in which every direction contains countless reiterations of the pleasure and luxury of the place and its patrons, they also produce a space particularly suited to surveillance and discipline, as patrons have no choice but to understand that their every move is reflected and watched by other patrons, just as they themselves observe the performances of their peers.

The presence of such social controls built into other-spaces serves a regulatory function that fundamentally undermines any sense that other-space is a uniquely liberatory space. Kevin Hetherington argues that such other-spaces do, in fact, "have their own codes, rules and symbols and they generate their own relations of power" even when they appear to be outside the usual codes and rules.[31] While it seems clear that sites like Sherry's, the Pullman cars, the Broadway parade, and the theater constitute emergent spaces for new forms of conspicuous consumption, and as such are ordered according to alternative social codes, they do not exist outside rules altogether. Indeed, it should by now be clear that although the regulation might appear different, other-spaces are highly disciplined and exist in symbiotic relation to dominant society. David Harvey makes a related point, arguing that the concept of heterotopia is problematic because "it presumes that connections to the dominant social order are or can be severed, attenuated or, as in the prison, totally inverted."[32] In other words, Harvey argues that nondialectical accounts of heterotopia mistakenly presume that "difference" constitutes an "outside" to established social relations.

Instead, however, it seems more likely that each other-space is an example of the internal contradictions of the larger social structure, in which, as Bertell Ollman argues, "each part [is] viewable as a relational microcosm of the whole."[33] In other words, other-space does not appear outside of, or despite, dominant cultural organization but instead emerges as a fundamental component of capitalist social relations. In staging heterotopic spaces as emerging sites of luxury, consumption, and consumer desire, then, Dreiser's novel emphasizes that the production of other-space is itself internal to the social reproduction of capitalism. Indeed, the difference between the restraint and thrift that characterizes the Hanson household and Carrie's own longing for luxury and pleasure is a manifestation of the internal contradictions of the same system. The industrial economy that requires long hours of labor and a household economy of scarcity at the Hanson flat are also responsible for the mass production of consumer goods that inspire Carrie's longing for fashion and luxury.

Moreover, neither Foucault nor Soja adequately accounts for how some spaces get designated as "ordinary" or "everyday" in order to set off differing spaces as "other." The very concept of other-space, in the territorial form proposed by Foucault and Soja, relies on a normative understanding of so-called ordinary space as anchored and fixed in certain sites rather than consisting in spatial experiences within the flux of social relations. After all, the servility that is required from the African American employees who staff Sherry's and act as porters on the Pullman car is likely not particularly different from the deference that is required of them in other white public spaces: the restaurant and train surely do not constitute anything like a heterotopia or thirdspace for these workers. Dreiser's careful account of the social production of space makes it clear that the differences between alternative space and so-called ordinary space are neither objective nor neutral: they carry material, ethical, and social stakes that shift and change according to one's lived experience.

Sister Carrie clearly challenges the notion that other-space is fixed, stable, and territorial. Broadway, for example, which at most times is everyday space inhabited by workaday people and even paupers like Hurstwood, is, at intervals, transformed into the other-place of fashion's throng. It is important to note the transience of this particular other-space, where an aura of enchantment descends upon an otherwise ordinary site, transforming the codes governing social behavior for a period of time, before lifting and leaving the site as it was before. Dreiser also foregrounds Carrie's own shifting experience of the spaces she herself inhabits over the course of the novel. Carrie's movements through various spaces over the course of the novel expose the limits of Foucault's and Soja's territorially defined versions of other-space by pointing out that the more Carrie moves in the rarified spaces of the theater, the promenade, the restaurant, and ultimately the luxury hotel, the less 'other' the social ordering of those spaces is for her. Indeed, it seems that the more that Carrie begins to move in the world of fashion's throng, the Casino theater, and restaurants like Sherry's, the more they begin to be, for her, not other-spaces of alternate social ordering, but instead the typical and routine spaces of her daily life. This normalization of what Carrie initially experienced as other-spaces culminates in her taking up residence in a luxury hotel. Once Carrie permanently moves into the luxury hotel, are we to understand that she experiences it as a site of alternative social ordering? On the contrary, it seems that it becomes her new "ordinary."

It appears, then, that any meaningful designation of other-space space must be understood as shifting and contingent—as experience-centered and processual rather than site-centered and fixed. Significantly, then, Dreiser's spatial imagination in *Sister Carrie* suggests that in contrast to the territorial accounts of heterotopia that currently predominate, we need to develop dialectical models of other-space that can account for the shifting and contingent nature of lived experience. Further inquiry is necessary into the processes by which lived experiences of space are subject to change over time—how the persistence and ascendancy of other-space eventually results in the obliteration of its status as heterotopic as it gradually shift into being experienced as ordinary space.

The Novel and the World

Like other-spaces, novels are produced by and within a culture that they do not transparently reflect. Indeed, novels often reflect back a world that is familiar enough to be recognizable to readers but different enough to be experienced as jarring or unsettling. *Sister Carrie* is a microcosm of the material world and all its contradictory relations and is simultaneously an altered and interpreted version of that world. This is perhaps best visible in the phenomenon of Carrie's simultaneous occupation of the seemingly contradictory roles of both "lost girl" and celebrity—two emerging figures of particular resonance in the United States at the turn of the twentieth century.

Melanie England argues that Dreiser's novel illustrates a cultural sea-change in which the promise of "factory wages, streetcars, and a myriad of shops crammed with ready-made goods enticed many young women," including Carrie herself, "to abandon country domesticity for the excitement and opportunities offered by city life."[34] However, the excitement of city life included social mixing on urban thoroughfares that, as Priscilla Wald points out, provided opportunities for "anonymity and dangerous attractions," opening up possibilities for an "unattached woman to disappear" entirely.[35] Indeed, at the moment of *Sister Carrie*'s publication, the United States was in the midst of a mounting panic about the disappearance of hundreds of young women who, like Carrie, moved from rural towns to nearby cities only to disappear forever shortly thereafter. Public alarm over these "lost girls," as they were called, who were presumed to be dead or ensnared by sex trafficking, prompted numerous newspaper stories, pamphlets, and books and eventually culminated in the passage of the Mann Act in 1910. Historian Frederick Grittner argues that the panic over the lost girls was, in part, the result of rapid urbanization and "a nation undergoing dislocations as young women moved to the city to find work" in patterns that defied established gender expectations.[36] Such is Carrie's own story. She travels from her country home into the city, where she is vaguely dissatisfied with the home life offered by her sister and brother-in-law, and is easily lured from her sister's flat by the prospect of pleasure offered to her by a strange man.[37] As far as her family can tell, Carrie disappears forever into the mean streets after only a few short weeks in Chicago, leaving only a brief note tucked under Minnie's hairbrush. From this moment forward, the break is complete, and Carrie never meets or communicates with her family again. She disappears, entirely and permanently, into the city and in their eyes becomes one of the lost girl statistics.

But from the reader's point of view, of course, Carrie's story is rather different. Upon "disappearing" into the streets, she begins a slow but steady social and economic ascent until by the end of the novel she emerges as a full-fledged celebrity whose residence in a luxury hotel serves as adequate advertisement for the hotel and whose name and image are emblazoned upon the cityscape itself. It seems clear that one reason Carrie's transformation startled audiences is that the reading public was used to understanding the lost girl phenomenon as it was portrayed in newspaper headlines—as a frightening deviation or aberration from the social fabric that held people together in small, knowable communities like Columbia City. There was no existing cultural narrative to explain Carrie's position as both lost girl *and* rising star.

The dearth of available cultural explanations for Carrie's situation is perhaps most evident in the legends that have grown up around

Doubleday's supposedly forced publication of the novel and its subsequent poor sales. These accounts have emphasized that the novel received terrible reviews, largely predicated on readers' inability to process or accept the possibility of Carrie as both lost girl *and* celebrity, as ruined *and* successful.[38] The *Detroit Free Press*, for example, declared that the novel is about Carrie's "fall in the eyes of others," by which the reviewer presumably means the novel's reading audience, for cognizance of any such "fall" certainly forms no part of the novel's internal plot. Despite this incongruity, however, numerous other reviews make similar claims about Carrie's moral status, averring, as does the *Churchman*, that the novel is an "unvarnished tale of the downfall of a poor girl," while the *New York Commercial Advertiser* concludes that Carrie is "unredeemed by even a touch of [. . .] basic honesty and inner charm."[39] All these reviews are strangely at odds with the novel's absolutely clear depiction of Carrie finding no moral fault with herself, suffering no sorrow or punishment in consequence of her sexual couplings, and meeting neither judgment nor condemnation from others. The conclusions drawn by these reviews, then, are the product of existing social sensibilities, not the reasoning forwarded by the novel itself. The lost girl is judged to be "fallen" by the novel's original reviewers according to nineteenth-century codes of moral character that were in the process of becoming residual by the early twentieth century, while Carrie's rise uniquely belongs to the kind of success that is only possible in an emerging mass consumer culture. Such, at least, has been the more recent critical assessment of the novel that, following Philip Fisher's lead, tends to focus on "the rise of Carrie by means of the fall of Hurstwood," particularly as these two trajectories are born out economically.[40] Carrie herself is suspended between these two cultural moments, however, and it is important to see that both plots are simultaneously inscribed in Carrie as she appears in the novel.

Dreiser's inscription of both the lost girl and celebrity in Carrie suggests that the two are not separate and unrelated phenomena but are instead intimately part of the same cultural processes. Just as the Hansons' round of toil and Carrie's desire for pleasure are two manifestations of the same cultural processes, so are the lost girl and the celebrity. The lost girl is a product of capitalist urbanization, which continually brings new wage-seekers from the country into the city and simultaneously provides opportunities for anonymous encounters in the context of rapidly changing social mores that increasingly allow respectable young women to fraternize with strange men. The celebrity is a product of consumer culture's reconfiguration of personality as saleable commodity to be made and remade according to one's consumer goods. The interconnection of capital's various workings—thrusting individuals both up and down—is made visible

in the single body of Carrie, as she moves in and through a world characterized by the seeming contradictions between spaces of production and
consumption, spaces of labor and leisure, spaces of everyday and alternative orderings.[41]

As *Sister Carrie* reshapes the familiar taxonomies of urban experience,
it throws readers into an imaginative world in which the codes that govern readers' ordinary worldviews are not absent but are made differently
visible through the novel's induction of the reader into a very particular
viewpoint. One function of *Sister Carrie*'s fictional world, then, is to weave
a narrative in which two positions that common sense would dictate are
mutually contradictory are represented as being simultaneously occupi-
able. Betsy Klimasmith suggests that one important function of Dreiser's
novelistic space is to "allow [. . .] his readers to dwell imaginatively in
his novel, enabling them to reorganize their conceptions of environment
into ideas that become increasingly flexible, mobile, and amenable to the
notion of social change as the novel progresses."[42] Indeed, it is instructive
to think about the imaginative world of the novel itself as existing in productive tension with the world in which it circulates. Novels are, after all,
invented worlds in which collected possibilities unavailable in the actual
space of the world and people's experiences of fictive spaces can prompt
readers to reshape their sense of material city streets. Such reshaping is
precisely the cultural work in which *Sister Carrie* engages as it revises common perceptions about danger and failure in the cities through the figure
of Carrie herself.

Notes

1. Priscilla Wald, "Dreiser's Sociological Vision," in *The Cambridge Companion
   to Theodore Dreiser*, ed. Leonard Cassuto and Clare Virginia Eby (Cambridge:
   Cambridge University Press, 2004), 182.
2. See Amy G. Richter, *Home on the Rails: Women, the Railroad, and the Rise of
   Public Domesticity* (Chapel Hill: University of North Carolina Press, 2005).
3. Dreiser, *Sister Carrie* (New York: Penguin, 1994); hereafter cited parenthetically in the text.
4. Indeed, there is a longstanding convention of reading Carrie as lacking substantial selfhood, and the critical commonplace is that Dreiser's novel posits
   what Rachel Bowlby has called the "materially constituted self" (*Just Looking:
   Consumer Culture in Dreiser, Gissing, and Zola* [New York: Methuen, 1985],
   37). For example, Amy Kaplan argues that Carrie "believes that by dressing
   or playing a part she can actually be transformed into the glamorous creature
   of her fantasies" and suggests that "Carrie desires things not for their own
   qualities or for pleasures they afford, but for the new self-image they seem to

offer" (Kaplan, *The Social Construction of American Realism* [Chicago: University of Chicago Press, 1988], 149). Babak Elahi's *The Fabric of American Literary Realism* (Jefferson, NC: McFarland, 2009) extends these critical accounts and argues that Carrie's interest in *things*—in clothes in particular—actually results in the annihilation of selfhood. He says that Carrie's "pursuit of career, clothing, and costume turns her into value. She becomes immaterial" by becoming a living advertisement (107). In contrast, Jessica Van Slooten claims that a rather different dynamic is at play and asserts that Carrie actually has a "stable inner conception" of herself that exists independent of her interest in fashion and to which she is strongly allegiant throughout the novel ("Fashion, Money, and Romance in *The House of Mirth* and *Sister Carrie*," in *Styling Texts: Dress and Fashion in Literature*, ed. Cynthia Kuhn and Cindy Carlson [Youngstown, NY: Cambria Press, 2004], 251). Gavin Jones's *American Hungers* (Princeton, NJ: Princeton University Press, 2008) attempts to redirect this particular vein of Dreiser criticism away from the "inner workings of capitalist consumerism" and instead toward what he calls the novel's "theorization of poverty as a social condition partially distinct from the discourses of class" (64).

5. Bowlby, *Just Looking*, 61.
6. Peiss explains that the commercialization of leisure "defined recreation as a commodity" one purchases outside the home is a phenomenon that bubbles up into middle-class American culture via the culture of working class women like Carrie Meeber; see Peiss, *Cheap Amusements: Working Women and Leisure in Turn-of-the-Century New York* (Philadelphia: Temple University Press, 1987), 186. See also Beth Bailey's *From Front Porch to the Back Seat* (Baltimore: Johns Hopkins University Press, 1989) for documentation of similar transformations in the classed and gendered dynamics of romance, when public "dating" shifted the domestic location of "courtship into the world of the economy" in the early twentieth century (21).
7. Richter, *Home on the Rails*, 8.
8. Foucault, "Of Other Spaces," *diacritics* 16, no. 1 (1986): 25.
9. Richter, *Home on the Rails*, 27.
10. It is crucial to note, however, that such experiences were profoundly raced, and the growth of Jim Crow laws during the late nineteenth century severely circumscribed the rail experiences of African Americans. Many African Americans, particularly women, found themselves much more precariously situated. In *Home on the Rails*, Richter recounts how many middle-class black women "experienced anger, confusion, and fear" aboard trains where they were "temporarily denied their respectable identities" by white passengers and conductors who sometimes threatened and intimidated them (54). The railroads were also a major site of labor for many black Americans. Jack Santino's 1989 *Miles of Smiles, Years of Struggle* (Chicago: University of Chicago Press, 1989) documents the professional and personal stories of African American Pullman porters, and particularly focuses on the irony of the fact that although the porters successfully "challenge[d] the might of the industrial giant, the

Pullman Company, to form an unprecedented black labor union, they were served up to the public by the popular media in images of grinning, obsequious, scheming Uncle Toms" (115).

11. Richter, *Home on the Rails*, 78.

12. Alan Trachtenberg (in "Who Narrates? Dreiser's Presence in *Sister Carrie*," *New Essays on Sister Carrie*, ed. Donald Pitzer [Cambridge: Cambridge University Press, 1991], 87–122) gives an important reading of this passage that focuses on its insertion as Dreiser's own ironic commentary on the illusion and delusion of such hopes that the city is for toilers (as well as the inversion of day/night imagery).

13. Richter, *Home on the Rails*, 48.

14. In fact, Richter suggests, closely scrutinizing others on the train offered working class women and women of color opportunities to view and imitate white middle class women's behaviors that might, in turn, help establish them as "respectable" (see *Home on the Rails*, 40–50).

15. Richter, *Home on the Rails*, 49.

16. Ibid., 45. Richter gives numerous examples drawn from letters and diaries of women travelers who enthusiastically engaged in train sociability with male strangers and passed very pleasant times with them, despite the etiquette books and the cultural warnings for them not to do so. Richter suggests that "[t]he courtesies a man could offer to a woman sometimes led to extended conversations" and recounts the story of Caroline Dall, who recalls spending a day with "three gentlemen from Cincinnati . . . [who] got me a campstool, set me out on the rear platform, told me stories, and gathered me flowers all day." Richter notes there is "no suggestion of impropriety; she seems simply to have enjoyed the attention and the company that made 'the day [pass] like a festival'" (51).

17. Richter, *Home on the Rails*, 50.

18. In fact, Richter herself briefly points to *Sister Carrie* as a prototype for the kind of transformation that railway sociability engenders, saying, "*Sister Carrie* tells of a young woman's transformation within an urban world of strangers, and the railroad serves as the site where that process begins" (*Home on the Rails*, 15). Richter's space-based formulation (she says that trains shattered women's senses of self, and then reconstructed them over the course of the journey) adds a layer of complexity to the existing critical accounts of Carrie's self-formation through consumption.

19. Edward Soja, *Thirdspace: Journeys to Los Angeles and Other Real-and-Imagined Places* (Oxford: Blackwell, 1996), 56. There are a number of analyses of *Sister Carrie* that resonate with geographic articulations of other-space as both real and imagined, though they tend to focus on narration styles rather than on representations of space. June Howard argues "Dreiser is a kind of perpetual stranger [. . .] who moves through each point of view and portrays every character from within but remains with none and so sees every character from without as well. The reader's position in relation to the window of observation is constantly shifting; we, and the narrator, are both inside and outside"

(151). Trachtenberg's "Who Narrates? Dreiser's Presence in *Sister Carrie*" follows Howard, renaming what Howard had called the sentimental and realist narrating voices of the novel "an innovative fusion of narrative and discourse" (98), and suggesting that to tell this particular story, Dreiser needed to develop a voice that could speak simultaneously from different positions: "a voice capable of speaking both from within, as an intimate and familiar, and from without, as a critical but sympathetic commentator" (108).

20. Previous discussions of Carrie's desire have tended to focus on the making of Carrie's "sense of self." Philip Fisher's *Hard Facts: Setting and Form in the American Novel* (Oxford: Oxford University Press, 1985) argues that "[t]he display of goods behind a glass that we cross in fantasy defines the process of yearning, choosing, and imagining the transformations of the self by things, by others, and by places that the city proposes" (131), while Kaplan's *The Social Construction of American Realism* similarly argues that "the characters in *Sister Carrie* continually pursue an image of themselves as they might be—not as they are" (149).

21. Barbara Hochman, "A Portrait of the Artist as a Young Actress: The Rewards of Representation in *Sister Carrie*," in *New Essays on Sister Carrie*, ed. Donald Pizer (Cambridge: Cambridge University Press, 1991), 52. In *Hard Facts*, Phillip Fisher attributes the same sentiment to the city itself, but I argue the novel locates the source of this feeling more specifically in all the spaces that function as heterotopic sites, or spaces of alternative ordering, in the novel, which at certain points include the city streets for Carrie but more often are comprised by other, more contained spaces like the stage and the train. See also Hugh Witemeyer's now-dated but useful "Gaslight and Magic Lamp in *Sister Carrie*" (*PMLA* 86, no. 2 [1971]: 236–40), in which he argues that the figure of the stage "characterize[s] the mental processes of Dreiser's American dreamers. It also helps to illuminate the ironic discrepancy between such dreams and unaccommodating realities" (236).

22. Dreiser's digressions into descriptions of things like twilight have prompted a number of midcentury critics to assess his work as "bad writing." Later scholars, starting in the 1980s, tend to understand the sentimental versus realism split in Dreiser's writing to be his own deliberate commentary on literary style and consumer culture. Amy Kaplan, for example, argues, "just as domesticity is relocated in *Sister Carrie* from the stable home to rented spaces, sentimental language is divested of its traditional familial ties and reinvested in market-engendered values and consumer goods," linking both spatial experience and sentimental writing to the emerging consumer ethos (*Social Construction of American Realism*, 144). More recently, Jennifer Fleissner's *Women, Compulsion, Modernity* (Chicago: University of Chicago Press, 2004) mounts a compelling reversal of the critical commonplace that associates Carrie with sentimentalism and Hurstwood with realism. Instead Fleissner points to the constructed nature and gendered implications of understanding Carrie's growing economic independence as "fantasy" and unreality. "What does it mean," Fleissner asks, "that we explain this story of a woman's rise to economic independence over and over as a dream story?" (165).

23. Although I do not explicitly explore the department store as an other-site in the novel, many other critics have commented on it as a particular site of plea- sure in the novel, and have suggested that it functions in ways not unlike my own description of how other-spaces function. For example, Gail McDonald (in "The Mind of a Department Store: Reconfiguring Space in the Gilded Age," *Modern Language Quarterly* 63, no. 2 [2002], 227–49) argues that the depart- ment store serves as a fantasy space for Carrie in which shopping constitutes the search for "possible selves" (233). Similarly, Charles Harmon's "Cuteness and Capitalism in *Sister Carrie*" (*American Literary Realism* 32, no. 2 [2000], 125–39) identifies "The Fair"—the Chicago department store where Carrie shops—as being a site in which "Carrie's sense of self expands until it becomes weightless, unballasted, barely embodied" (126).
24. Indeed, that urban streets constituted sites of indifference was the prevailing sociological understanding at the turn of the century set forth by sociologists like Georg Simmel, who asserted that "reserve" and a "blasé outlook" mark urban citizens' attitudes toward each other on the streets in his essay "The Metropolis and Mental Life," in *The Urban Sociology Reader*, ed. Jan Lin and Christopher Mele (London: Routledge, 2005), 23–31.
25. Richard Lehan, "*Sister Carrie*: The City, the Self, and the Modes of Narrative Discourse," *New Essays on Sister Carrie*, ed. Donald Pizer (Cambridge: Cam- bridge University Press, 1991), 71.
26. Foucault, "Of Other Spaces," 26.
27. In fact, Sherry's was particularly well known for actually creating extraordi- nary fantasy worlds within its walls. Arguably the most extravagant of such creations occurred just two years after the publication of *Sister Carrie*, in which C. K. G. Billings had an upstairs ballroom decorated as a garden full of live plants in order to host thirty-six of his friends. The floor was laid with sod, and live birds flitted around the room while the men dined astride three dozen horses, who had been brought upstairs via elevator. Each horse had a tray table attached to its saddle and a saddlebag full of champagne.
28. Foucault, "Of Other Spaces," 24.
29. Ibid., 24; Soja, *Thirdspace*, 70. Foucault also acknowledges what he calls "heterotopias of deviation," by which he means "rest homes and psychiatric hospitals, and of course prisons" in which those whose behavior is judged deviant are contained apart from the general community (25). But he de- emphasizes the significance of this category in favor of focusing on the opti- mistic aspects of heterotopias that are "real space, as perfect, as meticulous, as well arranged as ours is messy, ill constructed, and jumbled" (27).
30. Caren J. Town, "The House of Mirrors: Carrie, Lily, and the Reflected Self," *Modern Language Studies* 24, no. 3 (1994): 44.
31. Kevin Hetherington, *The Badlands of Modernity: Heterotopia and Social Ordering* (London: Routledge, 1997), 24.
32. David Harvey, *Spaces of Hope* (Berkeley: University of California Press, 2000), 184. More disturbingly, Harvey points out that the sheen of liberation that is associated with heterotopia is the presumption that "whatever happens in

such spaces of 'Otherness' is of interest and even in some sense 'acceptable,' or 'appropriate,'" which is simply not the case. Harvey points out that the "concentration camp, the factory [. . .] Jonestown, the militia camps" are all heterotopic sites of difference about which there is little to celebrate (185).

33. Bertrall Ollman, *Dialectical Investigations* (London: Routledge, 1993), 37.

34. Melanie England, "Thoroughly Modern Carrie: Theodore Dreiser, Modernism, and the Historical Moment," *Midamerica* 32 (2005): 88.

35. Wald, "Dreiser's Sociological Vision," 182.

36. Frederick Grittner, *White Slavery: Myth, Ideology, and American Law* (New York: Garland, 1990), 64.

37. In *At Home in the City: Urban Domesticity in American Literature and Culture, 1850–1930* (Durham, NH: University of New Hampshire Press, 2005), Betsy Klimasmith argues that Dreiser's novel figures the erosion of "the role that traditional domestic and familiar relations play" in the development of modern urban subjecthood. This erosion takes place, Klimasmith suggests, through "heterotopic urban spaces such as the apartment, the stage, the restaurant, and Broadway," all of which aid Carrie in peeling her interests away from domestic space and which form, Klimasmith claims, the basis on which Carrie is able to "thrive in urban space" (144–5).

38. See Nina Markov, "Reading and the Material Girl: Educating *Sister Carrie*," *Critical Sense* 10, no. 1 (2002): 19–58, for an extended account of the classed nature of the novel's reception and reviews, which she argues mirrors the novel's depiction of the classed relationship between Carrie and Ames. Marsha S. Moyer's "Dreiser, *Sister Carrie*, and Mrs. Doubleday" (in *Theodor Dreiser and American Culture*, ed. Yoshinobu Hakutani [Newark: University of Delaware Press, 2000], 39–55) gives a fascinating account of how the popularity of the myth of "Mrs. Doubleday as the evil power attempting to squelch the successful reception of Dreiser's first novel" (39) is a manifestation of the "foregrounding issues of sexual freedom or repression" in order to "mask economic, class, and power struggles" (51).

39. All reviews are quoted from Jack Salzman's 1972 collection of reviews of *Sister Carrie, Theodore Dreiser: The Critical Reception* (New York: D. Lewis, 1972), 1–24. Also see Florence Dore's *The Novel and the Obscene: Sexual Subjects in American Modernism* (Palo Alto, CA: Stanford University Press, 2005), in which her chapter on Dreiser argues that not only has the concept of censorship been important to the novel's publication history, but "censorship [. . .] significantly structures the novel formally" (13).

40. See Fisher, *Hard Facts*, 170. While my own account focuses almost exclusively on Carrie's upward trajectory, there is a substantial body of criticism concerned with Hurstwood's decline. See, for example, see Jones's *American Hungers*, which argues that a "rhetoric of pauperism" results in Hurstwood being deliberately kept at arms' length from the reader (86). Karl Zender's "Walking Away from the Impossible Thing: Identity and Denial in *Sister Carrie*," in *Studies in the Novel* 30, no. 1 (1998), argues that analyses of Hurstwood have typically overlooked the importance of his character

traits in favor of explaining his decline through the genre of naturalism or realism.

41. *Sister Carrie* similarly reformulates the stakes of cross-class mixing and contact on urban streets—a phenomenon around which also circulated much contemporary anxiety at the time of *Sister Carrie*'s publication. Near the novel's end, Carrie's encounter with Hurstwood on the street in front of the casino is the closest the novel ever gets to a conventional "gaslight tour" of New York. When Carrie first notices Hurstwood, she sees a "shabby, baggy figure"—a "seemingly hungry stranger" who is "edging so close" to her that she feels discomfort and fear as she stands in front of the casino, which is ablaze with her name and image in electric lights (477). But as it turns out, this vagrant begging on the streets is no stranger: it is Hurstwood, her estranged husband and kin. Just as Carrie is both lost girl and celebrity, Dreiser figures Hurstwood as both frightening stranger on the street and kin—two subject positions that in many ways also seem incompatible with each other.

42. Klimasmith, *At Home in the City*, 146.

10

Furrowing the Soil with His Pen

Derek Walcott's Topography of the English Countryside

Joanna Johnson

Press one foot on the soil of England and the phantoms spring. Poets, naturalists, novelists have harrowed and hallowed it for centuries with their furrowing pens as steadily as its yeomen once did with the plough.

—Derek Walcott, "The Garden Path: V. S. Naipaul"[1]

One icon of British heritage has a profoundly British cast. That is the landscape. Nowhere else is landscape so freighted as legacy. Nowhere else does the very term suggest not just scenery and *genre de vie*, but quintessential national virtues.

—David Lowenthal, "The Island Garden:
English Landscape and British Identity"[2]

Given Nobel Laureate Derek Walcott's intense concern with the physical and geographical aspects of his native Caribbean and other North American locations, it is perhaps surprising this concern is not mirrored in his poetical depictions of England. In fact, Walcott refers to the English rural landscape quite sparingly; any engagement with English pastoral tradition is instead via his prose writings or poetry that pay overt and deliberate homage to English poets themselves, or through his writing style, where he reflects the meter, rhythm, or language of English pastoral poetry. While this lack of concern and rejection of the English countryside (symbolically often seen as the epitome of Englishness) as subject matter might not otherwise be so unusual in writers from former colonies such as St. Lucia—Walcott's birthplace and home—it is of note because in so many other respects his writing and poetry act in great homage to a classical and an English tradition. Especially through the formal characteristics of poetry, Walcott highly prizes the pastoral nature of the English poetical tradition, and thus his lack of attention toward descriptions of the English countryside becomes more marked. Moreover, where he does overtly engage with it and acknowledge its influence, Walcott usually sees the English rural landscape as hostile or unwelcoming. This chapter aims to explore the nature and significance of Walcott's resistance to overt engagement with the English countryside, where more usually, as Walcott himself understands in his own writing, "topography delineates its verse."[3]

Derek Walcott was born in 1930 in Castries, the capital of St. Lucia in the Caribbean,[4] one of three children born to his mother, Alix, a Methodist schoolteacher, and his father, Warwick, who worked as a clerk in a district court. Both sides of his family were of European and African descent (his maternal grandfather was an estate owner in Dutch St. Maarten, while his paternal grandfather was an Englishman who moved to Barbados to purchase a plantation) and were part of the "brown middle-class" of St. Lucia,[5] who primarily spoke English in a predominantly French-based, Creole-speaking island (though Walcott certainly also speaks the St. Lucian Creole and has written several poems and parts of poems in that language). Walcott has lived on several other Caribbean islands, most especially Jamaica (as an undergraduate at the University of the West Indies) and Trinidad (where he developed the Trinidad Theatre Workshop), as well as spending several years in North America, primarily teaching at universities in Boston and New York. Bruce King, Walcott's biographer, cautions that to think of Walcott as "black or West Indian can be as much a misleading generalization as that of a New World poet or any broad category that ignores the social specificity of a life, its many identities, and their relationships to their contexts [. . .]. If he is part 'black,' he is more than half 'white.'"[6] Walcott's own narrator in his Caribbean "Odyssean" mini-epic "The Schooner *Flight*" claims, "I have Dutch, nigger, and English in me / and either I'm nobody, or I'm a nation."[7] Walcott's negotiation of such a complex background and identity manifests itself throughout his writing: by way of response to his own question in an early poem "A Far Cry From Africa," "how choose / Between this Africa and the English tongue I love?"[8] Walcott has evidently chosen neither one above the other. His friend and fellow Nobel Laureate poet Seamus Heaney comments in his review of Walcott's 1979 collection *The Star-Apple Kingdom*, "From the beginning he has never simplified or sold short. Africa and England are in him."[9] Walcott reclaims the language for himself and embraces and "rebuk[es] proprietary claims" on the English language.[10]

His great volume of work, which includes both poetry and plays, spans decades—from his first publications, such as *25 Poems* (1948), to the latest collection, *White Egrets* (2010), via such masterworks as the book-length poems *Another Life* (1973), *Omeros* (1990), after which he won the 1992 Nobel Prize in Literature "for a poetic oeuvre of great luminosity, sustained by a historical vision, the outcome of a multicultural commitment,"[11] and *Tiepolo's Hound* (2000). Becoming Nobel Laureate in 1992, coupled with his well-publicized friendships and connections with other world-renowned Nobel-winning poets, such as Heaney and Joseph Brodsky, has meant Walcott's readership extends far beyond a Caribbean audience. But to see his work outside of a Caribbean context is to miss vital parts of it. To be sure, he loves the English tongue, and grew up crafting the language from very early on, but he is quick to point out, for example, the iambic pentameter of Shakespeare "is very Caribbean,"[12] and he embraces this Caribbean rhythm in his poetry.

Not only does his native Caribbean feature via the language, but it also features via description of the landscape.[13] Sarah Phillips Casteel, in *Second Arrivals: Landscape and Belonging in Contemporary Writing of the Americas*, observes that "Caribbean writers are noted for their emphasis on landscape" but the aesthetic is usually "less receptive to the pastoral."[14] Instead, they "pursue less European modes of landscape representation that reach beyond the bounds of realism"[15] and write of the kind of Caribbean landscapes that are not fixed and "passive" but possess a "resonance,"[16] as Guyanese writer and theorist Wilson Harris has termed it. Descriptions of the physicality of the surroundings, including island topography, vegetation, and physical features of the landscape, especially along with the surrounding sea, constitute crucial parts of Walcott's poetry. Perhaps especially because of Walcott's "painter's eye for color and light," which "informs his poetic descriptions of landscape," his "descriptive mastery of landscape . . . [is] always more than mere description, deepening into metaphor."[17] Walcott's "painterly" eye allows him to describe in intricate detail colors, scenes, landscape, and physical surroundings, even though eventually he favored the word over the canvas, and his "pen replaced a brush."[18] Vivid, resonant description is certainly evident in Walcott's views of his native Caribbean, and although to a lesser extent, description of the topography and physical surroundings are also in his North American and European landscapes, for example in the rural France of *Tiepolo's Hound* (2000). Traditional views of England's landscape, however, appear harder to discern.

From early in his life, Walcott was introduced to the topography of the English countryside through his father's paintings of Cotman and Turner that hung on the wall of his childhood home and also apparently from a small blue notebook entitled "The English Topographical Draughts-men," which Walcott mentions both in *Another Life* and in *Tiepolo's Hound*.[19] Walcott is typical of most writers from former British colonies in that he would have seen and read extensively about England and the English countryside long before he actually saw them for himself. Thus much of his experience of the English landscape and representations of it would be (at least in earlier instances) refracted ones. Later works that describe England's landscape would come from firsthand accounts, but still by then, the myth of the immutable nature of the countryside might be expected to exert a hold and influence on his writing. One notable example of how Walcott in fact embraces the usually problematic nature of what Guyanese writer David Dabydeen has described as the colonial writer's limitations of learning to describe a tropical landscape in "English romanticist images" is with the daffodil (a common flower in England, but not in the Caribbean),[20] a flower that has come to symbolize the enforced colonial education. Caribbean writers Jean Rhys, Jamaica Kincaid, and even V. S. Naipaul have all written of their discomfort in varying degrees at being asked as schoolchildren to imagine and write about the English flower they had never seen but knew most commonly from being made to study Wordsworth's poem, "I Wandered Lonely As a Cloud." The poem famously begins in this way:

I wandered lonely as a Cloud
That floats on high o'er Vales and Hills,
When all at once I saw a crowd
A host, of golden Daffodils.

The use of these well-known first lines of Wordsworth's "daffodils poem" in Caribbean schoolrooms is an example of the hegemony of colo-nial discourse, where Caribbean schoolchildren were made to memorize a poem about a landscape, and specifically a type of flower, they had never seen and were not able to relate to. Not all reactions to the daffodils were so hostile, however, and Walcott, as he details in his 1974 essay "The Muse of History," saw it differently: "like any colonial child, I was taught English literature as my natural inheritance. Forget the snow and the daffodils. They were real, more real than the heat and oleander, perhaps, because they lived on the page, in imagination, and therefore in memory."[21] While other Caribbean writers viewed the daffodil with suspicion, representative of the control and imposition of the motherland's discourse over its colonies and symbolic of the hegemonic imperial power in the Caribbean, Walcott pre-fers to embrace the literary "power of a shared imagination."[22] He finds the landscape of his imagination to be more powerful than the physical landscape that actually surrounds him in the Caribbean.

To visualize the English countryside is often to conjure up such images of the Romantic era, of Wordsworth waxing lyrical having come upon a field of daffodils or of Constable's Hay Wain. These images constitute and construct part of the myth of England's countryside, a myth that obscures what has been termed the "dark side" of the landscape.[23] Raymond Williams's 1973 seminal work *The Country and the City* is a framework with which to understand this myth of countryside in England—that is, a place far removed from any rural wilderness or pure organic space yet a place that has for centuries been depicted and understood as a place of solace, of healing, of restfulness, or as a mythical, organic, and unsullied place, where one can go to be "at one" with nature and where there is a constant retrospection to a supposedly purer and simpler time. As Williams points out, such traditional views of the English countryside are as false as they are complicit in covering up the misery and poverty of much of its working class population and not least its colonial history. As he has famously remarked, "A working country is hardly ever a landscape."[24] Edward Said has subsequently reminded us that, for example, the English Georgian stately homes such as the fictional Mansfield Park and their rural surrounds would have been places that were constructed from the exploitation and enslavement of others.[25]

More recent examinations of the way landscape works as a cultural practice are in line with W. J. T. Mitchell's work in *Landscape and Power*.[26] Mitchell suggests that we "change landscape from a noun to a verb," that "we think of landscape [. . .] as a process by which social and subjective identities are formed," and that we consider "not just what landscape 'is' or 'means' but what it does, how it works as a cultural practice."[27] We can thus understand landscape as a cultural practice that reflects and naturalizes man-made intervention but also that becomes and reifies it. But despite a growing acknowledgment and awareness of the strong ideological underpinnings that shape the English countryside, even today the "English landscape tradition continues to view 'England' as a unit whose nature is essential and unquestioned."[28] Moreover, constructions of rural England are inextricably bound up with and "provide the basis for an understanding of Englishness."[29] In Britain, cultural and ideological questions of race and class are still especially subject to what Matthew Johnson has identified (borrowing Stefan Collini's terminology) a "muffling inclusiveness," where "debate about [ideas of Englishness and Britishness] is implicit and inflected rather than overt and strident."[30] As such, any debates to be had about the English landscape are stymied by a historical tendency to tightly "draw boundaries" around a calm and idyllic English landscape, boundaries that mean "the Empire gets left out, or more accurately, Britain's colonies are simultaneously inscribed and erased."[31] These tightly drawn boundaries around the supposedly essential and unquestioned nature of "England" means it also remains exclusive: the overwhelming majority of the population in rural areas is white.[32] For Trinidadian writer V. S. Naipaul to choose to live in the English countryside, as he has done for several decades, is "the equivalent of a Soviet dissident going home to Gorky, of a thirties Jew finding rest in Berlin, of a Bantu celebrating the delights of Johannesburg," as Walcott has astutely remarked.[33] Walcott, characteristically, disrupts what would otherwise be exclusive or subject to muffling inclusiveness by writing that challenges such a view.

Walcott's "sound colonial education"[34]—as his narrator Shabine in his 1979 poem "The Schooner *Flight*" terms it—has certainly given him the tools to write his poetry with the kinds of formal characteristics associated with "classical" or English traditional form in the "tongue that [he loves],"[35] enabling him to "[delight] in [those] forms he has inherited."[36] With his high regard and attention to traditional poetical form, his borrowing of specific lines, as well as his homages via specific poems and dedications, Walcott's poetry shows much evidence of this classical tradition, and his poetry is often a weave of borrowed allusions and quotations. One example is in the beginning of "The Schooner *Flight*," which Walcott has specifically acknowledged he sees as an "act of homage"[37] toward Thomas Langland's *Piers Ploughman* ("The Schooner *Flight*" begins "in idle August, while the sea soft,"[38] which replicates the rhythm and alliteration of the first line of Langland's *Piers Ploughman*: "In a somer seson, whan softe was the sonne"[39]). The rhythm and meter of the two lines is the same, along with the use of "soft" and the alliteration of the "s" sound in both lines. In part VI of the same poem, "The Sailor Sings Back to the Casuarinas," Walcott evokes a particularly English poem, "Old Man," by the Georgian poet Edward Thomas, who is often associated with a very rural and provincial Englishness.[40] Thomas questions the name of the shrub, "Old Man, or Lads-Love, / in the name there's nothing / To one that knows not Lads-Love, or Old Man,"[41] and in Walcott's poem, the narrator Shabine comments on the importance of the labeling of the local casuarinas trees as cedars or cypresses: even though they are just trees "with nothing else in mind," if "we live like our names our masters please, / by careful mimicry might become men."[42] Both poems reflect a preoccupation with the names and labeling of the "thing" itself, where the nomenclature reflects its ideological underpinning. As Walcott writes, "you would have to be colonial to know the difference, / to know the pain of history words contain."[43]

Another English poet who has been particularly influential on Walcott is W. H. Auden, someone whom Walcott "regarded as a mentor":[44] one specific poem is entitled "Eulogy to W. H. Auden" and employs the formal characteristics of Auden (such as use of the quatrain in the second and third sections of the poem) and is a poem in which Walcott again notes the "Empire's wrong" even as he makes his "first communion with the English tongue."[45] As Baugh writes, the "Audenesque poems of this period [*The Arkansas Testament*, 1988] are a mature repayment of Walcott's apprenticeship to Auden."[46] These homages and "repayments" (in whole poems, rhythm and meter, or in direct quotation) show Walcott's indebtedness and regard for an English and classical tradition. Especially relevant here is that this English and classical tradition is one, as the epigraph by Walcott to this chapter shows, that is indebted to the pastoral poets. Walcott understands this strong bond between England's poets and the countryside: "Boundless as its empire became, England remained an island, a manageable garden to every one of its poets, every one of whom is a pastoralist," where "still the provinciality of English poetry through Langland, Shakespeare, Spenser, Milton, Marvell, Pope, Keats, Wordsworth, Hardy, the Georgians, Thomas, is its pride."[47] Highly pastoral in its form, "culture and agriculture are synonyms [in England],"[48] where "[n]o other literature is so botanical as English, so seeded with delight and melancholy in the seasons."[49]

Yet, too, Walcott is aware of the complexity of the English countryside: in the same essay, he also recognizes a "malicious midden" in more recent accounts of the landscape,[50] where England's garden has "succumbed to the despair of Hamlet, 'an unweeded garden that grows to seed / things rank and gross in nature.'"[51] Walcott's views of England often tend toward suspicion; he has apparently always had a very difficult relationship with England, where, according to his biographer Bruce King, he feels "unease."[52] For Walcott, England is a place where "hereditary in each boy" is always the red "stain" of Empire "that spreads invisibly."[53]

One early poem, "Ruins of a Great House," published in Walcott's first major collection, *In a Green Night* (1962), is a work that reflects these "typical" Walcott characteristics: a poem that both draws on the English poetic tradition in an "Eliot-like weave of quotations and illusions,"[54] according to Walcott scholar Edward Baugh, yet also resists easy lauding of its countryside. The poem is an account of one of the many great houses built in the Caribbean during the colonial period, now derelict and symbolic of the now-defunct empire. These houses were the residences of the slave owners and plantation owners, and their present-day demise reflects the passing of that long-gone era, reflected in the beginning epigraph to the poem taken from Sir Thomas Browne's *Urn Burial*: "it cannot be long before we lie down in darkness, / and have our light in ashes."[55] This reflection on the temporary nature of life and of mortality continues into the next lines, where only the "disjecta membra"[56] of the house's ruins remain. The "leprosy of empire"[57] precedes the lines "Farewell green fields, / Farewell ye happy groves!"[58] Adapted from William Blake's poem "Night," the pastoral lines are a sentimental view of the countryside: a shepherd is going home at the end of the day, the sheep are in the fields, and the night is closing in. Thus in his use of these lines, Walcott alludes to the way empire has drawn to a close, the great house now in ruins and a remnant of empire, its decay figurative of the end of the colonial era. Yet the lines also reflect a symbolic rejection of a mythical view of the English countryside. The farewell is not just Walcott's message to the colonial influence of the great house; it can also be read as a rejection of the sentimentality that often otherwise accompanies poetical representations of the English countryside. This poem, in its validation of the language but not of a sentimental view of the countryside, is a characteristic example of Walcott's view and treatment of England's rural landscape. Walcott scholar Edward Baugh notes that a later poem, "The Bright Field," "brings back to mind 'Ruins of a Great House,' written some twenty years earlier, and a comparison of the two shows how Walcott is continuously working over his basic themes and yet not just repeating himself."[59]

Walcott's relationship to the landscape is especially revealed in two other of his poems, "Homage to Edward Thomas" (*The Gulf and Other Poems*, 1969) and "Midsummer, England" (*Sea Grapes*, 1976). Both works evince an unease with the English countryside and contain aspects that challenge a traditional pastoral and sentimental mode. Although both contain specifically pastoral and somewhat peaceful imagery, they reveal Walcott's equivocal relationship with the rural landscape. "Homage to Edward Thomas" is Walcott's tribute to the poet about whom Walcott has said he'd "leave the vicinity" if he heard a bad word said—as Walcott puts it, "[H]e's absolutely clear water."[60] According to Walcott, Thomas's writing is one of the English writers whose prose "brings us to tears in its natural affections."[61] Walcott values his meter, his rhythm, his clarity, and his formality, and, as we have seen, Walcott's own poetry reflects those attributes, not least in the "Homage to Edward Thomas" itself. Thomas is usually regarded as a very "English" poet (even though he in fact often identified himself as Welsh and has Welsh connections) because of his pastoral and provincial depictions: his most famous poem, "Adlestrop,"[62] wistfully remembers a deserted country railway station at the height of the English summer, and one that is certainly a work "seeded with delight and melancholy."[63]

Walcott's homage reflects the ambiguity of what England's garden ideologically represents; in the poem, we see the contrast of the formality and informality, as Walcott terms it, of the topography of England. The formality of the meter of the poem—the fourteen-line sonnet, iambic pentameter with Elizabethan rhyme scheme[64]—along with description of the dourly timbered manor house are both juxtaposed with the "sinuous"[65] and less-rigid Downs. The lines once thought of as tenuous are now "dissoluble," ones that "harden in their indifference."[66] The poem reflects both the subtlety and longevity of Thomas's prose, delighting in its form yet aware of the "indifference" of the pastoral Sussex down. Here language and landscape are intertwined—a place where "topography delineates its verse,"[67] as Walcott sees it. The garden is subtly scented, and at once is both "hedged or loosely-grown,"[68] an apparent contradiction reflecting the ambiguity and unease with his subject matter. Baugh sees Thomas's formality as an ideal and a "balance to luxuriance" for Walcott;[69] as well, I see this tension of the contradictions as a manifestation of the complexity of the subject matter for Walcott, one where the landscape is "in vocal contour."[70] I read "Homage to Edward Thomas" as a poem that reflects Walcott's insistence on immaculate form yet also never quite allows for an unproblematic view of the English landscape.

Another earlier poem, "Midsummer, England" (*Sea Grapes*, 1976) also uses the English countryside, this time around Henley on Thames, specifically as its subject matter. The scene is described at first as where "the legendary landscapes are alive" and where "Great summer takes its ease."[71] But the poem soon recognizes the taint of its imperial past, the "fear of darkness entering England's vein, / the noble monuments pissed on by rain," where a "great cloud's shadow grows close / as the past, a chill that intrudes / under the heat, under the centuries."[72] Lines that start by glorifying the beauty of the English landscape are soon infused with a darker core, where the "prodigious" summer produces a "black fruit."[73] In "Midsummer, England," riots of tropical color flare up amid the neat fields that have been "trimmed by centuries of reticence."[74] The muffling inclusiveness of England's rural communities is disrupted and challenged by its imperial legacy, here represented as the bright tropical squares of color, showing an English countryside whose supposed "legendary landscapes" are no longer alive but corrupted with the dark tide of imperial blood.

Moreover, "Midsummer, England" feels especially hostile and dark when juxtaposed with another Walcott "Midsummer" poem in the same collection, this time of a Caribbean landscape: "Midsummer, Tobago."[75] This Caribbean-set poem is an easy, short piece that revels in its own brevity and lightness, delights in a drowsy sleepiness, and is sparse and direct: "Broad sun-stoned beaches / White heat" and "scorched yellow palms / from the summer-sleeping house / allow the speaker to be drowsing through August."[76] England's hostility seems especially sharp when contrasted with this sleepy and restful Tobago scene.

Just as the tone of "Midsummer, Tobago" reveals the extent to which its companion piece, "Midsummer, England" is its opposite, comparing

Walcott's descriptions of the English countryside to other neighboring rural scenes, in Wales, for example, reveals how different his views of "non-English" landscapes are. Walcott prefers Wales (and Ireland) to England,[77] both of which parallel the West Indies in that they occupy a marginal position in relation to the colonial centre. And certainly in Wales, Walcott is able to identify with and "[recognize] the colonial condition."[78] But more than that, his two poems specifically about Wales (one simply called "Wales," published in *The Fortunate Traveller* (1981), and the other, "Streams," from *The Arkansas Testament* (1987) do evoke a very peaceful sense of the countryside with a much more restful tone. Here the rain doesn't "piss on" the countryside as it did in Henley; instead, it gently prods the sheep in a landscape "so windswept it refreshes" and where "pastures brighten with news."[79] In "Streams" the poet is reminded of his "mother's voice / in all its widowed, timbered strength"[80] (we have already seen this use of the heteronym timbre/timber in "Homage to Edward Thomas"). Wales is resilient and strong, where hard rocks, rusty gorges, and cold rustling gorse are defiant in the face of the elements rather than corrupted or fearful. Both these poems—"Streams" and "Wales"—show what Baugh describes as the intertwining of language, culture, and landscape. Rocks as hard as consonants, alliterative hills, and rain-vowelled shales sing of a language shared, and thus the landscape is like "bread to the mouth,"[81] a comforting one. For Walcott, Wales, unlike England, offers beauty, solace, and resilience.

One of Walcott's most unequivocal rejections of any fondness or regard toward England comes in his 1984 volume of poems titled *Midsummer*, a collection that recounts various episodes around the globe at the midsummer point. Here, any accounts of the English countryside reveal it to be quite unappealing: they depict drizzly mud-covered scenes, where a "gray English road hissed emptily," and Walcott confesses to "hating" the fable of wheezing English beeches.[82] This is an England that appears deeply unpleasant for Walcott, where "[s]omething branched in that countryside," with its old roads "brown as blood."[83] Against a backdrop of the infamous Brixton riots a couple of years previously,[84] Walcott's account of England firmly "closes the child's fairytale of an antic England, fairy rings, thatched cottages fenced with dog roses."[85] Walcott's English countryside lies far from any fairytale or mythical representation here. Yet even though the landscape might not hold any romanticism for Walcott, the English language itself continues to exert its hold on him: "the green oak of English is a murmurous cathedral / where some took umbrage, some peace, but every shade, all, / helped widen its shadow."[86]

The final poem I examine here is one from Walcott's most recent collection, *White Egrets* (2010), "A London Afternoon," and I think it is notable for its departure in tone from previous accounts. In the second section of the two-part poem, Walcott wonders what the narrow greasy streets of London with their pizza joints and ping and rattle of slot machines have to do with the England of his fifth-form anthology, an England that he remembers has the "scent and symmetry of Wyatt, Surrey."[87] Walcott writes, "spring grass and roiling clouds dapple a county / with lines like a rutted road stuck in the memory / of a skylark's unheard song, a bounty / pungent as clover, the creak of a country cart / in Constable or John Clare."[88] This is a view of the English countryside that, even as it acknowledges it came from a childhood anthology and thus a colonially refracted one, evokes a very peaceful image, where his love of the language now allows him to see beyond the red stain of the Empire on his schoolroom's map, and one where "words clear the page like a burst of sparrows over a hedge."[89] Walcott has not written of such images in earlier work without finding them to be false, or where the stain of the Empire encroaches too much for him to see the beauty evident here. I find these latest images of England's verse and countryside to be much more restful than in earlier poems, where Walcott's tone seems to be far more conciliatory toward the countryside, a mellower tone that is representative of the collection as a whole. In this part of the poem, we can better recognize the "literature so seeded with delight and melancholy"[90] that Walcott believes exists in England, yet up until now has not been present in his own poetry.

Still, this latest poem is an exception to the earlier poems I have discussed here and is not reflective of the rest of Walcott's depictions of England. Perhaps now that his mind is an "ageing sea,"[91] as he wistfully admits in "A London Afternoon," he has mellowed his views somewhat from those of his young student days and beyond. Walcott's biographer tells the story that when Walcott was a young undergraduate at the University of the West Indies in Mona, he was forced to hear how the Jamaican landscape compared unfavorably to the English landscape by his then professor, Professor Croston, an Englishman.[92] Travelling through Bog Walk scenic valley in Jamaica, Walcott remembers Croston responding to a comment that the valley was beautiful by saying "it is like a meaner sort of Wye Valley." Several years later, recounting this experience at a reading of the Star Apple Kingdom in Trinidad, Walcott said he felt it was as though the Jamaican landscape could "break its arse trying, but it would never quite achieve the effort required." He said it "typified the kind of experience we have been subjected to in every single nerve-end and aspect of our lives as colonials—a life of humiliation even in a remark like that."[93] Walcott was understandably very annoyed by this offhand and throwaway remark of the Englishman, and the poet's subsequent accounts of the English countryside have never served to underscore that particular myth.

Whether the motivation has been specific or whether it reflects a wider political challenge to the inherent dominative mode, Walcott has never written the English rural landscape as glowingly pastoral or in the "sense sublime" of William Wordsworth and his other poetical forebears. Although Walcott's own pen furrows the soil just as steadily as it does for the English writers to whom he refers and reveres, it does not reify the myth of the purity of the countryside; rather, it exposes that myth. In its unwillingness to engage directly with glowing descriptions of England's supposed green and pleasant land, Walcott's writing positions itself on the margins, challenging the discourses that shore up the long-held concept of the rural as an unsullied, organic, or natural space and encroaching upon the muffling inclusiveness of the English countryside. In doing so, Walcott shows that topography may delineate England's verse, but his own English topography bids farewell to green fields and happy groves with a "chill that intrudes."

Notes

1. Derek Walcott, "The Garden Path: V. S. Naipaul," *What The Twilight Says* (London: Faber and Faber, 1998), 121.
2. David Lowenthal, "The Island Garden: English Landscape and British Identity," in *History, Nationhood and the Question of Britain*, ed. Helen Brocklehurst and Robert Phillips (New York: Palgrave Macmillan, 2004), 137.
3. Derek Walcott, "Homage to Edward Thomas," *Collected Poems* (New York: Farrar, Straus & Giroux, 1986), 103.
4. The island changed rule over fourteen times between Britain and France from 1660 to 1803. St. Lucia was British from 1803 until its full independence in 1979. The warring over the island gave rise to it being popularly known as the "Helen of the West Indies." "Culturally and linguistically the island [. . .] until recently remained French or French Creole" (Bruce King, *Derek Walcott: A Caribbean Life* [Oxford: Oxford University Press, 2000], 5), but British rule since 1803 meant English then became the language of the "elite, the civil service, the educated," though the French-based Creole was "known by everyone" (Ibid., 6).
5. King, *Derek Walcott*, 4.
6. Ibid., 5
7. Walcott, *Collected Poems*, 346.
8. Ibid., 18.
9. Seamus Heaney quoted in Frank McMahon's, "Ambiguous Gifts: Seamus Heaney's Oxford Professorship of Poetry," *Oxford Art Journal* 13, no. 2 (1990): 4.
10. McMahon, "Ambiguous Gifts," 4.
11. King, *Derek Walcott*, 537–38.

12. Derek Walcott, "Introduction to 'The Schooner *Flight*'" (BBC Radio 3, September 27, 1991).

13. Writing about the landscape of the islands of the Caribbean would necessarily include the surrounding sea, and Walcott devotes himself to this, too: for example, "The Sea is History" (*The Star-Apple Kingdom*, 1979), as the title of one poem states. *Omeros* (1990) includes Homeric elements, and is a kind of Caribbean *Odyssey*, finishing with the line, "the sea was still going on" (*Omeros*, 325), while some of the last lines of "The Schooner *Flight*" have Shabine reflecting that "My first friend was the sea. / Now is my last" (*Collected Poems*, 361).

14. Sarah Phillips Casteel, *Second Arrivals: Landscape and Belonging in Contemporary Writing of the Americas* (Charlottesville: University of Virginia Press, 2007), 13.

15. Ibid.

16. Ibid, 14.

17. Edward Baugh, introduction to *Selected Poems* by Derek Walcott, ed. Edward Baugh (New York: Farrar, Straus & Giroux, 2007), xiv-xv.

18. Derek Walcott, *Tiepolo's Hound* (New York: Farrar, Straus & Giroux, 2000), 19.

19. Walcott, *Collected Poems*, 202, and Walcott, *Hound*, 11, respectively.

20. David Dabydeen, "West Indian Writers in Britain," *Voices of the Crossing: The Impact of Britain on Writers from Asia, the Caribbean and Africa*, ed. Ferdinand Dennis and Nasem Khan (London: Serpent's Tail, 2000), 67.

21. Derek Walcott, "The Muse of History," in *What the Twilight Says* (London: Faber and Faber, 1998), 62.

22. Ibid.

23. John Barrell, *The Dark Side of the Landscape: The Rural Poor in English Painting 1730–1840* (Cambridge: Cambridge University Press, 1983).

24. Raymond Williams, *The Country and the City* (Oxford: Oxford University Press, 1975), 120.

25. Edward Said, *Culture and Imperialism* (New York: Knopf, 1993).

26. W. J. T. Mitchell, *Landscape and Power*, 2nd ed. (Chicago: University of Chicago Press, 2002), 1.

27. Ibid.

28. Matthew Johnson, *Ideas of Landscape* (Oxford: Blackwell, 2007), 186.

29. Robert Burden and Stephan Kohl, *Landscape and Englishness* (Amsterdam: Rodopi, 2006), back cover. It is outside the scope of this investigation to deal with an intense examination of what constitutes "Englishness." Such, more thorough, examinations of Englishness and national identity would include, within a postcolonial context, Simon Gikandi's *Maps of Englishness: Writing Identity in the Culture of Colonialism* (New York: Columbia University Press, 1996), Ian Baucom's *Out of Place: Englishness, Empire, and the Locations of Identity* (Princeton, NJ: Princeton University Press, 1999), and Krishnan Kumar's *The Making of English National Identity* (Cambridge: Cambridge University Press, 2003), which deals with the English identity "enigma."

30. Johnson, *Landscape*, 168.

31. Matthew Johnson, "Muffling Inclusiveness: Some Notes Towards an Archaeology of the British," in *Archaeologies of the British: Explorations of Identity in Great Britain and Its Colonies,* ed. Susan Lawrence (London: Routledge, 2003), 28.
32. According to UK National Statistics (2001), ethnic minorities constituted 29 percent of London's population, compared to just 2 percent in the southwest (a predominantly rural area) of England (http://www.statistics.gov.uk/cci/nugget.asp?id=263).
33. Walcott, "The Garden Path," 131.
34. Walcott, *Collected Poems,* 346.
35. Walcott, "A Far Cry," *Collected Poems,* 18.
36. Baugh, *Selected Poems,* xv.
37. Walcott, "Commentary" (audio recording).
38. Walcott, *Collected Poems,* 345.
39. Prologue, Line 1, Version B Text.
40. Thomas's most well-known poem is "Adlestrop"—see also note 59.
41. Edward Thomas, "Old Man," http://www.bbc.co.uk/worldservice/arts/features/poems/adcock.shtml.
42. Walcott, *Collected Poems,* 354.
43. Ibid., 353.
44. Baugh, *Selected Poems,* xiii.
45. Derek Walcott, *The Arkansas Testament* (London: Faber and Faber, 1988), 63–64.
46. Baugh, *Derek Walcott* (Cambridge: Cambridge University Press, 2006), 176.
47. Walcott, "The Garden Path," 121–22.
48. Ibid., 122.
49. Ibid., 121.
50. Ibid.
51. Ibid.
52. King, *Derek Walcott,* 490.
53. Derek Walcott, "A London Afternoon," *White Egrets* (London: Faber and Faber, 2010), 44.
54. Baugh, *Derek Walcott,* 43.
55. Walcott, *Collected Poems,* 19.
56. Ibid.
57. Ibid.
58. Ibid.
59. Baugh, *Derek Walcott,* 107.
60. Ibid. 46.
61. Walcott, "The Garden Path," 122.
62. In fact, Adlestrop lies between Wales and England, a place "in between."
63. Walcott, "The Garden Path," 121.
64. A Shakespearean sonnet rhyme scheme is usually three quatrains, *a-b-a-b, c-d-c-d, e-f-e-f,* with the last two lines as a rhyming couplet, *g-g.*
65. Walcott, *Collected Poems,* 103.
66. Ibid.

67. Ibid.

68. Ibid.

69. Baugh, *Derek Walcott*, 46.

70. Tyler Hoffman, *Robert Frost and the Politics of Poetry* (Hanover, NH: Middlebury College Press, 2001), 219.

71. Derek Walcott, *Sea Grapes* (New York: Farrar Straus & Giroux, 1976), 67.

72. Ibid.

73. Ibid.

74. Ibid.

75. Ibid., 72.

76. Ibid.

77. King, *Derek Walcott*, 586.

78. Walcott, *The Arkansas Testament*, 81.

79. Ibid., 80.

80. Ibid.

81. Derek Walcott, *The Fortunate Traveller* (London: Faber and Faber, 1982), 87.

82. Derek Walcott, *Midsummer* (New York: Farrar, Straus & Giroux, 1984), xxxix.

83. Ibid.

84. Social, economic, and racial inner-city tensions had led to what was later termed "the worst outbreak of disorder in the UK this century": BBC "On This Day," November 25, 1981, http://news.bbc.co.uk/onthisday/hi/dates/stories/november/25/newsid_2546000/2546233.stm.

85. Walcott, *Midsummer*, xxiii.

86. Ibid., lii.

87. Walcott, *White Egrets*, 45.

88. Ibid.

89. Ibid.

90. Walcott, "The Garden Path," 121.

91. Walcott, "A London Afternoon," 45.

92. King, *Derek Walcott*, 87.

93. Ibid.

11

Global Positioning from Spain

Mapping Identity in African American Narratives of Travel

Maria C. Ramos

The Western Global Imaginary and Spain

To be a functioning and organic part of something is to be almost unconscious of it. I was a part, intimate and inseparable, of the Western world, but I seldom had had to account for my Westernness, had rarely found myself in situations which had challenged me to do so. (Even in Asia and Africa I had known where my world ended and where theirs began. But Spain was baffling; it looked and seemed Western, but it did not act or feel Western.) Since I now felt most strongly, in fact, *knew* that Spain was not a Western nation, what then did being Western mean?

—Richard Wright, *Pagan Spain*[1]

In the last section of his 1957 travelogue, *Pagan Spain*, Richard Wright develops the provocative thesis of his book that "though Spain was geographically a part of Europe, [and] it had had just enough Western aspects of life to make [him] feel a little at home, [. . .] it was not the West."[2] On the surface, Wright's account of three trips to Spain during 1954 and 1955 appears to reproduce the discourse of Spanish exceptionalism—that is, that Spain is essentially different from the rest of Europe.[3] Indeed, Wright goes as far as calling Spain "pagan," placing Spain not only developmentally before modernity but even before Christianity. Wright's view of Spain could easily be interpreted as consistent with an Anglo and Anglo-American vision that

has painted Spain as a backward or primitive space.[4] Yet a careful consideration of this passage, and the larger discussion of geographic metaphors of
identity, can lead to a more complicated interpretation of Wright's vision.

The description of Spain as decidedly un-Western illustrates the complex process of attributing identities to various geographical spaces within
the context of travel. It reveals a perception of elsewhere (in this case, Spain,
designated along with Asia and Africa as not Western) in relation to a home
space (which Wright labels the West). The mapping of a foreign space and
an eventual return to a familiar home are expected conventions of the
genre of travel writing. Moreover, it is generally assumed that, even if the
journey might lead to some unexpected experiences, the locations of home
and elsewhere will remain essentially fixed and recognizable throughout a
travel narrative. Wright, for example, apparently expected to engage difference in his travels to Africa and Asia, despite his belief that as a black man
he will have insider knowledge of these other locations. His travels to these
places, therefore, leave his sense of geographical identity intact. Yet Spain
"was baffling." In his mapping of Spain, Wright finds the lines between
home and abroad are blurred, causing him to reflect on the geographical
categories of identity he is employing. For Wright, being in Spain poses the
unexpected challenge of defining his own home, his sense of his Western
identity, by forcing him to "account for [his] Westernness."

Wright's assertion about Spain reveals both the significance and the
problematic nature of the geographic concepts he has inherited in their
function as identity categories. The geographical concepts of West and
non-West are laden with value judgments despite being commonly used
to refer to specific spaces and people as if these terms refer to knowable
and unified identities. Wright's need to define his own perspective on what
"being Western" means, for example, shows that this term is more slip-
pery than it at first appears. Wright acknowledges that the "West" is not
a specific place but an identity associated with particular ideologies—for
Wright, the epistemology of secular humanism. Yet as a directional term,
west has meaning only in relation to other spaces. One can look or travel
west from a particular position, but west is not a place. By consciously
articulating a category of identity that derives meaning only in relation to
other categories, other constructed concepts, Wright counters an understanding of identity that depends on a static understanding of geography.
Wright has defined identity as a set of relations rather than a set of fixed
characteristics.

The complexity of identity through relation is further exposed in the
travels of a figure such as Wright. As a black man in the 1950s, Wright
is not "at home" in his home, the United States, nor is he a citizen of
France, his location of exile. His blackness places his own relationship to

Westernness in question from the perspective of many in a racialized West because of the relationship of blackness to Africa. Yet when Wright travels to Ghana and Indonesia, travels narrated in *Black Power* (1954) and *The Color Curtain* (1956) respectively, Wright is clearly perceived by others as a Westerner and an American. Wright's own position as insider/outsider—part of, yet different from, the West—reflects the position he creates for Spain—a position that is paradoxically both outside and at the very heart of the West. This liminal space creates room for him to contemplate the relation between geography and the construction of identity categories.

Wright's work points to the legacy of the geographic knowledge of early modern Europe. The language of West and non-West reflects the global imaginary that resulted from developments in early modern European cartography. Early modern maps developed amid the need for mapping areas of the world (including the Americas) that were being opened up to colonizing forces within Europe, the emergence of technology and arts that permitted realistic representations of the world, and the growth of geography as an "objective" scientific discipline.[5] These maps, therefore, created the geographic knowledge and modern world view of their European makers. Alongside the need to represent the newly "discovered" Americas in relation to colonizing Europe, we witness the rise of the West as a geographic and ideological concept.[6] In addition, western Europe's relations to other places can be discerned in this global imaginary. Various continents are represented as discrete entities inhabited by people with distinct—and, outside of Europe, often primitive—characteristics, supporting the national and racial identities crucial for the colonizing project.

Wright is not the only African American author to write a travel narrative about Spain that wrestles with inherited geographic metaphors of identity in productive ways. A number of other well-known African American writers also produced significant travel writing about Spain during the first half of the twentieth century, among them Claude McKay, Langston Hughes, and Frank Yerby.[7] Spain, at first, seems an unlikely subject for so many African American writers. It did not have the liberal appeal of France or the radical appeal of the Soviet Union, nor was it a recognizably diasporic site such as the Caribbean or South America. Yet Spain allowed these writers to rethink identity construction, particularly with respect to contested modern racial and national identities of the time. Its history of Arab-Berber rule from the eighth through the fifteenth centuries, in particular, became the main lens through which they viewed Spain. The result is that Spain's liminal position geographically (between Europe and Africa), historically and culturally (between West and East), and politically (between liberal secularism and a totalitarian religious state), permits challenges to the geopolitics of the early modern European mapping of the world and, therefore, the politics of identity that accompanies it. Building on recent scholarship that has shifted frameworks for understanding cultural processes from ones based on history to ones based on space or geography,[8] this chapter will examine the alternative global imaginary mapped in these African American travel narratives of Spain and suggest an updated geographic metaphor for understanding the processes of identity construction, particularly for people on the move.

Challenging the Global Imaginary:
Spain and the Trans-Mediterranean

Spain's peculiar position in Europe allows for a reorientation of our global imaginary. Harlem Renaissance writer Claude McKay and midcentury popular novelist Frank Yerby both engage in this remapping; however, they do this by figuring Spain as a representative space rather than as an exceptional one. Anticipating the basin-centered thinking central to late twentieth-century theories of the Black Atlantic and circum-Pacific studies,[9] Yerby and McKay map Spain within a trans-Mediterranean network that debunks the notions of westward progress and, indeed, western Europe as a distinct location. Both authors invoke the history of medieval Spain to undermine the West's myths about itself.

Frank Yerby's 1965 novel *An Odor of Sanctity* provides insight into the concept of the trans-Mediterranean.[10] This novel draws the reader into a drama that locates the roots of the European Renaissance in the historical integration of the East into Europe through Spain. Subtitled *A Novel of Medieval Moorish Spain*, the novel is centered on the epic journey of its hero, a Christian Goth named Alaric, throughout the Iberian peninsula and North Africa during the ninth century, key years of Arab-Berber dominance in the South. The novel highlights the political and social exchanges between the Christian, Muslim, and Jewish cultures present during the medieval period within the southern Iberian peninsula, or al-Andalus, as well as in North Africa and the Levant.

Alaric is raised in a Gothic household that abhors the Muslim presence in Spain and proclaims a northern Gothic ethnic superiority. His first journey south to the heart of the Islamic empire in Córdoba upsets this perspective on the "foreign" invader. Alaric's first impression of Córdoba is of a magical city—"everything [is] a wonder," including the shops, artisan work, architecture, and a copy house in which books were reproduced. He is embarrassed by his own culture when his guide asks him, "Do not you infidels have the like?"[11] When he finally reaches the Alcázar, Alaric is led not directly to the emir but through "a richly carved double door of Lebanese cedar" to what he eventually discovers is a bath with marble floors and columns, alabaster walls; jade and porphyry urns, plants, and a pool "out of whose center a sizable fountain played."[12]

The bath Alaric encounters is an apt symbol of what he admires in the culture as a whole. Rather than being isolated and backward, Córdoba, and more generally al-Andalus, is a lively site in a system of global exchange. It is culturally complex, with a mix of people loosely joined under the Islamic rule and at the same time consciously and actively integrated into a larger network of sites that cross space and time.[13] The bath contains materials and technologies from locations all around the Mediterranean, including North Africa and the Levant. The overwhelming effect on Alaric derives from his realization that centuries of technology and craftsmanship have been harnessed, honed, and brought to a central location by the al-Rahman court of al-Andalus. The Islamic court is praised for the technological advancement it brings to Europe, including glassworks, waterworks, and paper, as well as refinement in the arts and an interest in gathering ancient texts. Through their efforts and funding, the learning of the Greeks and Romans is accessed, translated, and developed to bring the European continent out of its cultural dark ages. Yerby reverses the stereotypes of North and South, challenging the myth of northern European superiority, exposing the "other" roots of the European Renaissance.

Yerby's novel, as historical fiction based in al-Andalus, subverts the conceptual map that uses the Mediterranean to divide North from South and East from West. In its place, Yerby provides a map that is more flexible and reflective of change over time. Instead of distinct continents, Yerby maps a trans-Mediterranean network of sites, each connected to the others through various routes and over time. In other words, rather than highlighting the particular territorial or cultural boundaries emphasized in early modern European cartography, Yerby's map focuses on connections between sites that have always already been in contact with others.[14] Alaric recognizes what such a conceptual map suggests: these sites have always been related, and the brilliance of the emir's court is its willingness to learn from others. The reverse of this is what he condemns most in his own culture—its dismissal of others and their ways of life because of its confidence in its own superiority and truth.

Like Yerby, Claude McKay's work maps Spain as part of the trans-Mediterranean that challenges a Western geographical narrative. In his travel memoir *A Long Way from Home* (1937), McKay notes an "African streak" in Spanish culture that whets his appetite for visiting Africa.[15] Then when he travels to Africa, he expresses a longing to return to Spain. Presence in one location and culture crystallizes a perspective on the other even

as they are intimately tied to each other. Within the narration of his movements between the two spaces, McKay figures the relationship between
Spain and Africa as a cultural conversation, an exchange of ideas and influence over time amid colonial enterprises. And McKay, too, broadens the
scope of the conversation by demonstrating that it encompasses a larger
geographical area, including vast stretches to the east (Baghdad), south
(sub-Saharan Africa), north (Europe), and west (the Americas). McKay's
representation of any one location, then, is always defined through its relation to spaces around it.

His city poems, several of which he includes in his memoir, illustrate the
geographical imaginary at the heart of his method of representing Spain.
"Tetuán," for example, chronicles the history of empire and exchange
between North Africa and Spain. The poem begins not with a vision of
Tetuán, as one would expect, but with a vision of the Alhambra in Granada,
the location of the Islamic empire's last stronghold in the Iberian peninsula:

> The conquering Moor an homage paid to Spain
> And the Alhambra lifted up its towers!
> Africa's fingers tipped with miracles,
> And quivering with Arabian designs.[16]

In these lines, the invasion of Spain by North Africans is transformed
into a "tribute" to the peninsula, and the physical mark left by the invading force, the Alhambra, is praised for its beauty. The construction of this
palace is represented as an African miracle on European soil, one whose
inspiration was not solely from the South (Africa), but also from an East
(Arabia) that had penetrated Africa. When Tetuán is finally introduced
in the second half of the poem, McKay envisions a city built at the end
of the fifteenth century by refugees from the Catholic conquest of Anda-
lucía: "a fort of struggle and strife, / Where chagrined Andalusian Moors
retired."[17] Yet rather than a humble retreat, this city is a "repaid [...]
tribute" from Spain, who brings to it "a fountain bubbling with new life"
and "filled its sparkling with flamenco laughter."[18] This final image is
a beautiful "mosaic," a blending of the two cultures already themselves
blended.

In a poetic tribute to "Fez," McKay also connects Spain to the near East.
McKay begins the poem with another displacement of cities: "Mine eyes
saw Fez, my heart exclaimed Baghdad / In Africa."[19] Strikingly, the poem
about the "heart of Morocco" ends with a vision of the city that links its
"beauty African in shape and form, / With glowing fire of Andalusian
eyes."[20] He paints a similarly vivid (if not thoroughly "Orientalized") version of Fez in his memoir:

In Fez I felt that I was walking all the time on a magic carpet. [. . .] I was invited to princely marriage feasts to eat *cous-cous* from the common dish with stately old "turbans," to drink *thé a la menthe* in cool gardens, to intimate *flamenco* dancing of fatmas in the *garconnieres* of *fondouks*. [. . .] For my days were fully occupied in sampling the treasures of the city; [. . .] following the Afro-Oriental bargaining; feeling the color of the accent of the story-tellers in the market places. [. . .] For the first time in my life I felt myself singularly free of color consciousness.[21]

McKay figuratively and linguistically demonstrates a "magic carpet ride" through an Afro-Euro-Oriental marketplace, a space of so much color that he ironically finally feels "free of color consciousness." McKay's representation of the dynamic multiculturalism that characterizes the trans-Mediterranean is a rejection of the European version of colonization as a civilizing process led by the West. Though no supporter of colonial politics, McKay nevertheless appreciate the cultures created through migrations of people and the beauty that cultural mixing can bring. Modern national borders cannot hold against the power of such a history of migrations that, despite the violence of empire, surprisingly has one positive outcome: McKay notes the beauty of what can be created when difference is encountered. The West is only a brief historical moment embedded in a longer history of global markets, including the circulations of ideas and people oriented eastward.[22]

Individual Identification: The Moor's Return

Just as attention to McKay and Yerby's mapping of Spain reveals a subversion of the traditional geographic identities within the European global imaginary, Langston Hughes's reporting on the Spanish Civil War shows the importance of the figure of the Moor for thinking about individual identity construction through Spain. Hughes traveled to Spain in 1937 to cover the International Brigades for the *Baltimore Afro-American*.[23] Hughes uses his perspective on the Spanish situation to reflect on the relationship between local, national, and international struggles, particularly struggles that involve racial identities. His work attempts to create a geopolitics of black struggle from a global perspective that does not erase local particularities. Despite focusing on the political present of the Spanish Civil War, Hughes finds an approach for his project in the figure of the Moor from Spain's past. The representation of the Moor offers on an individual level the opportunity to rethink identity construction that the geographical category of Spain offers on a global level.

Recent analyses of English Renaissance renderings of the Moor explore how medieval and Renaissance European expressions of race vacillate between conceptions of cultural or religious difference and biological difference. During the Crusades, for example, both sides were constituted of diverse peoples, but each was seen as a distinct group.[24] Blackness functioned as a spiritual metaphor, expressing religious prejudice, but as contact with sub-Saharan Africa increased with the slave trade, it increasingly referred to physical blackness as a marker of an inner difference. During the Renaissance, Moorishness, originally designating Muslim identity, became associated with physical blackness despite the fact that the North African Arab-Berbers were not necessarily dark skinned. The essence of the Moorish difference is remarkably unstable—this figure can be Muslim/Arab or Black/African—resulting in a multivalent conception of the Moor.[25]

In Hughes's reporting from the Spanish civil war, the Moor appears in several contexts and from more than one perspective: the Moor appears as the Moroccan conscripts fighting in Franco's Army of Africa, the Spaniard, and kin to black Americans. The flexibility of the Moor's identity is central to his work as is its association with a variety of differences—that is, the ease with which it can be associated with many "others." We can see him use this figure in a number of ways as he reflects on racial politics in both Spain and the United States.

Two central questions in Hughes's reporting directly address black American soldiers fighting for the Spanish republic: "With so many unsolved problems in America," Hughes asks, "why would a Negro come way over to Spain to help solve Spain's problems—perhaps with his very life?"[26] Hughes uses a series of interviews with soldiers to explain, for a African American audience, what connection they might have to a national conflict so far away. One American college student draws the links for him: "Negro college students must realize the connection between the international situation and our problems at home. [. . .] Right here in Madrid, I've seen how Fascists destroy schools and libraries."[27] In addition, Hughes is concerned about how black fighters would be received given General Franco's use of Moroccan troops. But Hughes concludes from both his observations and interviews that black fighters are indeed welcomed into the Republican army and by its supporters. He suspects that Spain's past, those "traces of Moorish blood from the days of the Mohammedan conquest,"[28] accounts for the contemporary Spanish openness to people of color. He mentions the variety of colors one can see among the Spanish people, from the "pure-blooded Negroes from the colonies in Africa" to the "copper colored Gypsies."[29] This construction of Spain as already Africanized biologically is, of course, dependent upon the racial construction of the Moors as physically dark.

Hughes's work also shows concern about how this color will be per-ceived abroad. He, like several other African American reporters who pub-lished articles on the Spanish conflict, expressed the fear that Franco's use of North African troops would open the door for racism as a mode of attacking Franco.[30] He attempts to balance a condemnation of Franco with a sympathetic view of the Moroccan troops by placing them, as present-day Moors, in the context of colonialism in Africa. In "Letter from Spain: Addressed to Alabama" (1937), the best known of his Spanish political poems, one can observe a complicated reflection on these issues.[31] This dialect ballad is framed as a letter from an African American fighter for the republican army, Johnny, to a correspondent at home in Alabama, whom he refers to as "Brother." The narrative in the poem dramatizes a conversa-tion between this soldier and a "wounded Moor" from Franco's army. The poem narrates Johnny's coming to consciousness of the similarity between his own situation and that of the Moroccan soldier, despite being on oppo-site sides in the war.

Hughes attempts to connect Johnny, "the Moor," and the brother at home through color as an expression of his international politics.[32] Several times throughout the poem Johnny likens himself to the Moor through color, twice referring to the Moroccan soldier as being "just as dark as me."[33] Johnny's identification with the dying soldier may begin with color, but it develops on a deeper historical level. The soldier's claim of having been "nabbed" in his land and taken to Spain resonates with the language of slav-ery used later in the poem to describe colonial rule in Africa. This would, of course, invoke the transatlantic slave trade for the American reader. As Johnny looks from the Spanish conflict to the dying Moroccan soldier to Africa and back home to the United States, he collapses the various spaces related to these national identities. All are connected through the image of the "Moor," a flexible construction whose many imagined facets can be used to create a series of alliances despite Hughes's attentiveness to alterity within diaspora—that is, the differences among the trio in the poem.[34] The Moor's shifting racial/national identity against the background of a nation attempting to redefine itself in new terms allows Hughes to build a series of connections and alliances in his attempt to articulate a broader geopolitics. This figure in the poem links local and global by connecting various geog-raphies and the past and present, including the multiple figures meeting in Spain in the poem.

The Moor, as an unstable construction of difference that can signify various temporal and geographic identities, is intimately connected to both Spanish identity and history that these African American writers use as a canvas upon which to project various ideas of difference. The figure of the Moor is manipulated by each writer for his own purposes—either to create similarities between himself and those that once inhabited Spain under the Arab-Berber empire, to debunk the myth of racial purity in Europe, or to explore the connection of Spain and the rest of the West to the South and East. Each of these authors sets up his own relationship with Moorishness and Spain. Through these relations, through the act of relating to others, they define their own identities.

Recalculating: GPS as a Metaphor for Identity Construction

Examining these writers' attempts to counter the European global imaginary, and the identities associated with it, exposes the difficulties of letting go of such geographic identities despite their faults. Our geographical imagination is still important to the ways in which we orient ourselves in the world; we associate ourselves with various locations and groups. I am, therefore, suggesting an updated geographic metaphor suitable to help us rethink traditional geographic and identity boundaries in the ways these writers encourage.

The contemporary technology of Global Positioning Systems (GPS) is a useful metaphor through which to understand the identity construction and global imaginary being mapped in these texts. By appropriating the language of this recent technology, despite its being anachronistic to these writers' works, I hope to provide a way of understanding the impulses at work in these maps and further the usefulness of geographic metaphors for thinking through the future of identity politics and our relations to others, particularly across national borders. As writers departing from inherited maps, they lacked mapping language adequate to explain what they were creating. GPS provides a vocabulary and model that I believe is implied in their works. Just as travel is a matter of shifting physical position from one space to another, identity construction can be seen as a matter of positioning one's sense of self in relation to a globalized world system. A brief introduction to the basics of global positioning will illustrate what makes it such a useful metaphor.

GPS is not a map but a process used in the act of mapmaking. It uses a series of satellites orbiting the earth as reference points to determine the location of a specific receiver on the earth. The process of calculating the receiver's position, called triangulation, requires determining the distance between the receiver and at least three orbiting satellites at the same time. From this information, the precise location of the receiver on the earth can be determined.[35]

One way this metaphor is useful for understanding identity construction is in the use of triangulation to determine a receiver's location. If we imagine the receiver as an individual, then that individual's location can only be determined through a calculation of his or her relation to a number of satellites, each representing one of any number of categories of identification. For example, a person might need to weigh the relative importance of (or distance from) several identity categories that work together to determine his or her own subject location. An individual might find that in lived experience, the racial designation of black is shaped by the gender identification of woman or by a specific nationality. In this case, the individual is calculating his or her location/identity in relation to three identity categories simultaneously, just as the receiver measures its distance from a number of satellites to determine its location. Another individual might contemplate the meaning of racial identity by calculating his or her relation to a specific set of racial categories available in a given time and place. As has been argued in Asian-American and U.S. Latino/a studies, racial designations such as Asian or Latino/a have often been developed in relation to a dominant white-black dynamic, creating a triangulation in which one's racial status is negotiated through its relation to these other racial categories.[36]

Moreover, the GPS model can accommodate the effects of an individual's movement through space as well. Just as a receiver that is in motion will need to recalculate the distance between itself and each of the reference satellites to know its position, so a person recalculates his or her relationship to the terms of identification as that person travels from one culturally conceived space to another. A black writer, such as Wright, for example, might not feel very "American" in the United States given the conditions of segregation in the first half of the twentieth century; the relationship to a racial identity is too strong. However, when traveling abroad, Wright at times finds that the relation to the United States comes much closer. In Indonesia he finds himself associated with Americanness rather than with people oppressed by Western empire.

Finally, a third dynamic that this model accounts for is that the satellites themselves are in motion over time. Similarly, globalization, which involves the constant movement of people, ideas, and markets around the world, renders unstable the very categories we have used as points of identification. The borders surrounding stable geographical concepts and identities—nations, regions, continents—are beginning to blur and are as contested as they are reified. These categories are themselves better understood as a series of relations to ideas than as static lists of traits. This means that the model can help us recognize the changes in the various categories of identity to which we see ourselves in relation.

The most common experience many have with GPS is with in-car navigation systems. What makes in-car GPS systems particularly compelling as a model for identity construction is that the system constantly updates and recalculates its position, its perspective on a possible map of locations (including possible routes), in response to ongoing changes in the location of the receiver as it moves through space over time. The constant use of triangulation to compute location means that location is always determined in relation to other objects.

One can see how the figure of the Moor illustrates such a model; its identity depends on the perspective or location from which it is viewed and the identity categories to which it is related. When viewed from medieval Catholic Spain, the Muslim religious identity is emphasized. In fact, the focus on the Moor's relation to a religious category is so important, and flexible, that it is even applied to the newly encountered indigenous peoples of the Americas, whom the Spanish conquerors referred to as American Moors—the Moor's relation to Africanness becomes unnecessary as long as he is associated with a territory considered foreign to Europe. Yet from the Anglo empire, defining itself in relation to the Spanish empire, the Moor was physically black, making the Anglo relation to an African identity more important than the religious one. The Spanish empire was represented as racially tainted by Moors as well as morally blackened. And later, the Moor is perceived by many in the West as romantically associated with a nostalgic view of the Oriental East, exotic and linked to the past. The Moor becomes a figure in the European global imaginary that can be constructed in relation to a number of identity categories depending on the time and place from which it is viewed.[37]

The strength of this model is that can take into account that which the traditional metaphor of the two-dimensional map cannot. On a traditional map, the home space, the perspective through which the map is constructed, is clearly indicated and the spaces abroad are demarcated through boundary lines, whether nationally or regionally constructed. What GPS makes plain is that one can only determine one's position by calculating the relation to a number of categories at once and this is done while these reference points are moving. In addition, as one travels in space, one must recalculate the distance from the various satellites anew. This reflects the multiplicity and intersectionality of identity described in postmodern thought. Through GPS, we can see the fluid nature of several different dynamics operating simultaneously. This can be wildly disorienting, yet it also creates possibilities, possibilities of shaping identities in ways that focus on the very relations we wish to cultivate and to disrupt.

Given this, when one subject encounters another, as we see in the case of the Moor, we find ourselves at the nexus of a complicated system of identifications. When this is taken into account, any conversation between two involves a complex web of relations.

An Uncanny Look at Home: Spain as a Cautionary Tale

Like the other writers considered here, Richard Wright figures the Other as central to the mapping of Spain in his travelogue. Yet even as he describes the grounds of Spanish difference, he reveals a double reality: Spain is simultaneously at the very heart of the West. Commenting on a part of his translation of the Francoist *Formacion Politica* regarding Spain's place in the world and its destiny, Wright exclaims, "I was staring at the mouth, at the veritable fount of Western history."[38] Wright's double reading evokes the notion of the uncanny that critics such as Julia Kristeva borrow from Freud. For Kristeva, the recognition of the foreigner within the state (or the parallel recognition of the difference of the Other) exposes the fiction of the homogeneity of the group (or the unity of the self).[39] The stranger outside ultimately mirrors the stranger within.

In the end, therefore, *Pagan Spain* is a cautionary tale for the West. The accusations of irrationality often launched at the non-Western world really hide the Western world's own irrational behavior. Wright implies as much in mapping Spain as part of a network of totalitarianism—likening Franco's government to the racist regime in Mississippi, Perón's police state in Buenos Aires, and the U.S. Communist Party. In addition, at the end of *The Color Curtain* (1956), Wright warns that prevailing Western cold war modes of relating to the Third World are destructive. The West, he argues, takes a great risk by not honestly and ethically engaging with the nations at the Bandung Conference.[40] In both this work and *Pagan Spain*, he compares the way Spanish conquerors approached Native Americans and the way the West now approaches the Third World, making this three-world construction of the globe an updated colonial map. If the West insists on its own way, insists that it possesses the Truth rather than entering into conversation with others, it will be fighting, as the Spaniards did, against a group that will unify on common ground and that would rather die than be defeated.[41] In the final words of the book, Wright pictures the Spaniard stuck in an imperialistic mindset: "Convinced beyond all counter persuasion that he possesses a metaphysical mandate to chastise all of those whom he considers the 'morally moribund,' the 'spiritually inept,' the 'biologically botched,' the Spaniard would scorn the rich infinities of possibility looming before the eyes of men, he would stifle the hearts responding to the call of a high courage, and he would thwart the will's desire for a new wisdom."[42] This could describe the attitude historically promoted in any of the European colonial powers, but more significantly, it is not far from attitudes toward those in the burgeoning movements in Africa and Asia found in the United States in Wright's time and in our own.

If we take seriously the GPS model of identity, one that reflects post-modern provisionality of identity, the most stable part of the model is the set of calculations used to measure distances, the method of determining relations. This suggests that while one might need to constantly recalculate one's relation to various ideas, what remains stable is the method of relating to others. Identity, then, is a matter of *how* one relates to others. This concept of identity has the possibility of reinvigorating an identity politics.[43] As Wright suggests, this would call for an ethical approach to intercultural communication that works by understanding others' views and differences with a critical eye on the self, a relation of equality, in which each side engages in the dialogue, translation, and evaluation of ideas. Each must express its own positions but also listen to the other's translation of what it hears and sees. Such a form of communication is required if we wish engagement with others to be educational and certainly if we wish to employ these interactions in a political understanding of the world. Yet it can also help to build the potential of identity politics of which Wright was so skeptical. It can help us move beyond the identity categories—without denying the lived experience of them—to the kind of inventive alliances that Wright envisions.

Notes

1. Richard Wright, *Pagan Spain* (Jackson: University Press of Mississippi, 2002), 228.
2. Ibid.
3. The idea of Spanish exceptionalism can be traced back several centuries, while twentieth-century work of political scientists such as Howard J. Wiarda popularized within academia the theory that Spain and Portugal have developed differently from the rest of Western Europe. The Iberian difference is attributed to a number of factors: the geographic separation from the rest of Europe by the Pyrenees, a lack of Enlightenment and industrialization, the embrace of Catholicism and, later, fascism, and influence of the Muslim rule of al-Andalus from the eighth to the fifteenth centuries. See Howard J. Wiarda, "Spain 2000: A Normal Country?" *Mediterranean Quarterly* 11, no. 3 (2000): 30–61. So pervasive has the idea of Spain's difference been that in 1964 the Minister of Information and Tourism under General Francisco Franco used the slogan "Spain is Different" in its campaign materials to promote Spain as a tourist destination. See Eugenia Afinoguénova and Jaume Martí-Olivella, "A Nation under Tourists' Eyes: Tourism and Identity Discourses in Spain," in *Spain Is (Still) Different: Tourism and Discourse in Spanish Identity*, ed. Eugenia Afinoguénova and Jaume Martí-Olivella (Lanham, MD: Lexington Books, 2008), xi.
4. Maria DeGuzmán, *Spain's Long Shadow: The Black Legend, Off-Whiteness, and Anglo-American Empire* (Minneapolis: University of Minnesota Press, 2005).

5. For more on the history of early modern cartography and representational strategies of maps, see J. B. Harley and David Woodward, eds., *History of Cartography*, vols. 1 and 3 (Chicago: University of Chicago Press, 1987, 2007); Denis Wood and John Fels, *The Power of Maps* (New York: Guilford Press, 1992); Christian Jacob, *The Sovereign Map: Theoretical Approaches in Cartography throughout History*, trans. Tom Conley (Chicago: University of Chicago Press, 2006).

6. Enrique Dussel argues that the end of Islamic rule in Western Europe and the reorientation of its sights in exploration of the Americas shift the European conception of itself from being surrounded by the Islamic world to being the center of a world moving westward. The "West" develops as it transforms "other subjects and peoples into its objects and instruments for its own Europeanizing, civilizing, and modernizing purposes." Enrique Dussel, *The Invention of the Americas: Eclipse of "the Other" and the Myth of Modernity*, trans. Michael D. Barber (New York: Continuum, 1995), 90.

7. Nella Larsen, Arthur Schomburg, Chester Himes, and Dorothy Peterson also left documents of their travel to Spain. Himes, Peterson, and Frank Yerby all chose to settle there permanently. In addition, Spain served as inspiration to midcentury jazz such as Miles Davis's 1960 album *Sketches of Spain*.

8. See, for example, Edward W. Soja, *Postmodern Geographies: The Reassertion of Space in Critical Social Theory* (London: Verso, 1989); Walter Mignolo, *The Darker Side of the Renaissance: Literacy, Territoriality, Colonization* (Ann Arbor: University of Michigan Press, 1995); Laura Doyle and Laura A. Winkiel, eds., *Geomodernisms: Race, Modernism, Modernity* (Bloomington: Indiana University Press, 2005).

9. A notable example is Paul Gilroy's *The Black Atlantic: Modernity and Double Consciousness* (Cambridge, MA: Harvard University Press, 1993).

10. Frank Yerby, *An Odor of Sanctity: A Novel of Moorish Spain* (New York: Dial Press, 1965).

11. Ibid., 51.

12. Ibid., 55.

13. Yerby emphasizes the diversity within the Arab-Berber empire, explaining in the prologue that the term "Moor" is nearly meaningless because of the range of cultures to which it refers. Ibid., vi.

14. This anticipates James Clifford's concept of "traveling cultures." See James Clifford, *Routes: Travel and Translation in the Late Twentieth Century* (Cambridge, MA: Harvard University Press, 1997).

15. Claude McKay, *A Long Way from Home*, ed. Gene Andrew Jarrett (New Brunswick, NJ: Rutgers University Press, 2007; orig. 1937), 228.

16. Claude McKay, "Tetuán," lines 1–4, in *A Long Way from Home*, 236.

17. Ibid., lines 10–11.

18. Ibid., lines 9, 12, 14.

19. Claude McKay, "Fez," lines 1–2, in *Complete Poems: Claude McKay*, ed. William J. Maxwell (Urbana: University of Illinois, 2004), 226.

20. Ibid., lines 13–14.

21. McKay, *A Long Way from Home*, 229–230.
22. McKay's work has much in common with contemporary world-systems theo-rists who take a long view of the interactions between varying parts of the globe. These theorists doubt any belief in essentially "different" civilizations whose fates are determined independently. In particular, it is reminiscent of Frank's *ReORIENT*, which views the rise of "the West" as merely one economic blip within an essentially Eastern-oriented world market. See Andre Gunder Frank, *ReORIENT: Global Economy in the Asian Age* (Berkeley: University of California Press, 1998).
23. Hughes later used the series of essays and poems published for the papers as the basis of the section on Spain in his autobiography *I Wonder as I Wander: An Autobiographical Journey* [1956], ed. Arnold Rampersad (New York: Hill and Wang, 1993).
24. Ania Loomba, *Shakespeare, Race, and Colonialism* (New York: Oxford University Press, 2002), 25.
25. Ibid., 93.
26. Hughes, *I Wonder as I Wander*, 243.
27. Ibid., 368. Michael Thurston places Hughes's work in the larger context of the political and aesthetic factions of Harlem, explaining Hughes's own effort to develop a racial and class revolutionary politics that would tran-scend these local squabbles. See Michael Thurston, "All Together Black and White: Langston Hughes," *Making Something Happen: American Political Poetry between the World Wars* (Chapel Hill: University of North Carolina, 2001), 86–134.
28. Hughes, *I Wonder as I Wander*, 351.
29. Ibid.
30. Social worker Thyra Edwards and Edward Strong both published articles expressing similar concerns: Thyra Edwards, "Moors in the Spanish War," *Opportunity* 16 (1938): 84–85; Edward Strong, "I Visited Spain," *The Crisis* (December 1936), 358–59.
31. This poem was first published in the *Volunteer for Liberty* in 1937 and subse-quently republished in *The Daily Worker* in 1938.
32. Thurston views Hughes's work on Spain as typical of black press coverage of Spain as influenced by leftist politics. See Michael Thurston, "'Bombed in Spain': Langston Hughes, the Black Press, and the Spanish Civil War," in *The Black Press: New Literary and Historical Essays*, ed. Todd Vogel (New Bruns-wick. NJ: Rutgers University Press, 2001), 140–41.
33. Hughes, "Letter from Spain: Addressed to Alabama," lines 2, 24, in *I Wonder as I Wander*, 353.
34. Johnny can understand what the wounded Moor says only through a transla-tor, and his moment of diasporic recognition is undermined by the death of the soldier at the end of the poem and Johnny's inability to convey his revo-lutionary politics to his new compatriot before that death. See Brent Hayes Edwards, "Langston Hughes and the Futures of Diaspora," *American Literary History* 19, no. 3 (2007): 689–711.

35. A useful explanation of how GPS works can be found at "GPS Tutorial," Trimble Worldwide, http://www.trimble.com/gps.

36. Shu-Mei Shih discusses racial triangulation in her discussion of racialization as a series of comparative relations. See Shu-Mei Shih, "Comparative Racialization: An Introduction," *PMLA* 123, no. 5 (October 2008): 1350.

37. Timothy Marr argues that the combination of Islam and Africa in the figure of the Moor provided a unique transnational identity available for performance by mid-twentieth-century African Americans "because its heterogeneity confounds the continental categories of race and religion that have constituted hegemonic definitions of nation and hemisphere" ("'Out of This World': Islamic Irruptions in the Literary Americas," *American Literary History* 18, no. 3 [2006]: 524). He traces the performance of a cosmopolitan Moorish or "Moroccan" identity from the early twentieth-century promotion of the Moorish Science Temple among African Americans to the "transnational empowerment that reversion to Islam provided to jazz musicians and members of the Nation of Islam" (523), quoting Dizzy Gillespie's account of a jazz musician saying "Man, if you join the Muslim faith, you ain't colored no more" (543).

38. Wright, *Pagan Spain*, 29.

39. Julia Kristeva, *Strangers to Ourselves*, trans. Leon S. Roudiez (New York: Columbia University Press, 1991), 17–20, 103.

40. The Bandung Conference, in April 1955, was a gathering of representatives of Asian and African states, most of which were newly independent, to discuss the future of the decolonizing world. Wright wrote *The Color Curtain* (1956) about the conference after his trips to Spain but before finishing the manuscript *of Pagan Spain* (1957).

41. Wright, *Pagan Spain*, 217–18.

42. Ibid., 288.

43. Wright experiments with such alliances when he links the oppressed within Spain, to, whether they are women, Protestants, Gypsies, Catalan nationalists, and so on, to blacks in the United States by referring to them "white negroes." See M. Lynn Weiss, *Gertrude Stein and Richard Wright: The Poetics and Politics of Modernism* (Jackson: University Press of Mississippi, 1998), 34.

12

The Space of Transgression

A Geocritical Study of Albert Camus's "The Adulterous Wife"

Brigitte Le Juez

The title of Albert Camus's 1957 collection of short stories to which "The Adulterous Wife" belongs, *Exile and the Kingdom*,[1] indicates that the characters of the six texts that form the volume are all defined by their relationship with the space in which they evolve. The terms exile and kingdom designate experiences both physical and spiritual (which can also be interpreted as both horizontal and vertical). This thematic link between the stories constitutes in itself the spatial unity of the book. Isabelle Daunais contends that, in Camus's work, exile places the observing protagonists outside the place they occupy in reality, and that the kingdom is that rare moment when the space they desire to occupy and the space they actually occupy are one and the same.[2] However, one further dimension needs to be taken into account: the passage from one to the other. Through an analysis of "The Adulterous Wife," I would like to argue that the movement from one to the other is in fact a transgressive one and that it is therefore attached to different kinds of moral considerations.

The reference to adultery in the title of the story immediately brings the idea of moral transgression to mind. Yet transgression (etymologically "stepping beyond or across") is first and foremost a spatial concept. It can refer to the violation of a command or law (if a divine law, it is synonymous with sin), to the infringement of a duty (e.g., the nonfulfillment of an obligation), or to the exceeding of due boundaries or limits, such as a misbehavior. These denotations, which are all evoked in some way in "The

Adulterous Wife," refer to the encroachment of well-defined bounds and imply a possible moral judgment.[3] In this story, the transgression, likened to adultery, is only mentioned in the title, and, remarkably, it is not the kind of transgression that would normally be associated with infidelity, as it is neither presented as a misdemeanor nor committed with another person. The climactic moment is experienced with the desert instead. Space being at the heart of this foretold contravention, I propose to analyze Camus's text geocritically.

"The Adulterous Wife," which opens *Exile and the Kingdom*, takes place in Algeria in the fifties. It describes the journey undertaken by a *pied-noir*[4] couple, Marcel and Janine, both middle aged, from their coastal city to the interior of the country—that is, southward from the north of the country to the edge of the Sahara. This journey, which Janine has never undertaken before, takes them quite far away from their comfortable French-style existence and into a world inhabited by Arabs—a space seemingly silent, empty, and hostile.

At the beginning of the story, observed from the bus in which Marcel and Janine are travelling, the landscape seems blurred by a sand-carrying wind, and Janine has an overall impression of her surroundings as made purely of stone. As she cannot identify with anything she sees, her thoughts begin to wander, and considerations about her youth and the choices she made, which explain where she is now, come to light. Thus the forward, spatial movement of the bus is in opposition to the backward, temporal direction of Janine's thoughts. Nevertheless, both have in common a difficulty in advancing smoothly and often stumble over unexpected obstacles: lack of visibility and sand for the bus, and Marcel's frequently negative interjections for Janine. The relationship between the topographical and the personal is therefore established from the outset.

Janine is profoundly disturbed by this displacement from her familiar shelter. The homeboundness she deplores about her life, but that she accepts passively, has made her shy of any type of adventure, and clearly neither she nor Marcel (who thinks poorly of the Arabs) have made any effort to learn about the native Arabic or Berber cultures (a distinction they don't even make). As John Cruickshank underlines, Camus had already observed in *L'Envers et l'endroit* (*Betwixt and Between*, also translated as *The Wrong Side and the Right Side*, 1937) that travel temporarily takes away the masks behind which we normally hide, and it can provide us, in certain circumstances, with a staggering revelation of our fundamental loneliness: "One is confronted with an unfamiliar self through contact with an unfamiliar outside world."[5] Janine wishes Marcel had not insisted on taking her with him, yet this trip through unknown territory is about to crucially reveal her profound lack of contentment with her life.

As soon as the journey begins, she experiences her dislocation in physical terms: she feels frozen, heavy, and cramped, and her senses are attacked by elements new to her, making her feel generally insecure and uncomfortable. "A fly circled feebly for a moment toward the raised windows of the bus. Oddly, it came and went in silence, in exhausted flight. Janine lost sight of it, then saw it land on her husband's motionless hand. It was cold. The fly trembled at every gust of sandy wind that scratched against the windows" (1). This sense of confinement engenders thoughts of her own captive circumstances, of her life with Marcel: "They lived above the boutique in three rooms decorated with Arab hangings and middle-class furniture. They had not had children. The years had passed in the shadows they had maintained behind the half-closed shutters. Summer, the beaches, the drives, even the sky were long ago" (3). An absence of light, warmth, and horizon dominate Janine's conventional, bourgeois, urban setting. By contrast, the increasing emptiness and brightness that surround the bus trigger her long-delayed introspection. Janine progressively comes to the conclusion that she has given up her life for a false sense of security to protect herself from loneliness, but that marriage, which she believed would provide against it, has in fact had the opposite effect.

Janine never before questioned her Western values regarding the relationship between men and women, and she has felt the need to be attractive and to be looked after. But now she realizes that this need is only a fallacy and the root of the very dependency that has smothered her life. Her ordinary world is precisely the space where she cannot belong, where she has no clear identity, where she is invisible—"in the shade of the arcades of this half-native, half-European quarter" (3). Little by little Janine comes to compare the situation she did not choose wisely with what she truly yearns for: "Twenty-five years were nothing, it seemed to her only yesterday that she was hesitating between a free life and marriage, only yesterday that she had felt such anguish at the thought that perhaps one day she would grow old alone" (2). "Free life," the only alternative for her to marriage, is what she has not allowed herself to reconsider, a mistake that has kept her in "exile." It therefore becomes synonymous with "the kingdom," as she eventually comes to realize when faced with the desert.

In *A Thousand Plateaus*, Gilles Deleuze and Félix Guattari have contrasted city living, *hadara*, and nomadic living, *badiya*, according to Ibn Khaldūn's fourteenth-century work. The former is "striated" or gridded, with all kinds of lines and barriers, whereas the latter is "smooth" or open ended, and further smoothened by mobility. *Hadara* is the space "allocated," "according to determinate intervals, assigned breaks" (walls, enclosures, etc.), whereas for the *badiya* "one 'distributes' oneself in an open space, according to frequencies and in the course of one's crossings."[6]

Bertrand Westphal adds that the "smooth space" rouses an essential yearning, which may be considered nostalgic or incantatory, away from the "striated," which is everywhere.[7]

Janine's original resistance to movement (and to breaking the barriers
in her life) is followed, as she reaches her destination, by her embracing the
vast expanse of the "smooth space" that the desert represents. On her first
night in the oasis, a strong sense of anguish overwhelms her and wakes her
in her sleep: "She was not happy, she was going to die, in fact, without being
delivered. Her heart was in pain, she was suffocating under an immense
weight, which she suddenly discovered she had been dragging around for
twenty years. Now she was struggling under it with all her might" (14).
That same night Janine leaves her husband asleep in their hotel room, runs
to the rooftop of a fort from which they discovered a view of the desert
earlier, and there she experiences the liberation she has been craving: "She
was breathing deeply, she forgot the cold, the weight of beings, the insane
or static life, the long anguish of living and dying. [. . .] She seemed to
be recovering her roots, and the sap rose anew in her body, which was no
longer trembling" (15).

This stepping out of a striated space into an open, smooth one is Janine's
transgression, and it is described as an orgasmic experience: "Then, with an
unbearable sweetness, the waters of the night began to fill Janine, submerg-
ing the cold, rising gradually to the dark centre of her being, and overflow-
ing wave upon wave to her moaning mouth. A moment later, the whole
sky stretched out above her as she lay with her back against the cold earth"
(16). Although she tries to return to the hotel room as stealthily as she had
slipped out, she finds herself "weeping uncontrollably," to the bewilder-
ment of her husband suddenly awake, and the light he turns on slaps her
"full in the face" (16)—the only hint to a possible form of judgment coming either from him or from her. Indeed, the "smooth space" has enabled
Janine to answer one her own questions regarding "love": "The only joy
[Marcel] gave her was the knowledge that she was needed. He probably
did not love her. Love, even hatred, does not have this closed face. But what
was its face? They made love at night, without seeing each other, groping
in the dark. Was there a love other than one in darkness, a love that would
cry out in broad daylight?" (13). Her conservative approach to life has pre-
vented her from fulfilling the essential core of her personality—that of a
sensual woman, who needs genuine affection more than material security.
The movement from city space to open space had brought a shift of perspective in Janine's outlook, allowing her to finally question the meaning
of her existence and identify her true desires, which, she finds out, can
only be realized on a terrain where her husband does not belong—hence
her "adultery."[8]

Westphal's methodology for examining interactions between human and literary spaces, promotes the inclusion of different yet complementary perspectives, namely multifocalization, polysensoriality, stratigraphy, and intertextuality, which taken together allow diverse points of view to be gathered in order to establish the literary space: "The premise of geocritical analysis resides in the comparison of several perspectives which refine, feed of and enrich each other."[9] This involves the perspectives found not only in the text but also around it, whether preceding it or following it. Adopting this approach allows us to investigate other aspects of "The Adulterous Wife."

As a short story, Camus's text does not provide a range of narrative points of view. The omniscient narrator, who offers the protagonist's perspective in a third-person narrative, although he remains anonymous, is most probably the author himself. Indeed, in the preface for the first edition of the story (1954) Camus wrote, "In Laghouat I met the characters of this story. I am not certain, of course, that their day ended as I have told it. Doubtless they did not go forth to the desert. But *I* went, some hours after that, and during all that time their image pursued me and challenged what I saw."[10] This is an interesting posture for Camus: not only does he create a work of fiction out of a personal experience, but the work of fiction in the making influences his own perception of a real space at the time he experiences it. Amazingly, this also brings him to opt for a feminine perspective. As Brian T. Fitch has highlighted before, Janine is the only female protagonist in all of Camus's fiction to be not only central but also the character "whose inner experience—her thoughts and emotions—are shared directly by the reader."[11] This apparent departure of Camus from his own frames of reference not only suits our transgression theme, but it also introduces the idea that Janine is a peripheral figure in Camus's fiction.

From the very start of the story, she is portrayed in a marginal position. As a woman in a male-dominated place (the space of the town, and that of the bus, are masculine, and she feels physically out of place in both), as a French presence in Arabic surroundings (and in troubled times between the two communities), she represents an odd female presence in between patriarchal societies. The desert that fascinates her to the point of epiphany, on the other hand, is inhabited by Tuaregs, pastoralist nomads who live according to a matrilineal (and, as found with some groups, matriarchal) system. Although unaware of this, Janine strongly wishes to belong to that land where women hold a clearly defined and important role within their community. Her body responds harmoniously to their space, in contrast to her awkwardness on the bus and in the town. But to access this kingdom, Janine must step beyond the patriarchal, striated space—and turn her back on her husband's world.

Janine shares a common trait with the natives: silence. Her perspective, as mentioned before, is not offered to us in direct speech. She says very little throughout the journey, like the Arabs and the Berbers she encounters. After she has seen the desert for the first time, she hears its "mute call" in the night (14), to which she responds by going to the fort, silently and alone. Her quietness is the result of years of submission to the patriarchal order. Equally, the natives have had to submit to the French order. However, they carry their muteness with a kind of pride and sometimes defiance. Interestingly, these voiceless figures will transgress the French male-dominated world at some point and in their own way; Janine does so by experiencing an intense communion with the cosmos, the natives, by reclaiming their land later—a point to which I will return.

Janine has progressively opened her eyes on new ways of being. She now envisages new points of view and no longer just her predicament. Above all, what she discovered during her journey, in increasingly desert surroundings, are attitudes and lifestyles unknown to city dwellers:

> Suddenly, she started. On the embankment, just next to the bus, stood motionless covered shapes. Beneath the hoods of the burnooses, and behind a rampart of veils, only their eyes could be seen. Mute, appearing out of nowhere, they gazed at the travellers. "Shepherds," Marcel said. (5) [...]

> In the heart of a woman brought here by chance alone, a knot tightened by years, habit and boredom was slowly loosening. She looked at the nomad encampment. [...] [N]othing was moving among the black tents, and yet she could think only of them, of their existence, which she had hardly known until today. Homeless, remote from the world, they were a handful of men wandering through the vast territory her gaze had discovered [...]. Since the beginning, on the dry earth of this measureless land scraped to the bone, a few men ceaselessly made their way, possessing nothing but serving no one, the destitute and free lords of a strange kingdom. (11)

These reflections show that Janine is effectively removing all the layers of conventions and prejudices, accumulated over the years, and that have blinded her for so long. At that moment, she only knows "that this kingdom had been promised to her from time immemorial, and that it would never be hers, never again. . . . What would she do from now on but drag herself into sleep, into death?" (11–12). Hope is therefore removed as soon as its presence has been felt. The smooth, open-ended, nomad space is not for the likes of Janine, who belongs to city living. According to Deleuze and Guattari, "Movement in [the striated space] is confined as by gravity to a horizontal plane, and limited by the order of that plane to preset paths between fixed and identifiable points."[12] Janine will not go further than the fort.

Camus maps Janine's world by combining representations of places: on one hand, the nonidentified coastal town where she normally lives (possibly Algiers as it is north in almost a direct line to where the couple ends up) and, on the other, the clearly identified town and oasis of Laghouat and its surroundings (where she has never been before).

When looking at a map of Laghouat as it was when Camus visited in the 1950s, we may imagine that Janine and Marcel's hotel is the Hôtel Transatlantique, as it is situated in the oasis and it faces Fort Morand, from which Janine possibly discovers the desert (neither place is precisely named in the story). Moreover, this hotel is on the northwest side of the town, which was the European quarter (the hotel's owner is French in the story), where streets with arcades could be found, harboring shops, the kind in which Marcel finds business to conduct—"the bus stopped in front of the adobe arcades of a hotel with dirt-streaked windows" (6). It is worth noting that the European houses in this area replaced native dwellings, hence also, partly, the disdain of some of the inhabitants. The central street, named Avenue Cassaigne, previously known as "route d'Alger," must be the "long street flanked by low houses" (5), through which the bus arrives. Janine can see "a graceful yellow minaret above the houses. To her left, the first palm trees of the oasis stood out" (6), and indeed the map indicates a couple of mosques in the vicinity and the oasis spread on both sides of the street.[13] Local places of state interest have been given French names, which the map delineates precisely, but the oasis and the desert that lie further are unmeasured and unnamed, with little circles indicating palm tree tops and sand—a good illustration of the difference between striated and smooth spaces. These cartographic details bring together diverse elements, which allow for a new approach of the literary space in "The Adulterous Wife."

Indeed, this lack of geographical precision is significant of the protagonist's state of mind. Janine's familiar space is imprecise because *she* is indifferent to the place where she lives. The journey southward (possibly following the Trans-Sahara Highway but also remaining unnamed) is an in-between space, which for Janine remains nondescript. But details of Laghouat, a town not only new but fascinating to her, are given more clearly. This is further confirmation of her past unhappiness, and it also indicates that, as a result, she has constantly projected herself into the future. About her life with Marcel, "No, nothing was the way she had imagined" (3). Similarly, during the trip, she declares, "Here they were now, and really, nothing was the way she had imagined" (4). Both instances translate disappointments. Finally, when they arrive in Laghouat, she reiterates this feeling:[14] "Nothing was the way she had imagined" (6), but this time, she is more happily surprised as the musical sounds coming from the oasis have already begun to appease her. However, at that point, she is still at an intermediary stage, where she must give up all her preconceived ideas, and, in the process, betray the life that her husband, possibly with good intentions, has built for her.

What Camus creates with his story is a dual space made of both an imprecise, partial rendering of a place synonymous with gloom, but one the reader can realistically imagine, and a cartographically exact description of a real space, which is in fact associated with a vision. Camus thus reverses the expected order of visibility: the striated space, though in principle well documented, is vague, and the smooth space, left open, is clear—although one could also argue that Laghouat is both and that Camus sees in a striated space the possibility of creating a smooth one (a notion with which Deleuze and Guattari would agree). Nevertheless, the sum of both represents the parameters of Camus's own literary space, where his character will be transformed: a space both historical (it carries its own political and architectural connotations) and timeless (it stirs the imagination of the protagonist in a way that erases her ordinary reality). It corresponds to what Westphal identifies as an interface: a line that enables the real and the fictional to communicate.

The various references to Janine's senses belong to this interface. At the outset, the narrator denies her sight: there is a sand storm, and fog is also mentioned. Janine's visual perception of her new surroundings is therefore hindered. Hearing, however, is most acute. She is highly aware of the screeching of the wind, of the rain of sand on the windows, and upon their arrival in Laghouat, of the guttural cries around her: all harsh sounds that add to her extreme malaise. But soon she becomes aware of the "murmur of a river [. . .] raised by the wind in the palm trees [. . .] the gentle voice of the waters becoming the whistling of waves" (6). This is the first sign of well being, identifying a change of mood.

Moreover, physical sensations are constant in the text. I have already mentioned her discomfort during the journey, but her uneasiness continues after she has arrived. In the hotel room she wonders "where to put her bag or herself," and later in the dining room she remarks that "she would have liked to take up less space" (7). This reminds us of her iterative observation of the thinness of the natives earlier. Janine, who had so far taken pride in her "tall, full, fleshy and still desirable" (3) body, now seems to wish to be less conspicuous. "Now she felt too tall, too heavy, and too white for this world she had just entered" (12). In the first shop they visit, she moves "aside so as not to block the light" (8). Yet the people around her in Laghouat are all men and none of them seems to notice her: "They turned that [tan, thin] face toward the foreign woman, they did not see her, and then, lightly and silently, they passed around her as her ankles swelled" (10). Janine's relationship with both the land and its inhabitants is therefore captured through her physical response to them, and her bodily sensations tell her she does not fit in.

What Janine does not quite understand, though, is that the men's attitude may have nothing to do with the fact that she is a woman. In reality, they ignore her husband in the same way. Here, in the heart of the country, perceptions of the French are more likely to be influenced by politics. This brings us to the wider context of the story and to an essential element of geocritical analysis—that is, to considerations emphasizing the "observed space."[15]

Laghouat is an important town in Algeria, and as mentioned before it is situated at the edge of the Sahara desert. Its name means "house surrounded with gardens," which is in itself a spatial description. Laghouat under French rule proved to be one of the hot spots of Algerian nationalism. This is hinted at by Camus in the passage where an Arab treats Marcel and Janine as if they were invisible, forcing them to move themselves and their trunk out of his way: "Although they were surrounded by the empty space of the square, he walked directly toward the trunk, without seeing it, without seeing them [. . .]. 'They think they can get away with anything now,' [Marcel] said" (9). As Mary L. Pratt reminds us, the stories of *Exile and the Kingdom* were written "between 1952–54, the tense and violent years preceding the outbreak of the French-Algerian war, [and] appeared in collection in 1957, at the height of the conflict."[16] In Laghouat the French are not treated with special favors, not even as travelers, and especially not those who, like Marcel, hope to engage in commercial activities. The demand for buyers puts salesmen in a position of economic need, and the Algerians make sure there is no ambiguity as to who has the upper hand in such matters. As Marcel and Janine visit the first shop on their arrival in Laghouat, Marcel becomes irritated by what he perceives as the Arabs' disrespect:

> The odour of wool and spices floating through the room emerged behind the scent of tea when the old merchant placed the teapot on the counter and greeted them.
>
> Marcel spoke rapidly in that low voice he used when talking business. Then he opened his trunk, displayed cloth and silks [. . .]. He got excited, raised his voice, laughed inanely, like a woman who wants to please and doubts herself. [. . .] The old man shook his head, passed the tea platter to the two Arabs behind him, and said only a few words that seem to discourage Marcel. [. . .] "They think they're God himself," Marcel said, "but they do business too! Life is hard for everyone." (8)

Clearly, by refusing to acknowledge the difference between his means and theirs, Marcel confirms his lack of understanding, or interest, certainly of respect, for the natives whose language he has never bothered to learn—which reduces him to gestures during his negotiation attempts with the Algerian traders.

The fort that dominates Laghouat is itself a constant reminder of French power, and it is clear, as Pratt points out, that "Janine's personal crisis is invoked by the social situation as much as by nature."[17] The social comfort that represented for Janine a form of security began to disappear as soon as she found herself on the bus amid native passengers—that is, on an equal par, a position she did not relish: "The bus was full of Arabs who *seemed* to be asleep, buried in their burnooses. [. . .] Their silence, their impassiveness, weighed on Janine" (1–2, my emphasis). Janine is vaguely aware of a potential danger, a feeling justified, even for a *pied-noir* who does not follow political issues, such as herself, by a sense that things might be about to change. That this should be so is implicitly indicated in the natural, yet seemingly hostile, elements as described in "The Adulterous Wife." Furthermore, as mentioned earlier, Camus himself was acutely sensitive to the town of Laghouat and its surroundings, and some of his descriptions remind us of details found in Orientalist art: "the *blue* and *white* roofs of the Arab village overlapped, stained by the blood-*red* spots of peppers drying in the sun" (10, my emphasis). Laghouat is thus seen as having bled under French fire.

Possibly relevant details pertaining to Camus's perception of Laghouat should be brought in at this point. After Algeria was conquered, it quickly became a subject of fascination for French Orientalist artists. Eugène Fromentin, one of the best known among them on the subject of Algeria, created an ideal picture of Laghouat in his book *Un été dans le Sahara* (*A Summer in the Sahara*, 1857). During his visit, Fromentin went to the top of its fort, and his impressions were as full of admiration for the landscape as Janine's: "I pass my best hours, those that one day I will miss the most, on the heights [. . .], facing that enormous horizon free in all directions, a horizon without obstacles to block one's view, rising above everything, from east to west, from south to north, mountains, town, oasis and desert."[18] Fromentin's experience inspired him to compose one of his most famous paintings, *Une rue à El-Laghouat* (*A Street in El-Laghouat*, Douai, Musée de la Chartreuse, 1859).[19] Charles Baudelaire, Théophile Gautier, and Maxime Du Camp, among others, praised it very highly in its day, and other Orientalists after Fromentin visited and painted Laghouat; for example, Gustave Guillaumet (*Laghouat, Sahara algérien*, Paris: Musée d'Orsay, 1879) and Etienne Dinet (*Une rue à Laghouat*, Paris: Musée d'Orsay, 1887).[20]

Camus, who was knowledgeable about and appreciative of the arts, had to be familiar with those representations before he headed for Laghouat. And what he could not ignore was the fact that a century before he visited the town, and not long before Fromentin headed there (in fact it was the main reason for Fromentin's journey), Laghouat had fallen victim to a terrible and bloody battle that had killed many civilians. When Fromentin arrived there were still corpses lying around. Camus's own visit was delayed by trouble that had started around the centenary celebrations of the siege.[21] Camus's experience of this trip, as noted before, influenced his writing of at least a first outline of "The Adulterous Wife." He had arrived on December 14, it was as cold and windy as described in the story, and he was fascinated by the desert light and the black tents of the nomads. He spent the next day wandering through the oasis alone, which may have given him the opportunity to immerse himself in its history.[22]

The subject of war brings us back to the Tuaregs. It is important to note that, in the late nineteenth century, they resisted the French colonial invasion of their Saharan homelands, and that, among the different names they still use for themselves, one finds "Imashaghen," which means "the Free People"—reminiscent of Janine's description of them. Their presence in the text can be seen, therefore, as another implicit mention of the political dimension of the story, referring to the first signs of an imminent war of independence, a war aimed at regaining one's land; a war, and Camus might have sensed it since he refused Janine access to that ideal land, that the Algerians would win.

In "The Adulterous Wife," Janine is portrayed as a transgressor all along—transgressor of the social order, of the patriarchal order, and, as the title signifies, of a divine law. By choosing a title with biblical connotations, Camus gave his protagonist what was then perceived as a reprehensible posture for a woman, not only because of its sexual implications, but also because it described a woman capable of thinking and feeling beyond her husband. Janine discovers she is bereft of land, of freedom, of love, and of identity—which prevents her from belonging to the kingdom. As a representative of the settlers' community, Janine's failure is indicative of the fact that the colonizers were in exile, away from their original land, which they could not recreate, and never fully accepted in the one they occupied. As history has confirmed, the *pieds-noirs* would indeed have to leave Algeria at the end of the War of Independence in 1962, including those who had lived in Algeria for several generations and who found themselves in a kind of limbo, that same indeterminate position Janine inhabits at the end of the story. Hence her tears and her cryptic last words to Marcel: "'It's nothing, darling,' she said, 'it's nothing'" (16).[23]

Notes

1. Albert Camus, *Exile and the Kingdom*, trans. by Carol Cosman (London: Penguin, 2006); page numbers given in parentheses hereafter. The original French text is *L'Exil et le royaume* (Paris: Gallimard, 1957). It may be worth noting that an earlier, and much quoted, translation by Justin O'Brien translated the title of the story "La Femme adultère" as "The Adulterous Woman" (*Exile and the Kingdom*, New York: Knopf, 1958).
2. Isabelle Daunais, "L'Expérience de l'espace dans les nouvelles de Camus," *The French Review* 67, no. 1 (October 1993): 47.
3. Moreover, as Bertrand Westphal observes, space can be considered transgressive in itself because it is never fixed. It fluctuates, seized by forces provoking a constant oscillation. See Bertrand Westphal, "Approches méthodologiques de la transgression spatiale," in *Primerjalna književnost*; Special issue in English: "Literature and Space. Spaces of Transgressiveness," edited by Jola Škulj and Darja Pavlič, http://www.zrc-sazu.si/sdpk/PKrevija/2004-Literature&Space.htm#Bertrand%20Westphal (accessed July 7, 2010).
4. The term *pieds-noirs* refers to French nationals living in Algeria.
5. John Cruickshank, *Albert Camus and the Literature of Revolt* (Westport, CT: Greenwood Press, 1959), 28.
6. Gilles Deleuze and Félix Guattari, *A Thousand Plateaus*, trans. Brian Massumi (Minneapolis: University of Minnesota Press, 2005), 481.
7. Bertrand Westphal, *La Géocritique. Réel, fiction, espace* (Paris: Minuit, 2007), 263.
8. Elizabeth Appleby has a different take on the idea of Janine's so-called adultery here and suggests that "in marrying Marcel, she was unfaithful to herself": http://crisolenguas.uprrp.edu/Articles/ElizabethAppleby.pdf (accessed August, 29, 2010), 6.
9. Westphal, *Géocritique*, 187 (my translation).
10. Cited in Herbert R. Lottman, *Camus: A Biography* (London: Picador, 1979), 523.
11. Brian T. Fitch, "La Femme adultère: a microcosm of Camus's solipsistic universe," in *Albert Camus' L'Exil et le royaume: The Third Decade*, ed. Anthony Rizzuto (Toronto: Les Editions Paratexte, 1988), 117.
12. Deleuze and Guattari, *Thousand Plateaus*, xiii.
13. Laghouat was then known is the 40,000-palm trees oasis. Regarding these factual geographical details, including the map, see "Laghouat, Selon les Guides Bleus, 1955," http://www.alger-roi.net/Alger/laghouat/textes/2_laghouat_guide_bleu.htm (accessed August 17, 2010).
14. I say "feeling" because the French original provides us with different verbs (*cru, imaginé,* and *attendu*) not translated here.
15. As Westphal points out in *La Géocritique*: "When one resorts to geocriticism one emphasizes more the observed space than the observers captured in their specificity" (212).
16. Mary L. Pratt, "Mapping Ideology: Gide, Camus, and Algeria," *College Literature* 8, no. 2 (Spring 1981): 165.

17. Ibid., 168.

18. Quoted in Anne-Marie Christin, "Space and Convention in Eugène Fromentin: The Algerian Experience," trans. Richard M. Berrong. *New Literary History* 15, no. 3 (Spring 1984): 562.

19. Known today as "Rue Bab el-Gharbi à Laghouat" ("the Bab El Gharbi Road"). See http://www.orientalist-art.org.uk/ef42.html (accessed August 20, 2010).

20. *De Delacroix à Renoir: l'Algérie des peintres* (Paris: Institut du Monde Arabe/ Editions Hazan, 2003), 178–79.

21. See Christine Margerrison, Mark Orme, and Lissa Lincoln, *Albert Camus in the 21st Century: A Reassessment of His Thinking at the Dawn of the New Millennium* (Amsterdam: Rodopi, 2008), 89.

22. Lottman, *Camus*, 517.

23. For an alternative reading of the end of the story, see Brian Duffy, "Journey to the Desert and Other Motifs in Albert Camus's 'La femme adultère' and Richard Ford's 'Abyss,'" *Revue de Littérature Comparée* 2 (2010): 77–90.

13

Affective Mapping in Lyric Poetry

Heather Yeung

Like the naturalist, the cartographer, or the surveyor, the poet's visual and aural engagement with a landscape seeks to map and determine spaces. However, the poet's eye is endowed with a freedom to observe and record sensations in addition to those that make up the concrete landscape. The poet thus communicates with a freedom of affect that the geographer or naturalist cannot notate, bridging the gap between the ready-to-hand of the observer in the natural setting, and the present-at-hand of the geographer or naturalist's detachedly observed phenomena or specimens. Through this freedom of vision and voice, the "I" (enunciating first person pronoun) and the "eye" (or angle of poetic vision) of the poem become necessarily interchangeable, producing a blurring between landscape and voice that the reader of the poem must subsequently negotiate, engaging affectively with the poem on a level different than that of its creator. Poetic voice and the space from which and about which enunciation occurs simultaneously demands and evades definition as the position of the first person pronoun and angle of vision shifts, and all too frequently the two major constituent elements of poetic experience—the poem read as stemming from an "I" (the implied speaker's or a personal or psychological point of view) and the poem as stemming from an "eye" (the mimetic constructions of landscape, theme, and image in the space of the poem)—are separated in criticism to facilitate an apparently stable understanding of the text in question.

It is my contention in this chapter that the manner in which we experience the poem is dependent on the natural blurring of the poem's enunciating "I" and/or "eye." This elision occurs not only at the level of writing but also at the level of reading the poem and is reliant on a movement back to the idea of a poem as being primarily of experience rather than as an object of knowledge. It moves away from ways of reading that, in their logo- or graphocentrism, do not accommodate the other life of poetry, as vocal performance, and takes into account the importance of the ontological as well as the epistemological approach to both criticism and the text. The poem is an open work as Eco defines it, its reader-dependent multiplicity of possibilities as much due to the "aesthetic stimuli" as to the "field of connoted meanings,"[1] where "poetic language involves at once the emotive use of references and the referential use of emotions."[2] A way of approaching reading that takes into account the simultaneous existence of the poem's (and, indeed therefore, the reader's) enunciating "I" and poetic "eye" is also one that is predicated on ideas of space rather than personality or theme.

The experience of reading a poem is an act that can only occur in the present, something that has led many critics of lyric poetry to emphasize a specifically poetic space of reading, which, due to the nonnarrative nature of the lyric, occurs apart from, or in a suspension from, conventionally perceived or linear time. As Northrop Frye writes, "in the lyric, then, we turn away from our ordinary, continuous, experience of space and time, or rather from a verbal mimesis of it."[3] This readerly act of suspending lived time and space (a sort of Coleridgian suspension of disbelief), is also a readerly surrender to a complicit and absolute becoming and allows for a reading of the lyric poem that emphasizes an experience of the poem dictated through a sympathetic relationship with the unfolding of the work itself. This sort of sympathetic relationship between reader/viewer and artwork is explained by Gilles Deleuze as "a virtual map, traced by art, superimposes itself on the real map, whose very contours are thus transformed."[4] This relationship is not only sympathetic but also reciprocal: the aesthetic experience is both transforming and transformative. This suspension or surrender of lived time and space is also an inherently ethical act inasmuch as it allows for an approach to the poem that is ungoverned by the power dialectic between personality and theme that is characteristic of much literary criticism.

The poem as experience may be split into several constituent elements: the reading act, identification, understanding, reflection, and analysis. Although this may seem to be a linear progression, it is less this than an accretion of experience and understanding through the experience of the work, facilitated by the surrender of the reader to the space of the poem and the openness of the work. The consequent reading of the poem will be ultimately unsuccessful unless the base for this reading, generated through these constituent elements, is not primarily a sympathetic one. The becoming of the poem must be accompanied by a simultaneous becoming on the part of the reader of the poem. Again, if this balance is not struck, we run the risk of destructively establishing binary power relations between reader and text, leading to a primacy either of text or of response in the resultant criticism. I would like to propose that a psychoanalytic approach to the poem provides us with a way to successfully redress this balance. The use of psychoanalysis as part of the methodology of affective mapping here is not meant to preclude one's approach to poems that are less than "personal" or "confessional." Indeed, this approach to the experience of poetry provides an inherently spatial groundwork for all subsequent analytical approaches. Later in this chapter, I offer a reading of Alice Oswald's volume *Dart* (2002), in which I hope to demonstrate some of the ways that affective mapping aids bridging the space between the "I" and "eye" of the lyric poem.

Too often, psychoanalysis is used in literary studies to find in the text particular pathologies analogous to known incidents in the writer's life or on the part of the fictional speaker of the poem. The process of trauma and recovery through the writing experience may be seen to find a parallel in the talking cure of psychoanalysis. Equally, the critic may see himself or herself take on the role of analyst to the text's analysand. All these approaches to literary studies through psychoanalysis are in some way reductive, as Jonathan Culler also observes:

> If critics devote themselves to identifying in literary works the forces and elements described in psychoanalytic theory, if they make psychoanalysis a source of themes, they restrict the impact of potentially valuable theoretical developments [. . .]. This body of work provides, among other things, an account of processes of textual transference by which critics find themselves uncannily repeating a displaced version of the narrative they are supposed to be comprehending—just as the psychoanalyst, through the process of transference, finds himself caught up in the re-enactment of the analysand's drama. *Contemporary psychoanalytic theory might have much to teach us about the logic of our interaction with texts but it is impoverished when it is treated as a repository of themes.*[5]

But what has this psychoanalytically indebted approach to literature to do with ideas of space in poetry? After all, the majority of psychoanalytic readings of poetry fall short of holistic in the ways Culler enumerates, leading to readings of even the most nonnarrative of poems as if within a narrative framework or as if evidence of the artistic expression of a particularly traumatic period in the writer's life. Both of these types of reading in some ways reduce the experience of the poem to the reader's ability to situate the poem within a narrative framework somehow exterior to the poem itself. In both cases, the critic finds himself or herself caught up in the analysand's (i.e., the poem's or the speaker's) drama, leading to a reading of the lyric poem that could be mistaken for one of a dramatic monologue. Concerned in the broadest way possible with interrelationships—relationships within the self and between the self and the world—psychoanalysis investigates and articulates these relationships in spatial terms. It thus contributes to our study of the lyric poem in a fundamental way, allowing us to bridge the gap between the critical idea of the poem in space and the idea of the poem as space, the position of the enunciating "I" and the poetic-visual "eye." The judicious use of many of the tenets of psychoanalysis in our analysis of the ideas of space in the experience of the lyric poem results in an ethically and critically balanced manner of reading of this highly experiential, nonnarrative, poetic form.

It is at this point that we return to the idea of poem as experience. Many literary critical approaches, even if they take this idea as a given, begin and end obsessed with understanding: understanding all the levels of meaning operating in the poem. And it is through understanding (or, indeed, not understanding) the subject matter of the poem that we may form aesthetic value judgments about the poem in question. This manner of reading tends to discount the distinct lyric space of the poem and the lyric voice, intent instead on contextualization. It is a cognitive approach to the poem, which is emphasized in an approach to poetry that identifies only the textual phenomenon in the poetic experience. This is an important aspect of poetic, and indeed literary, analysis, but it is only a secondary aspect of the constituent elements of reading the lyric poem that I mention previously. Before understanding comes sympathy, even empathy, which leads to the continuation of the reading act. This primary element of reading continues even when methods of textual understanding kick in and is built out of the reader's sympathy, then empathy, for and with the lyric voice as he or she voices the poem. This process is affective rather than cognitive and is primarily identificatory in its functioning.

As Culler writes, "The fundamental aspect of lyric writing [is] to produce an apparently phenomenal world through the figure of voice."[6] The experience of the poem is rooted in identification with the poem's voice, and only then does this experience extend to understanding of the meaning of the poem's text. This is not to say that affective engagement with the voice of the poem is the same as the aesthetic experience of poetry whose sonorous base formed the theories of the French symbolist poets. Rather, affective engagement, with its concern with the voice of the poem, presupposes an element of literacy on the part of the reader but sees them as complicit in an act of voicing on which the foundations of the reading act are based. The poem's voice is embedded within the ventriloqual relationship between the reader and the text and is contingent on the reader's engagement with the "I" and "eye" of the poem simultaneously. Affect itself is an important element of the identification processes that voicing catalyses, even, as Steven Connor writes in *Dumbstruck: A Cultural History of Ventriloquism*, "psychological inquiry into the voice has tended to focus on the cognitive rather than the affective aspects of self-recognition."[7] This affective engagement is also intimately connected to the formation of aesthetic value judgments about a given poem, just as the affects are an important element of one's formation of ethical decisions in life. As Jonathan Flatley writes, "Affects process information as being essentially different from 'reason.' The affects serve a function [. . .] that thinking in itself cannot; thinking cannot make us *care* about things. This, if for no other reason, because of the central importance of this function for human life, it is worth emphasising that specific nature of affect."[8] For Flatley, "affect indicates something relational and transformative, [. . .] one is affected *by* people or things"[9] and it is through a process of affective mapping that one can begin to understand one's aesthetic experience.

The rise of affect in contemporary thought is both a part and the natural culmination of the important reanimation of ideas of space. Indeed, the majority of studies in affect are also directly concerned with space,[10] and affect has also become an important area of research in contemporary neuroscience, psychology, and psychoanalysis. It is in the affective realm that we can locate the aesthetic and ethical force of poetry as experience, which catalyses the transformative, moral, and cognitive aspects that characterize the theories surrounding poetry and poetics. It is in the affective realm that the important primary engagement with the world and/or work takes place. I would like to extend Flatley's thesis to the lyric poem, proposing that it is in our engagement with the lyric voice that we can locate the aesthetic and ethical force of poetry as experience as well as lay the groundwork for our experience of the poem as space and for our analysis of the manner in which space operates in the poem.

Lyric voice is a phenomenon that has been a given in the reading of poetry for hundreds of years but that is also permanently shrouded in some sort of mysticism—ideas of ultimate truth, oracular function, and possessive power. Yet the idea and experience of distinctive poetic voice is generally the overarching element through which the value judgments important to our conception of poetry are made. Bill Berkson makes this aspect of reading and assessing poetry very clear in an address to an audience at the Museum of Modern Art in New York:

> In poetry, we say it is a "voice" that does or doesn't come across to the ear. A contemporary translation of *The Seafarer* begins "This verse is my voice,

it is no fable"; and the rigors of "finding our own voice" are well known to workshop students, though lately the premium on individual quirks seems to be waning. At any rate, the voice of a good poet is liable to be just that, intimation of truthfulness that enters his work most without knowing; it exists in ratio to his conviction and beyond technique in the ordinary sense [. . .] [The] poem will always denote the poet's world. There is always more to say because there is always more to feel, and *vice versa*.[11]

Stripped of the comfortable ordering of narrative or historicity, the reader of the lyric poem relies first on voice in order to gain some semblance of identification with the poem in question. It is from this first identification with and of voice that the reader can then build a picture of the world of the poem. For many New Critics, the difficulty in pinning down the lyric voice led to an elevation of the idea of the "speaker" of the poem and often the readings of lyric poems as if dramatic monologues. For the more historically or biographically orientated critic, this need to identify with the poem's voice manifests itself in the association of the speaking "I" of the poem with the implied or critically constructed character of the poet. Where New Criticism and structuralism posit an eminently stable and representative text and author and builds criticism from this point, poststructuralism destabilizes the very notion of text, positing instead a set of infinitely generative possibilities. The words of the text, before any narrator or speaker is even considered, let alone an author, are constantly in process, constantly under question. Symbolism situates the latent force of the text not in its language but in the unconscious effect that the sound patterns formed by the phonemes, which make up the words of the text, have on the reader. However, to locate a "readerly" identification in either the constructed speaker of structural discourse or its opposites, the deconstructed text of poststructuralism and the sound patterns of symbolism, is to ignore completely the reciprocal nature of the experience of the poem. Reading is reduced to an ethics already polarized and predetermined, complicating the concept of lyric voice.

Between the different perspectives on lyric voice previously presented, there lies a point of stability, a single point at which, or process within which, it is possible to locate the act of primary identification with the lyric voice: the function of reading that makes "us *care* about things."[12] This primary (affective) process occurs within the act of voicing the poem, the consequent identification of the reader with the I/eye of the poem, and continues alongside all other elements of the reading act. I would like to emphasize at this point that there is a distinct difference between the lyric utterance and reading act and a "real world" speech act; this difference is often ignored in reader-response theory and in philosophies of reading, which invariably take all sorts of utterances as a form of intentional speech act. However, I would like to contend that the difference between lyric voice and all other types of voicing (reading and speaking) can be seen by looking at the qualitative difference between the idea of speaking and the idea of voicing a poem that lies in the suspended time and nonnarrative nature, or "space," of the lyric voice. The reader allows himself or herself to voice the poem, and thus form an initial level of engagement through identification with voice, which is apart from any sort of a priori assumptions of character or event.

The idea of voicing the poem is one that is a major constituent part of the experience of the lyric poem, and also one that establishes, at an initial stage of the reading process, the inherently spatial nature of the lyric poem. Steven Connor emphasizes the importance of voice in self-recognition, and for him this is an inherently spatialized and spatializing process:

> The voice is not merely orientated in space, it provides the dynamic grammar of orientation [. . .] When I speak, my voice shows me up as a being with a perspective, for whom orientation has significance [. . .] A voice also establishes me as an inside capable of recognising and being recognised by an outside. My voice comes from the inside of a body and radiates through a space which is exterior to and extends beyond that body. In moving from an interior to an exterior, and therefore marking out the relations of interior and exterior, a voice also announces and verifies the co-operation of bodies and the environments in which they have their being. The voice goes out into space, but also always, in its calling for a hearing, or the necessity of being heard, opens a space for itself to go out into, resound in, and return from. Even the unspoken voice clears an internal space equivalent to the actual differentiation of positions in space necessary to the speaker or hearer.[13]

This "complex feedback loop" of voicing is a process that leads to orientation and individuation.[14] This is the case whether the voicing is aloud or silent (as Connor states, "the unspoken voice [also] clears an internal space"), and recent studies in cognitive linguistics have demonstrated that the detection by a reader of syllabic stress patterns and lyric meaning is unaffected by whether the reading is aloud or silent.[15] In the experience of the lyric poem, the reader is doubly complicit in this process of voicing. The act of voicing the lyric poem involves a suspension of self on the part of the reader and a subsequent identification with and ventriloquism of the lyric voice. The autonomy of both poem and speaker is absolute, yet the process of voicing sees these autonomies become mutual. The reader will at once seek the voice of the poem and voice the poem. Voicing is not an appropriation, rather it is a process of primary identification. Voicing is primarily affective.

Didier Anzieu also links voice to primary identification. It is with the idea of a sonorous envelope that Anzieu makes his contribution to developmental psychoanalysis, and it is the sonorous envelope that influenced Steven Connor's formation of the idea of vocalic space. The sonorous envelope is the auditory equivalent to the highly visual Lacanian mirror stage or Freudian *fort-da* game. The approach to and the playing out of this developmental stage is primarily affective, a form of what the Kleinian psychoanalyst would call "projective identification." For Julia Kristeva, "affect is the internal correlate responsible for the positioning of the I in the exterior world [. . .]. Affect precedes and exceeds [Husserl's] predicative thesis,"[16] and indeed, the idea of affect is important in Kristeva's literary criticism, seen especially in the important formative space of the *chôra*. Yet the play of affect in the identificatory process of reading the lyric poem that I am trying to establish here differs from Kristeva's *chôra* inasmuch as Kristeva posits the *chôra* as a prelinguistic space of becoming. The spatial play of identification *with* and *against* is the same in both processes, but Kristeva's use of the *chôra* often forgets the linguistic origins of the work of literature that she seeks to use it to extrapolate. The affective experience of poetic voicing is, rather, simultaneously extralinguistic: affect as a phenomenon lies firmly outside the linguistic sphere and is inherently shaped by language, as it is language that the reader seeks to voice and seeks identification with. It is in this identificatory process and initial play of "I"-positioning in the process of voicing that we can see the development of a process that will, in adult life, be incorporated into self-identification and knowledge-formation: "[T]he bath of sounds into which the child sinks, and which, we may suggest, is recalled in later experiences in which individual identity is immersed in sound, is also a defining, limiting, shaping function."[17]

Affect is the first shaping element in both self and also any form of identification, but it is at the same time more difficult to pin down than the cognitive processes that precede it. Again, it is a question of location of force or ethical impulse. Brian Massumi sees in affective experience "a gap between *content* and *effect* [. . .]. This is not to say that there is no connection and no logic. What is meant here by the content of the image is its indexing to conventional meanings in an intersubjective context."[18] It is through the intersubjective element of the affective experience that we can draw a strong parallel with the experience of the poem, and indeed, intersubjectivity is a major element of lyric voicing: as the boundaries between reader and text blur in the act of voicing and the experience of the poem, the "reader" can locate the lyric voice. Through the theoretical intervention of psychoanalytic thought we know not only that this act of voicing is an inherently spatial one but also that it forms, patterns, and regulates subsequent experience. It is the ethical groundwork on which subsequent becomings may occur. And it is through the prior and ongoing experience of affective mapping and on the foundations laid by the sympathetic voicing of the poem that all subsequent "readings" of the poem may take place. In denying this important formative element of the experience of the poem, the reader risks positing into the space of the poem a cognitive map unrelated to the poem itself. In acknowledging the affective mechanisms at play in the process of reading and engaging with the lyric poem, the lyric voice remains uncolored by the interventions of narrative or dramatic monologue interpretations. At the same time the critic may discover and map the various interpretative possibilities exposed by the poem, conscious at all times of the many different types of space that are in operation, reaching an understanding of both the lyric voice and also the lyric poem.

But all this talk about lyric voice, readerly voicing, and the identification with and experience of the poem must have a more practical application than an abstract ethics of reading. How, for instance, in the contemporary lyric's nonnarrative form and frequent fluctuations and dissociations of voice and perspective are we to locate the part of the poem to voice? And indeed, how are we to gain the clear and coherent vocalic experience in our voicing of the poem without seeking recourse to the imposition of some idea of character or speaker on the voice or voices that we see and read in the poem? How are we to distinguish affective engagement and primary identification from the subsequent understanding and analysis also necessary to literary study? And what has this, really, to do with the space of the poem?

The problem of identification with the lyric poem without imposition of narrative lies in the specific, suspended, temporality of the lyric poem, which Culler sees as generated in the "memorable language" of the lyric poem, the "rhetorical transaction" between lyric poem in its written and spoken forms.[19] However, Culler too frequently elides the voice of the poem or lyric speaker and the act of voicing the selfsame poem, thus positing the lyric poem as a polar point within the power dynamic of poem-text and reader-performer. The affective engagement with the poem is not, however, the engagement of a performer with speech and audience but rather the engagement of the reader in the strange ventriloquism of the vocalic act and the affective identification with voice. This identificatory act is too personal to be performative. But again, where are we to locate this distinct lyric voice and voicing if it is not within the abstract time of lyric? I would like to contend that the space of enunciation that the voicing of the lyric poem opens up is one whose difficulty lies in the blurring of voice and perspective that makes the lyric poem at once a vocalic and a descriptive, but an eminently nonnarrative, poetic form.

In reading the lyric poem, critics too often make the split between the poem's language (or, as New Criticism would have it, the speaker) and the themes and images that are also contained by the poem, analyzing the latter as a creation of the former. However, if we do away with this dissociation, we are left with an enunciating "I" that is at the same time the "eye" of the poem. It is with this blurred I/eye that the voice of the poem can be located, avoiding narrative or dramatic imposition. The simultaneous immersion of reader and poem in the intersubjective space of the blurred I/eye forms the "defining, limiting, shaping function" that Anzieu's bath of sounds allows the infant and produces the "apparently phenomenal world" of the lyric poem. And the affective identification with this I/eye through the voicing of the poem is the germ of all subsequent critical engagement with the poem. Through an acknowledgement of the simultaneous and nondivided nature of the enunciating I/eye of the lyric poem, we see the difficulties of lyric "temporality" dispelled; the speaker, through the primary identification with *all* the constituent parts of the poetic experience, is thenceforth fully equipped to formulate a balanced understanding of the manners in which the poem operates on a critical level.

Alice Oswald's volume *Dart* presents us with a poetic field to which we may effectively apply an analysis of both the "readerly" and the "writerly" dimensions of affective mapping. What we are presented with in *Dart* is immediately geographical but is, moreover, intimately concerned with personality. *Dart* is not only a "soundmap" of the Devonian river; it is also "made from the language of people who live and work on Dart."[20] The poem aims to map the river through voice, creating, in the words of the poet herself, "a songline from source to sea."[21] Early reviews of Oswald's poetry note the lack of a distinct voice,[22] unable to find stability in the constant multiplicity of Oswald's "I" and "eye." However, it is the very fluidity of vocal performance of the enunciating I/eye in Oswald's poetry that makes it distinct; the first person pronoun and point of poetic vision is not the cardinal point at whose intervention understanding or stability is gained, rather, it is the designated point at which objects, characters, and events coexist. It is in Oswald's use of the first person pronoun that the reader-listener is most clearly placed, with the speaker, at the interstices of voice and event. It is the poem's voices that simultaneously demand and evade definition as the position of the first person pronoun shifts.

Dart's "foundry of sounds,"[23] "soundmap,"[24] or "songline"[25] plunges its reader into such a stream of sounds akin to that we have seen Connor and Anzieu construct around the vocalizing individual—immersing individual identity into a sonorous plurality out of which, through a process of delimitation, a specific sort of lyric subjectivity arises. It is the act of reading, or voicing, the poem that recreates a primal, affective state through the demand and evasion of definition or identification in both the poem's voices and its reader that makes *Dart* seem difficult. But if we can read the poem as a process of becoming, this identification anxiety is dispelled. We no longer feel compelled to answer the ontopoetic questions the poem so often poses, and instead, in voicing *Dart* and immersed in the sounds of word patterns, we can instead define, limit, and shape the voice of the poem. This is less a *symboliste* idea of voicing primal sounds than a process of immersion in the sound of word patterns and the idea of sound and the subsequent delimitation of *milieu* that is broadly analogous to the process of confusion and identification, which is in turn analogous to the manner in which *Dart*'s "sound beings" articulate the river's movement "from source to sea."[26] In these voicings *Dart* also simultaneously diverges from and questions the manner in which lyric voice is figured and read: on reading *Dart* we above all have to accept that Culler's figure of voice is at once single and multiple and is written intentionally so in order to produce an apparently phenomenal world as fluid as the "riverscape" that is its model. But rather than a segmented *Paterson*-like epic or a series of more conventional lyric vignettes as in Hughes's *River*, *Dart*'s riverscape presents us with a deconstructed, or exploded, lyric voice.

To map as verb, relating to the river's geography, the poem's trajectory, and the geography of the poem best sums up the manner in which we must engage with *Dart*'s voices. Mapping ties in very well with *Dart*'s vocalic becomings, with the circular nature of the poem's questioning of itself, its becomings, and the very idea of voice. It helps elucidate the difficulty inherent in the poem's multiple voices and single geography, the "word-marks, momentary trances / in the wind-script of the world's voices,"[27] the constantly changing field of vision and voice, or "I" and "eye." It is through this blurring that *Dart*'s vocal landscape, soundmap, or songline manifests itself as a constantly shifting vision and voice. It is with this blurred I/eye that the reader, or voicer, of the poem seeks, in the bath of sounds to identify, whose becomings the poem traces.

Mapping encompasses the many different ways in which we engage with the poem. First, there is the affective level, best described as the initial reaction to the lyric voice of the poem, made manifest in the initial act of voicing inherent in reading. It is primarily voice-based and related to the Connor/Anzieu idea of vocalic space and the process of becoming. Second, there are the multiple, different cognitive levels (and I allude primarily to Fredric Jameson's aesthetic here but also to the uses of the term in developmental psychology, anthropology, and cultural geography) that, in literary studies, would broadly justify our placing of the poem in relation to different and broader contexts, forming webs of echo and influence, and identifying forms and tropes, thus reading rather than voicing the poem. This is primarily text based, conscious of the elision in *Dart* of geographical space and the space of the poem; the poem follows the trajectory of the river and its confluences but at the same time creates itself. But the idea of becoming is important in both of these levels of mapping. Helpful here perhaps is the close of Niran Abbas's meditative definition of the idea of mapping in intellectual and social thought and praxis: "In describing and visualising otherwise hiding facts, maps set the stage for future work. Mapping, like poetry, is always a project in the making."[28]

Dart is immediately map-conscious, not just through the poet's description of the poem as a sound map, but also within the poem itself. The poem constantly questions who and where. The two questions are usually inextricable: the who, or voice as sound and movement, giving rise to and at the same time actualizing the where, or the changing vocalic location. Indeed, the poem both begins and ends with the same question ("who's that moving"),[29] positing voice and position at once. The map thus drawn is something that is vocal, mental, and physical; literal and metaphorical; and constantly in a state of revision. The poem begins by blurring all these things:

[the walker charts a] course through the swamp spaces
pulling distance around his shoulders
[...]
He consults his map. A huge rain-covered wilderness.
This must be the stones, the sudden movement,
the sound of frogs singing in the new year.
Who's this issuing from the earth?
[...] I've done all the walks, the Two
Moors way, the Tors, this long winding line the Dart
this secret buried in reeds at the beginning of sound I
won't let go of man under
his soakaway ears and his eye ledges working
into the drift of his thinking, wanting his heart
I keep you folded in my mack pocket and I've marked in red
where the peat passes are and the good sheep tracks[30]

Through some fluid shifts in grammar, the map carried by the walker we meet at the source of the poem becomes the space the walker navigates, the point at which the voice of the Dart is recognized, the charted course of the river, a cape, what is thought, seen, experienced. For Oswald, mapping in *Dart* is not orthodox but necessary in all its dimensions, and it is through the enunciation of voice, or voices, through the voicing and identification of the various I's/eyes in *Dart* that mapping of the soundscape takes place, the poems becomings are articulated, and the successful voicing of the poem, the composition of its voices, occurs. It is through the acknowledgement of the free, fragmented, or multiple voices and perspectives ("I's" and/or "eyes") of this, or any poem, as our profoundly unstable waymarkers at linguistic, imagistic, and narrative levels that a richer understanding of all the spatial elements of the given poetic topos occurs. Beginning and ending with itself, the ventriloqual process of poetic voicing emphasizes the manner in which the poetic I/eye is less fully mimetic than affective—a process, constant in its becoming, that turns around upon its own ground, leaving us, the reader, to continue to return, voice, and draw anew our affective map from the multiple different possibilities inherent in reading, or voicing, the phenomenal world of the poem.

Notes

1. Umberto Eco, *The Open Work*, trans. Anna Cancogni (Cambridge, MA: Harvard University Press, 1989), 37.
2. Ibid., 36.
3. Northrop Frye, "Approaching the Lyric," in *Lyric Poetry: Beyond New Criticism*, ed. Chaviva Hosek and Patricia Parker (Ithaca, NY: Cornell University Press, 1985), 31.
4. Gilles Deleuze, quoted in Russell West-Pavlov, *Space in Theory* (Amsterdam: Rodolpi, 2009), 227.
5. Jonathan Culler, *The Pursuit of Signs* (London: Routledge, 1981), 10, my emphasis.
6. Jonathan Culler, "Changes in the Study of Lyric," in *Lyric Poetry: Beyond New Criticism*, ed. Chaviva Hosek and Patricia Parker (Ithaca, NY: Cornell University Press, 1985), 50.
7. Steven Connor, *Dumbstruck: A Cultural History of Ventriloquism* (Oxford: Oxford University Press, 2000), 9.
8. Jonathan Flatley, *Affective Mapping: Melancholia and the Politics of Modernism* (Cambridge, MA: Harvard University Press, 2008), 200n9.
9. Ibid., 12.
10. See Flatley, *Affective Mapping*, and also Nigel Thrift, *Non-representational Theory: Space Politics Affect* (London: Routledge, 2007); Brian Massumi, *Parables of the Virtual: Movement Affect Sensation* (Durham, NC: Duke University Press, 2003); Joyce Davidson et al, *Emotional Geographies* (Aldershot: Ashgate, 2007).
11. Bill Berkson, "Afterword," in *In Memory of My Feelings: Frank O'Hara* (New York: MOMA, 2005).
12. Flatley, *Affective Mapping*, 200n9.
13. Connor, *Dumbstruck*, 6.
14. Ibid., 8.
15. See Ruth Campbell et al., "Stress in Silent Reading," *Language and Cognitive Processes* 6, no. 1 (1991): 29–47, and Reinier Plomp, *The Intelligent Ear: On the Nature of Sound Perception* (London: Psychology Press, 2001).

16. Julia Kristeva, "De l'affect ou 'L'intense profondeur des mots,'" *Esteriorità di Dio*, Facultà Teologica dell'Italia Settentrionale, Milan (February 23–24, 2010), 2.

17. Connor, *Dumbstruck*, 29.

18. Brian Massumi, *Parables for the Virtual: Movement, Affect, Sensation* (Durham, NC: Duke University Press, 2003), 24.

19. Jonathan Culler, "Why Lyric," *PMLA* 123, no. 1 (2008): 205.

20. Alice Oswald, *Dart* (London: Faber, 2002), vii.

21. Ibid.

22. See, for instance, Charles Bennet, "Current Literature 2002," *English Studies* 3 (2004): 230–40.

23. Oswald, *Dart*, 15.

24. Ibid., vii.

25. Ibid.

26. Alice Oswald, *A Sleepwalk on the Severn* (London: Faber 2009), 1; and Oswald, *Dart*, vii; respectively.

27. Oswald, *Dart*, 42.

28. Niran Abbas (intro.), *Mapping Michel Serres* (Ann Arbor: University of Michigan Press, 2005), 8.

29. Oswald, *Dart*, 1, 48.

30. Ibid., 1.

Contributors

Christine M. Battista teaches English at Binghamton University, specializing in American studies, ecofeminism, and theories of geography and space.

Rachel Collins teaches in the Department of English at Arcadia University. She is completing a book, *Toward a Literary Geography: Space and Social Consequence in American Fiction*.

Antoine Eche is an assistant professor of French at Mount Royal University. Formerly a researcher at the Université de Tours, Eche has also taught elsewhere in Canada, Scotland, and Cyprus. He is the coeditor of *Les genres littéraires et l'ambition anthropologique au XVIIIe siècle: Expériences et limites*, and the author of articles on travel narratives of the seventeenth and eighteenth centuries.

Joanna Johnson is a senior lecturer in the Department of English at the University of Miami. Her research involves representations of the English landscape in the work of Caribbean writers.

Brigitte Le Juez is a senior lecturer in comparative literature at Dublin City University. She is coeditor of *Modern French Short Fiction* and author of *Beckett before Beckett*. She has published essays on literary reception between France and Ireland, literature and film, and *ekphrasis*.

Peta Mitchell is lecturer in Writing in the School of English, Media Studies, and Art History at the University of Queensland. She is author of *Cartographic Strategies of Postmodernity*, as well as essays on spatial theory, metaphor, and twentieth-century literature.

Sten Pultz Moslund is a postdoctoral fellow at the University of Southern Denmark, specializing in postcolonial studies. He is the author of *Migration*

Literature and Hybridity: The Different Speeds of Transcultural Change and *Making Use of History.*

Eric Prieto is an associate professor of French and comparative literature at the University of California–Santa Barbara. His *Listening In: Music, Mind, and the Modernist Narrative* explored the interrelations of music and literature. He is currently working on a book titled *L'entre-deux: Literature, Geography, and the Postmodern Poetics of Place.*

Maria C. Ramos is an associate professor of English at J. Sargeant Reynolds Community College in Richmond, Virginia.

Maria Mercedes Ortiz Rodriguez, Profesora-Escuela de Estudios Literarios at the Universidad del Valle, is a literary scholar and anthropologist with a PhD in Spanish from the University of Iowa and a bachelor's degree from the Universidad Nacional de Colombia. She has also taught Spanish and Latin American literature at Bates College.

Jane Stadler is senior lecturer in Film and Media Studies at the School of English, Media Studies, and Art History, University of Queensland. She is author of *Pulling Focus* and coauthor of *Screen Media* (with Kelly McWilliam) and *Media and Society* (with Michael O'Shaughnessy).

Robert T. Tally Jr. teaches American and world literature at Texas State University. He is the author of *Melville, Mapping and Globalization: Literary Cartography in the American Baroque Writer* and *Kurt Vonnegut and the American Novel: A Postmodern Iconography.* He is also the translator of Bertrand Westphal's *Geocriticism: Real and Fictional Spaces.*

Michael K. Walonen is an assistant professor at Bethune-Cookman University, and the author of works on food, travel narrative, and identity in nineteenth-century America; translations of poems by Guillaume Apollinaire; and a book-length study of the social dynamics of space and place in the writings of the Tangier expatriate community.

Rebecca Weaver-Hightower is an associate professor of English at the University of North Dakota, specializing in postcolonial studies. The author of *Empire Islands: Castaways, Cannibals and Fantasies of Conquest,* she is also the book reviews editor of *The Journal of Commonwealth and Postcolonial Studies.*

Bertrand Westphal teaches comparative literature at the University of Limoges, where he leads the "Espaces humaines et interactions culturelles" research team. He is the author of *Geocriticism: Real and Fictional Spaces*, as well as other books on the Mediterranean and on Austrian literature.

Heather Yeung is a teaching assistant and is completing her PhD in the Department of English Studies at Durham University. Her thesis, "The Geometry of Space in Contemporary British Poetry," is sponsored by the Arts and Humanities Research Council.

Index

CPSIA information can be obtained at www.ICGtesting.com
Printed in the USA
BVOW03s0820311014

373078BV00017B/261/P